THE CHINA
BOOM AND ITS DISCONTENTS

THE CHINA
BOOM AND ITS DISCONTENTS

Ross **Garnaut** and Ligang **Song** (eds)

ANU
THE AUSTRALIAN NATIONAL UNIVERSITY

E PRESS

Asia Pacific Press at
The Australian National University

ANU

E PRESS

Co-Published by ANU E Press and Asia Pacific Press
The Australian National Unversity
Canberra ACT 0200, Australia
Email: anuepress@anu.edu.au
Web: http://epress.anu.edu.au

National Library of Australia Cataloguing-in-Publication entry

The China Boom and its Discontents.

Includes index.
ISBN 0 7315 3727 0
ISBN 1 9209 4241 6 (Online document)

1. Industrialization - China. 2. China - Economic policy -

2000- . 3. China - Commercial policy. 4. China - Economic

conditions - 2000- . I. Garnaut, Ross. II. Song, Ligang.

III. Title.

338.951

Editors: Davina McConnell and Bridget Maidment, Asia Pacific Press
Cover design: Annie Di Nallo Design

First edition © 2005 ANU E Press and Asia Pacific Press

Contents

Tables

Figures

Appendix tables

Abbreviations used in tables

n.a.	not applicable
..	not available
-	zero
.	insignificant

Abbreviations

AFTA   ASEAN Free Trade Area
ASEAN Association of Southeast Asian Nations
CCP   Chinese Communist Party
CIP   covered interest parity
CPI   Consumer Price Index
CSRC   China Securities Regulatory Commission
ETC   economic and trade commission
EU   European Union
FDI   foreign direct investment
FTA   free trade agreement
GATT   General Agreement on Tarriffs and Trade
GATS   General Agreement on Trade in Services
GDP   gross domestic product
HRS   Household Responsibility System
IMF   International Monetary Fund
IPO   initial public offering
MLSS   Ministry of Labour and Social Security
MNE   Multinational enterprises
MOFTEC Ministry of Foreign Trade and Economic Cooperation
NAFTA North American Free Trade Area
NBS   National Bureau of Statistics
NDFs   Non-deliverable forwards
NERI   National Economic Research Institute
NPL   Non-performing loan
NSSF   National Social Security Fund
OECD   Organisation for Economic Cooperation and Development
OLS   Ordinary least squares
OTC   over-the-counter
RMB   renminbi
SASAC State Asset Supervision and Administration Committee
SCRES State Commission for the Restructuring of the Economic System
SETC   State Economic and Trade Commission
SOE   state-owned enterprise
SRS   SOE Restructuring Survey
TEF   Trade and Economic Framework
TVEs   township and village enterprises
US   United States
WTO   World Trade Organization

Contributors

Prema-Chandra Athukorala is Professor of Economics, Division of Economics and Australia South Asia Research Centre, Research School of Pacific and Asian Studies, The Australian National University.

David Dickinson is Head of the Department of Economics, University of Birmingham.

Jianping Ding is Professor of Finance and Economics at Shanghai University and is Director of Research Center for Modern Finance (SUFE), Shanghai.

Cai Fang is Professor and Director of Institute of Population and Labour Economics, The Chinese Academy of Social Sciences.

Ross Garnaut is Professor of Economics, Research School of Pacific and Asian Studies, The Australian National University.

Hanene Hamdoun is a Research Assistant at the University of the Mediterranean, Aix-en-Provence, France.

Yiping Huang is the Chief Economist for Greater China at Citigroup.

Tao Kong is a PhD Candidate of Research School of Pacific and Asian Studies, The Australian National University.

Kunwang Li is Professor of International Economics and Trade at Nankai University.

Zhenya Liu is Professor of Economics at Renmin University of China.

Xin Meng is Associate Professor of Economics, Research School of Pacific and Asian Studies, The Australian National University.

Tim Murton is Acting Assistant Section Manager, Capacity Building, Department of Family and Community Services.

Ted Rule was formerly Managing Director of the Asian Infrastructure Fund. Currently, he is a company director in the high-tech sector in Sydney.

Ligang Song is Director of the China Economy and Business Program and Associate Professor at the Asia Pacific School of Economics and Government, The Australian National University.

Dewen Wang is Associate Professor at the Institute of Population and Labor Economics, Chinese Academy of Social Sciences.

Xiaolu Wang is Deputy Director and Senior Research Fellow at the National Economic Research Institute at the China Reform Foundation and a Visiting Fellow at the Asia Pacific School of Economics and Government, The Australian National University.

Mei Wen is a Senior Lecturer in the Department of Economics at the University of Sydney.

Sheng Yu is a PhD candidate at the Australia–Japan Research Centre, Asia Pacific School of Economics and Government, The Australian National University.

Ying Zheng is a PhD candidate at the Shanghai University of Finance and Economics.

Acknowledgments

The China Economy and Business Program gratefully acknowledge the financial support for China Update 2005 from the Australian government's development agency, AusAID, and the National Institute of Economics and Business (NIEB) of The Australian National University.

1

The China boom and its discontents

Ross Garnaut

Chinese economic growth is less problematic now than at any time since the beginnings of reform more than a quarter of a century ago.

Economic growth last year and this is proceeding at an annual rate around nine and a half per cent, which is the average rate of the reform period. The deflation of the early twenty-first century has ended, without being replaced by worrying degrees of inflationary pressure. Last year's concerns about excessive investment in state-owned heavy industry have been eased by restrictions on bank credit and a modest increase in interest rates. Current external payments have moved into surplus to an extent that is generating international anxieties, and which requires correction, but on a scale that can be corrected without dislocation. Direct foreign investment is high and increasing, contributing much to productivity growth. The private sector continues to grow rapidly, as a share of total activity as well as absolutely, with artificial restrictions on its expansion being removed progressively. The state-owned enterprises are shrinking steadily as a share of the economy, their number is falling absolutely with restructuring including sale into the private sector, and the financial performance of those which remain is improving with reform.

China is reaping large benefits from reform prompted by WTO membership, facilitating deeper integration into the international economy. Over the past year, China has overtaken Japan as the world's third largest participant in international trade. It continues to be the world's major destination for direct foreign investment. China's growth has systematically raised global prices of its main import products and reduced prices for its main exports. The world has come to see China as by far the most rapidly growing competitive threat and market opportunity.

These are amongst the characteristics of the Chinese economy in 2005. The international official and business communities are talking about a China boom, but they are actually feeling the huge but foreseeable impact of a very large economy on a path of rapid growth that is broadly familiar from earlier East Asian experience. The reality is business as normal.

The discontents of the apparent boom include Chinese who are participating less than their fellow citizens in the rising tide of prosperity. They include those who are exposed more than others to the risks and pressures for structural change in patterns of production that come with prosperity and success. They include foreigners subjected to the need for structural change as China expands its role in international business.

There have always been voices predicting inevitable failure of the vast contemporary Chinese experiment in reform and growth—a Leninist State presiding over the establishment of a modern market economy; the government of a backward, inward-looking society and economy aspiring to deeper integration into the international economy than most of the advanced industrial countries; and a population larger than the sum of all of the countries that have become rich since modern economic growth began in Britain a quarter of a millennium ago, aspiring to the attainment of the living standards of the world's most prosperous peoples within a couple of generations.

Those who said that Chinese reform would not succeed are already wrong. The debates about whether modern, internationally oriented growth could take root in China, at all or under Communist Party rule, have been settled by reality. The optimists in these debates were themselves wrong, because they were too timid in calling the scale and speed of China's economic transformation. The pessimists about China over the past quarter century—the legions of commentators who have said that the establishment of a modern economy in China was too large, too strange to any earlier precedents of history ever to succeed—are scrambling out of the dust bin of history.

But the wiser optimists about Chinese structural transformation and economic growth have always recognised that there would be exclusions and victims of prosperity, generating threats to stable economic growth if ways were not found to assuage their resentments. They always recognised that the modernisation of China, like that of the communities of Europe, North America, Japan and the smaller newly industrialised economies of East Asia before it, would have bumps in the road, false turns that would have to be reversed and corrected, and detours from the main path of economic, social and political transformation. They always recognised that the transformation of the authoritarian political system that would be nurtured by successful economic transformation would be fraught with risks to stability and from time to time to economic growth.

This book is mainly about some of the risks to and problems associated with the inexorable but uneven emergence of China as a high-income economy and modern society.

Garnaut and Huang in Chapter 2 seek to answer a question that has been on the minds of many economists, especially in the business sector. Can China's extraordinarily high investment levels continue to fuel growth? Or would the continuation of the high and rising investment rates of recent years—higher than any the world has ever seen, excepting only Singapore for a brief period in the 1980s—create problems that ended or slowed growth?

Garnaut and Huang reach the surprising (in the light of the current domestic and international economic discussion) conclusion that the correction of current imbalances may require higher rather than lower investment rates, and that this will be associated with higher rather than lower growth rates.

This is a conclusion that emerges from the application of standard economic analysis to contemporary Chinese data. China has underutilised resources of labour and human capital (Chapters 6 and 7), and some underutilised industrial capacity. Indeed, unemployment and underemployment represent large loss of economic opportunity and a large social and political problem. While there are some bottlenecks inhibiting economic expansion—for example in electric power and some forms of transportation—there is no general inflationary problem. A residential property boom is raising the costs of housing in some cities, but even in these places it is smaller than that in the large cities of the United States, Australia and Britain in recent years, and it is of modest importance on a national scale. The domestic economic imbalance is one of inadequate rather than excessive activity.

At the same time, China in 2005 is experiencing a large external payments surplus on both current and capital accounts—the latter partly speculative in response to the former and to the widespread expectation of currency appreciation. The huge and rapidly growing foreign exchange reserves—mostly invested in United States' financial assets at low rates of return—represent an opportunity forgone to expand current and future living standards in a country which is still far from meeting the aspirations for material progress of its people.

One can see the current account surplus as the excess of prodigiously high savings over very high investment. Chinese private and government consumption expenditure have both been rising rapidly, but not at the rate of incomes. Savings have been rising—partly as a precaution against old age and ill health; partly in response to rising private investment opportunities; but above all as consumer desires and preferences have lagged behind the increase in incomes. Various government policy measures to encourage consumption—more and longer holidays, new taxes on bank interest receipts—have had only marginal effects on the flood of savings.

The high savings in contemporary China are to a considerable extent the product of rapid growth itself. They would be affected to some degree by reforms to the financial sector that increased confidence in the security of and earnings on long-term savings, and allowed earlier access to higher quality private housing and consumer durables. But they are going to remain high for the foreseeable future, and may go higher with continued and possibly accelerating economic growth.

In Japan, a tendency towards huge excess of private incomes over consumption is offset in part by large fiscal deficits—to the extent that Japanese public debt, in absolute terms and as a share of GDP, is by far the highest of the advanced economies. China, with good reason, is deeply resistant to pursuing such a course. The good reasons begin with the potential for financial fragility in a developing economy with a weak financial sector. The state-owned banks owe their stability to state guarantees that would be fiscally demanding should they be called. It is prudent for the time being to nurture the fiscal capacity to stand by the banks. It is sensible as well to avoid the disincentives to economic activity that would be inherent in the need to raise large amounts of taxation revenue to service public debt.

There is scope for fiscal expansion at the margin, but the Chinese authorities are wise not to make expanding fiscal deficits a central part of economic development strategy. The expansion at the margin could nevertheless have a useful impact in raising demand, prospects for long-term growth and also incomes and lifetime prospects of low-income people. To generate all of these effects, increased government expenditure would need to be directed carefully towards the expansion of such public services as education in rural China, and for the children of migrants from rural China to the great cities.

The external payments surplus and the high rates of investment, much of it in export industries, and China's sustained high rates of economic growth, have led to calls from abroad to reduce investment and raise the foreign exchange value of the renminbi. The Chinese authorities responded to the international pressures, and to some domestic analysis that followed the path of the emerging international conventional wisdom, in July, by appreciating the renminbi by 2.1 per cent and shifting the currency peg from the US dollar to a basket of currencies of important trading partners. This followed a lift in regulated interest rates in 2004, designed to reduce investment and economic growth. A common macroeconomic prescription in China and abroad favours more monetary tightening and currency appreciation.

China's internal economic imbalances argue for more not less domestic expenditure. With limited scope for increases in public expenditure and private consumption in the short term, a substantial part of any expansion would need to be contributed from investment.

The impact of increased investment on Chinese growth prospects would depend greatly on the manner in which it was stimulated. An expansion of direct Government investment, and lending by state-owned banks to other state-owned businesses, along the lines of the Keynesian expansion that maintained growth at reasonable rates through the East Asian financial crisis, would perpetuate the current disappointing contribution of investment to long-term growth. If public expenditure expansion is to play a role, it would be much better for it to be focused on investment in human capital formation amongst lower-income Chinese. Financial sector reform, which would have the effect of facilitating increases in bank lending to the productive and rapidly growing private sector, and would generate better outcomes for productivity and economic growth than expanding state-owned enterprises' access to capital.

An increase in absorption would in itself reduce the external payments surplus and pressure for additional appreciation of the exchange rate. An acceleration of liberalisation of trade in goods and services—abolition of import quotas, reductions in tariffs, and removal of remaining constraints on current payments for tourism and other services—would have additional impacts in the same direction. These would seem to be the most productive first steps in moderating the external payments surpluses.

It is possible that excessive payments surpluses would remain after taking domestic expenditure expansion and trade and payments liberalisation to their prudent limits. Exchange rate appreciation would be useful as a third element in a strategy to establish an appropriate balance in external payments. The systemic changes announced in July after a long period of preparation strengthen the base for such adjustment.

The monetary authorities have been undertaking preparatory work towards a market-oriented foreign exchange system for a year and more. Major steps have included the authorisation of trade in a wide range of currencies and the encouragement of institutional development in the financial sector to facilitate active trade in foreign exchange. The much-heralded steps in July 2005, were not in themselves of decisive importance for economic adjustment—a small appreciation, the fixing of the renminbi's value daily against a basket of currencies, and the 'floating' of the currency within a daily band of plus and minus 0.3 per cent against a mid-point for the United States dollar. But they undoubtedly reduce the risks of, and bring closer, an eventual move towards a freely floating rate and capacity for economically meaningful exchange rate adjustment.

The change in the renminbi parity after a decade and more fixed firmly against the United States dollar may have the unwanted effect of encouraging speculation in anticipation of further and larger appreciation. The immediate economic effect of this would be to accelerate monetary expansion, thus contributing to the expenditure expansion that would be part of an optimal macro-economic strategy in current circumstances. It may bring forward the time when official China recognises the need for larger change in the foreign exchange regime and rate. Adjustment under speculative pressure along these lines is likely to carry more risks of over-shooting and more generally of instability than purposeful change in the settings of policy instruments affecting expenditure, liberalisation of trade and payments, and the exchange rate.

Through one mechanism or another, China is likely to see higher rates of investment and economic growth in the period ahead than over the past half dozen years. This will disappoint foreign commentators who have seen a large exchange rate adjustment as a means of reducing Chinese growth.

Ding and Zheng in Chapter 3 examine the exchange rate issue in more detail, and are generally cautious about the extent of exchange rate appreciation that could be sustained without major dampening effects on Chinese economic growth.

Chapters 4 and 5 look closely at the deep wellsprings of Chinese growth. Fang and Wang examine the contribution of favourable demographic factors in strong economic growth in East Asia over the past half-century. A high ratio of work-age to total population assists economic growth in a number of ways, and China has been a beneficiary through recent years and will remain so for a considerable period ahead. But a severe and unfavourable demographic transition will follow, as the offspring of the one-child policy in the reform era come to dominate the labour force, and as the children of the earlier era, living longer with improved nutrition and health services, survive through many years of retirement. China needs to do well economically in the years of favourable demographic balances, to support high living standards beyond.

Kong addresses one of the most important and elusive questions of economic development: what is the optimal political system for economic development, and how do China's institutions compare with what would work best. Her analysis demonstrates that neither an excessively weak State, nor one that is excessively dominant over the lives and decisions of its citizens, will produce strong, sustained economic growth. The Chinese State was too dominant and intrusive in the Maoist era. Despite the continuation of one-party rule through the reform period, there has in fact been considerable political liberalisation affecting the lives and decisions of ordinary people. This has been crucial to the success of market-oriented reform. It is a lesson of the global development experience that the optimal balance between the strength of the State and the autonomy of the individual changes with the progress of economic development. If Chinese growth is to be sustained over long periods, the political system will need to continue to evolve.

In Chapters 6 and 7, Wang, Song and Sheng discuss the important issues surrounding rural-urban migration and urbanisation in the process of economic growth. The availability of large amounts of labour that can move from agricultural to urban employment with little sacrifice of agricultural output is a source of resources for rapid, non-inflationary growth. Migration is an important mechanism for raising incomes of people resident in rural areas. But current policy settings in China deliver inadequate services and incomes to many people in and from rural areas. There is also a large backlog of investment in urban services that has to be corrected if migrants and their children are to participate fully in the opportunities in China's dynamic market economy.

In Chapters 9 and 12, Meng and Murton discuss aspects of the rapidly changing system of social security and welfare in urban China. Meng demonstrates, against the conventional wisdom in China and abroad, that the restructuring of state-owned enterprises has favourable effects over time on labour market outcomes and employees' welfare. Murton describes and assesses the effects of the far-reaching changes in social security arrangements that have been introduced alongside the disintegration of the old safety nets built around secure employment in state-owned enterprises.

Wen (Chapter 8), Liu, Hamdoun and Dickinson (Chapter 10) and Rule (Chapter 11) discuss corporate aspects of China's emerging market economy. The general picture is one of extraordinarily rapid evolution of Chinese enterprises, their governance, and the markets through which their ownership rights are traded. The scale of the task means that, despite extraordinary rates of change, much of the challenge of reform, structural change and institutional development still lies ahead. The pace of change means that there are risks of error and misjudgment that could have disruptive consequences. But the achievements so far are a source of confidence that Chinese development in these areas will over time meet the demanding requirements of continued rapid growth.

Finally, Athukorala in Chapter 13 and Li and Song in Chapter 14 discuss changes in the structure of Chinese foreign trade that are accompanying rapid, internationally-oriented economic growth. Athukorala draws attention to and analyses the increasingly important role of trade in components in China's export competitiveness. This is one reason why China's rapid economic growth is assisting and not detracting from the export performance of many of its East Asian neighbours. He cautions that the increasing importance of discriminatory bilateral trading arrangements may undermine this beneficent dimension of globalisation in the East Asian region, with harmful effects on Chinese export competitiveness, and more damaging effects on the economies that have received large benefits from the export of components to China's burgeoning export industries. Li and Song demonstrate more generally that Chinese trade expansion has contributed opportunities through export expansion and specialisation to other Asia Pacific economies, at the same time as it has placed them under great pressure for structural change.

The overall story of Chinese economic development in 2005 is one of immense stress, and of many problems associated with fundamental change inside China and amongst its trading partners. But this year more than at any earlier time in the reform period, it is a time of confidence that the challenges of change are being met, and that China is on course in its fast but long journey towards the productivity, incomes and living standards of the world's advanced economies.

2

The risks of investment-led growth

Ross Garnaut and Yiping Huang

High rates of Chinese economic growth in recent years have been associated with exceptionally high and rising rates of investment. This has led to discussion of whether growth that is so dependent on investment is sustainable.

Rising levels of investment have been a feature of the Chinese economy since the 1950s. Leaving aside the large surge of investment in the late 1950s, the ratio of investment to national production had reached and has continued at levels that were high by international standards by the early 1970s (Figure 2.1).

In the era of central planning, before 1978, investment was applied wastefully, and its positive effects on economic growth offset by low or negative total factor productivity growth. The waste reached its height during the 'Great Leap Forward' of the late 1950s, in which the investment share rose suddenly from around 20 per cent to over 30 per cent, and retreated as rapidly, bringing national economic performance down with it. This episode is proof of the possibility of growth deriving from high and rapidly increasing investment levels being unsustainable, and is etched in the Chinese public memory of the dangers of excessive and wrongly directed expansionary policies.

Since the commencement of reform, investment rates have remained high, and from the early 1980s resumed their upward tendency, in recent years reaching levels that are unprecedented in China and rare internationally. On three occasions since December 1978—in the enthusiasm of the beginnings of reform in 1979–80, in the febrile reform atmosphere of the late 1980s, and in the aftermath of Deng Xiaoping's exhortation during his famous visit to South China to accelerate reform

Figure 2.1 **Share of gross fixed capital formation in GDP in China, 1952– 2004** (per cent of GDP)

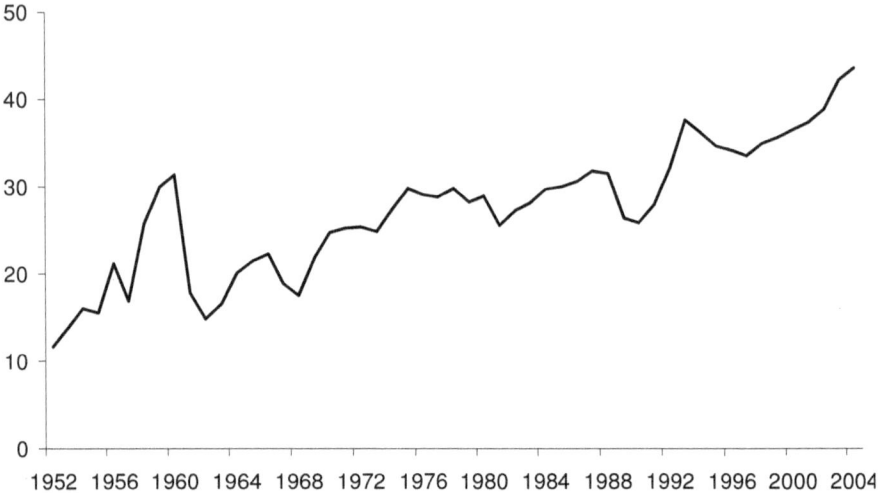

Source: National Bureau of Statistics (NBS), various issues. *China Population Statistic Yearbook*, China Statistics Press, Beijing. CEIC Database, 2005. Hong Kong. Available online at http://www.ceicdata.com/

after the post-Tiananmen uncertainty—investment ratios briefly rose above trend and triggered retrenchment and disruptive deceleration of growth.

The success of the retrenchment policies on each of these occasions meant that none of the investment bubbles of the reform had damaging consequences on anything like the scale of the Great Leap Forward. More generally, the main difference between the investment story in the modern and Maoist periods of Communist Party rule is that in the reform era, capital resources have been allocated in ways that generate reasonably high productivity growth, so that high investment contributes to strong growth in total product.

And yet the questions about the sustainability of investment-led growth continue to be asked. Why would high investment rates now be different from earlier spurts of Chinese investment that have come to grief? Wasn't the financial crisis in several East Asian economies in 1997–98 preceded by an investment boom? Isn't high investment leading to excess capacity, deflationary tendencies, and the threat of disruptive adjustment?

This chapter examines the phenomenon of investment-led growth in China. It analyses the risks to the sustainability of growth that have been identified by commentators on the economy, and seeks to address comprehensively the possible risks, including some that have received little attention. It examines the experience with high investment in other East Asian economies in periods of rapid growth.

The chapter concludes that high levels of investment themselves are consistent with continued rapid economic growth, but that some sources of high investment could contain seeds of instability, and some of the international structural implications of investment-led growth could be destabilising. It identifies policy adjustments that would improve the prospects for sustainably rapid growth built on high rates of investment.

Investment-led growth in China

The share of gross fixed capital formation in Chinese GDP has risen strongly through the reform era, from levels that were already relatively high levels by global standards. It moved up from an average of 29 per cent in the 1980s to 33 per cent in the 1990s. By 2004, it had risen to an historic high of 44 per cent.

Investment continues to rise more rapidly than total output, so that the ratio of investment to production will reach new highs in 2005. In the year to the June quarter, fixed asset investment increased 28.8 per cent in nominal terms, compared with the 9.4 per cent increase in real GDP or 14.2 per cent in nominal GDP.[1] Fixed investment has typically contributed around one third of the increase in domestic demand (Figure 2.2). This rose to over one half in 2003 and 2004.

All categories of business ownership have experienced strong investment growth: state-owned enterprises, collectively owned firms, direct foreign investments, and other private firms (Figure 2.3). The relative importance of each category has changed over time.

Private domestic and direct foreign investment have grown more rapidly than state and collective investment since the early 1990s. However, this general tendency was broken for a while in the aftermath of the East Asian financial crisis. The deterioration in the external environment for Chinese growth in the financial crisis coincided with a new round of structural reforms which removed large numbers of redundant workers from the payrolls of state-owned enterprises. This coincided with the establishment of market-based social welfare systems. Consumer expectations were weakened for a while, and national savings rose prodigiously, from 42 per cent of GDP in 1994–96 to 47 per cent in 2002–04. Special measures to boost consumption, including a 20 per cent tax on interest

Figure 2.2   **Contribution to GDP growth by different factors, 1979–2004** (per cent)

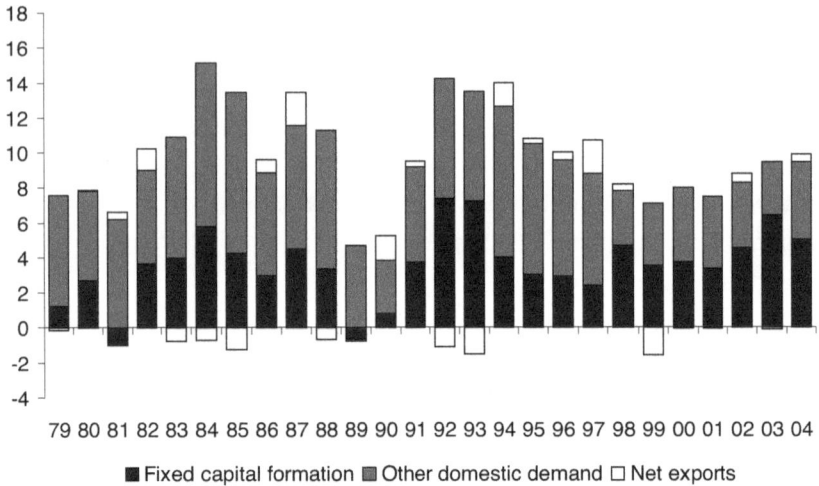

■ Fixed capital formation ■ Other domestic demand □ Net exports

Source: National Bureau of Statistics (NBS), various issues. *China Population Statistic Yearbook*, China Statistics Press, Beijing. CEIC, 2005. *CEIC Database*, Hong Kong. Available online at http://www.ceicdata.com/ and authors' estimation.

Figure 2.3   **Gross fixed capital formation by investor ownership, 1996– 2004** (per cent of GDP)

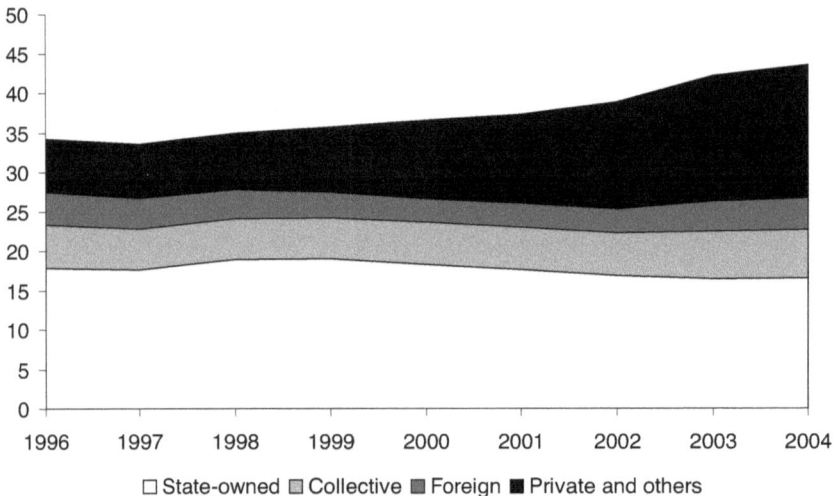

□ State-owned ▨ Collective ■ Foreign ■ Private and others

Source: Authors' estimation using data from National Bureau of Statistics (NBS), various issues. *China Population Statistic Yearbook*, China Statistics Press, Beijing.

earnings, did not stem the tide of rising savings. To maintain growth in domestic demand, employment and output, the authorities turned to the stimulation of investment, including through direct investment by the government and increased loans from state banks to other state-owned enterprises.

The restoration of international confidence in the East Asian growth story and recovery of the fortunes of Chinese businesses in Southeast Asia, Taiwan and Hong Kong after the financial crisis, and the boost in confidence from China's accession to the WTO in 2001, contributed to larger inflows of direct foreign investment, from US$41 billion in 2000 to US$61 billion in 2004. But while this level and rate of expansion of direct foreign investment was extraordinarily high by international standards in any historical era, this category of investment actually became relatively less important in the total through the early years of the twenty-first century. Over recent years, the domestic private sector has been by far the most important locus of investment growth (Figure 2.3 and Garnaut et al. 2005).

Looking more closely at recent years, there was a slump in the rate of increase in investment following the Keynesian expansion in the aftermath of the financial crisis, although with overall investment levels remaining high (Figure 2.4(a)). The year-on-year growth rates accelerated rapidly from early 2000, and tended to stabilise at 25–35 per cent from early 2003, although with a spike to over 50 per cent for two months at the beginning of 2004.

Rates of investment expansion have been high in all sectors, but at the peak of the boom in 2003–04 especially in iron and steel and some other heavy industries, and more generally in construction. Monetary policy was tightened in the first half of 2004 to take some of the heat out of the boom, and especially by restricting credit expansion to state-owned firms in metals, construction and other heavy industry. This adjustment was effective (Figure 2.4(b)). At the same time, there has been an acceleration of investment growth in energy and transport.

Comparative East Asian and international experience

Sustained rapid growth in East Asia has been characterised by rates of investment that are exceptionally high by international standards (Figure 2.5). Indeed, high rates of investment can be seen as the central feature of rapid growth in the East Asian manner, that took Japan and then Hong Kong, Taiwan, Singapore and Korea from low incomes to the frontiers of world productivity and incomes within a generation. China does not stand out sharply in this context: rates of investment rose to about 40 per cent in Japan at the height of heavy industrialisation in the late 1960s and early 1970s; the Korean ratio of investment to GDP has been at or above 30 per cent for several decades and peaked at 40 per cent in the late

5

Figure 2.4　**Growth of fixed asset investment in China** (per cent year-on-year)

(a) Acceleration then stabilisation of nominal fixed asset investment growth

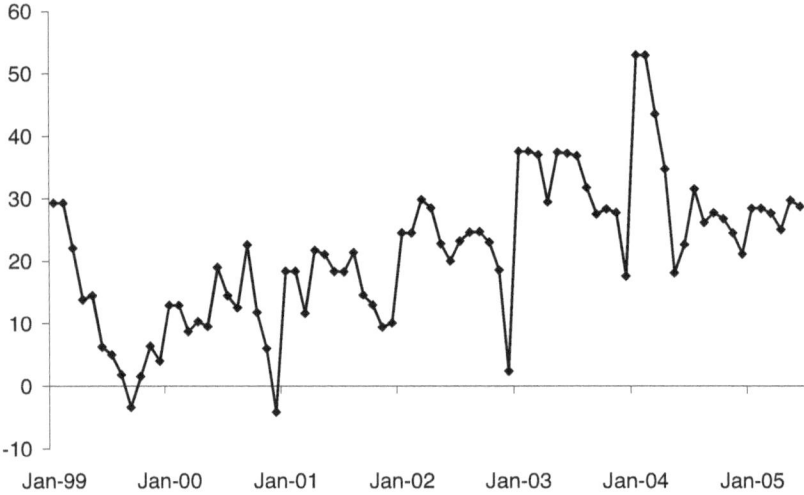

(b) Fixed asset investment growth in selected industries

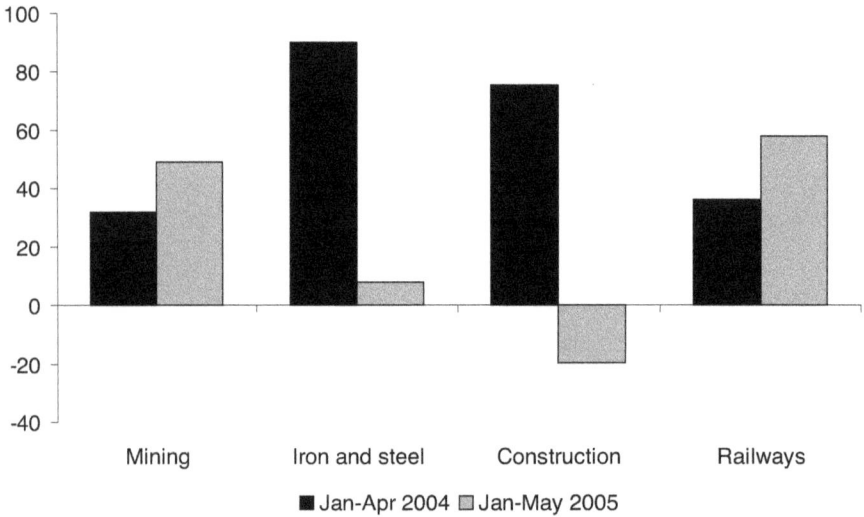

■ Jan-Apr 2004　□ Jan-May 2005

Source: Authors' estimation using data fromNational Bureau of Statistics (NBS), various issues. *China Population Statistic Yearbook*, China Statistics Press, Beijing.

1980s; Singapore's ratio was above China's for almost four decades until the end of the twentieth century and reached almost 50 per cent in the first half of the 1980s; and Thailand's and Malaysia's ratios exceeded 40 per cent for much of the decade prior to the financial crisis, and did not fall below China's until the crisis. It is only since 2003 that Chinese investment rates have been above earlier East Asian experience, and even then they have been below Singapore's at their height.

But China's (and earlier East Asian) investment rates do stand out in wider international context (Table 2.1 and Figures 2.5 (d), (e) and (f)). Chinese investment rates in the early twenty-first century were twice as high as the rest of the world taken as a whole. They had risen strongly from the 1990s, when rates had fallen in all other regions and major countries excepting alone the United States.

Did high investment rates elsewhere in East Asia generate problems for the sustainability of the economic growth that they generated?

The general story is that high investment rates were integrally related to the high growth itself. They were a necessary cause of high growth, and themselves were supported by that growth.

In several episodes in late twentieth century East Asian economic development, however, a period of exceptionally high investment preceded macroeconomic instability and a serious set-back for growth. One of these was a period of high investment in heavy industry in Korea in the late 1970s, followed by inflation and external imbalances, retrenchment and several years of lower growth. A

Table 2.1 **Saving and investment shares in the world, 1994–96 and 2002–04** (per cent of GDP)

	Gross national savings			Fixed capital formation		
	1994–96	2002–04	Change	1994–96	2002–04	Change
United States	15.9	13.8	−2.1	18.7	18.8	0.1
Australia	18.2	19.2	1.0	22.5	24.3	1.8
Other industrial economies	22.8	21.8	−1.0	22.2	20.7	−1.5
Major oil exporters*	27.6	30.4	2.8	22.7	20.4	−2.3
China	41.7	46.8	5.2	35.0	43.6	8.6
Latin America	17.6	20.1	2.5	22.7	19.5	−3.2
CEEMEA[a]	17.9	15.7	−2.2	23.7	23.4	−0.3
Asia Pacific[b]	25.2	25.7	0.5	34.4	23.1	−11.2

Note: [a] Bulgaria, Czech Republic, Hungary, Poland, Romania, Russia, Slovakia, Turkey, Ukraine, Algeria, Cote d'Ivoire, Egypt, Israel, Nigeria and South Africa. [b] (excluding China) Bangladesh, Hong Kong, India, Indonesia, Korea, Philippines, Singapore, Taiwan, Thailand and Vietnam
Source: International Monetary Fund (IMF), 2005. *International Financial Statistics*, IMF, Washington, DC. Citigroup, 2005. *Global Economic Outlook and Strategy*, Citigroup, Hong Kong.

Figure 2.5   **China's investment share in East Asian and international context** (per cent)

(a) China, Taiwan and Korea

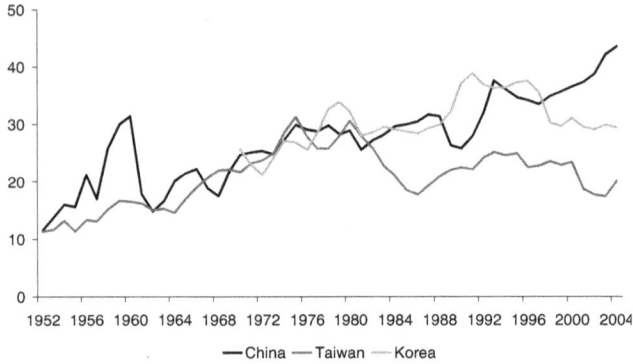

1952 1956 1960 1964 1968 1972 1976 1980 1984 1988 1992 1996 2000 2004
——China ——Taiwan ——Korea

(b) China, Singapore and Hong Kong

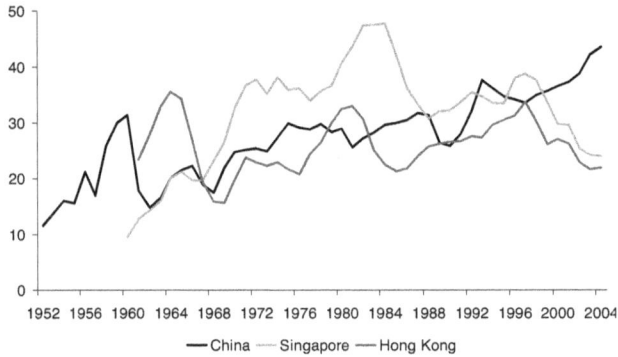

1952 1956 1960 1964 1968 1972 1976 1980 1984 1988 1992 1996 2000 2004
——China ——Singapore ——Hong Kong

(c) China, Thailand and Malaysia

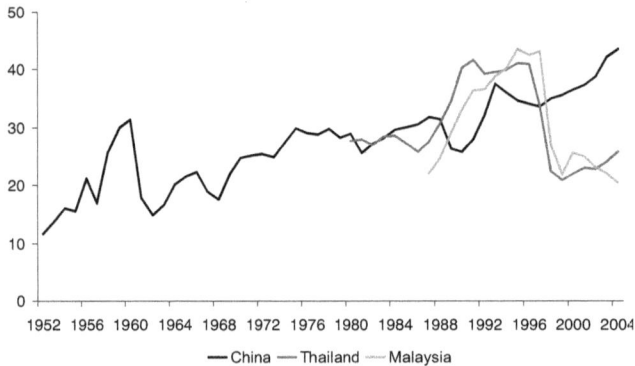

1952 1956 1960 1964 1968 1972 1976 1980 1984 1988 1992 1996 2000 2004
——China ——Thailand ——Malaysia

(d) China, Japan and India

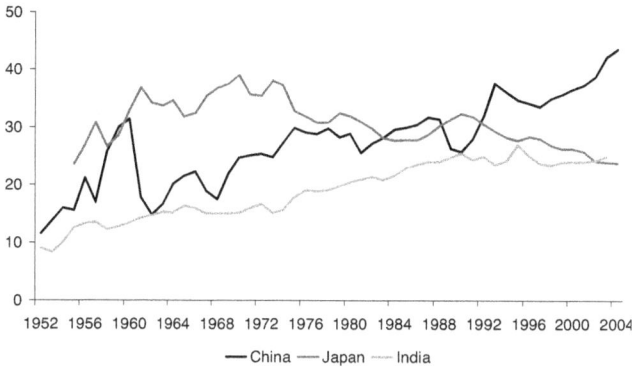

—China — Japan — India

(e) Brazil, Mexico and Turkey

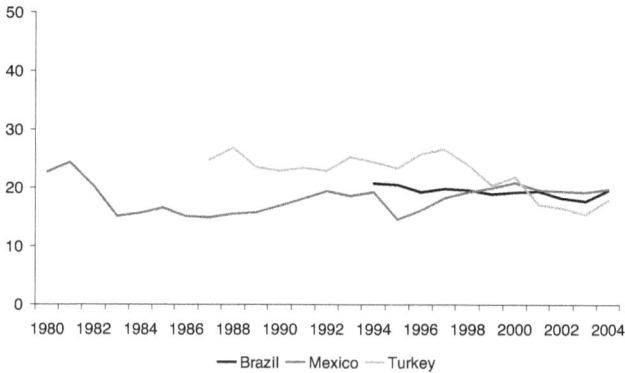

— Brazil — Mexico — Turkey

(f) The United States and Australia

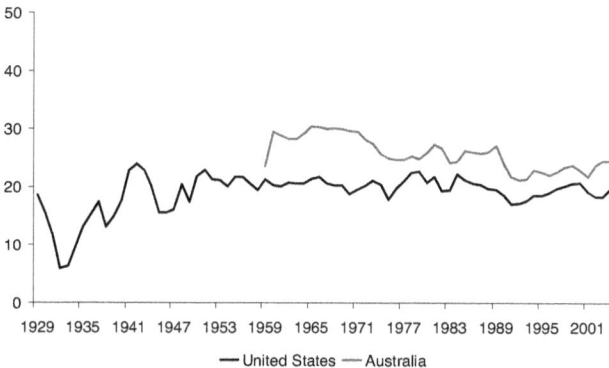

— United States — Australia

Note: The shares are gross fixed capital formation in GDP are all calculated from current price GDP expenditure data.
Source: CEIC, 2005. *CEIC Database*, Hong Kong. Available online at http://www.ceicdata.com/ and authors' estimates.

second was the expansion of investment in industries serving Japanese domestic demand in the late 1980s, followed by extended attrition of asset values and by economic stagnation. This was an extreme example of a common phenomenon: a period of exuberant expansion leading to what came to be known as a 'bubble economy'. A third was the experience of Korea and several Southeast Asian countries, notably Thailand and Indonesia, when more than ten years of high and rising investment, supporting decade-long growth at unprecedented rates for the Southeast Asian economies, was followed by financial crisis (Garnaut and McLeod 1998).

The lesson from East Asia is that high investment is a necessary but not a sufficient condition of sustained rapid growth. Pushed beyond prudent limits, high investment and growth can generate economic instability that threatens growth itself.

The question for us from the East Asian experience is whether China remains within the prudent limits of investment and growth, or whether recent increases in investment are likely to lead to retrenchment and in the worst-case instability. This is the same question that is raised by China's own history of spurts in investment leading to retrenchment and in the worst-case instability.

Finally, we should mention that some observers question the data on investment as a share of GDP, on the grounds that Chinese GDP is underestimated in the official data. This may be so, but there is no incontravertible reason to expect much larger underestimations in the GDP than in the investment data.

Why might investment-led growth be unsustainable in China?

If we move beyond analogy with other times in China and with other East Asian countries, what does economic analysis suggest about the relationship between exceptionally high investment and the sustainability of growth? In what ways might dependence on high rates of investment make rapid economic growth unsustainable? What is the validity of these arguments in favour of the unsustainability of investment-led growth?

The first argument is a matter of arithmetic. Obviously the share of investment in domestic product cannot rise without limit. Therefore if rapid growth comes with investment rising more rapidly than GDP, sooner or later this pattern must give way to one in which other sources of final demand are growing as rapidly as investment. This statement, of course, begs the question: what is the limit to the investment share of GDP? There is no obvious reason why this limit is binding now or soon. However, the current large excess of growth in investment over growth in other sources of demand suggests that early moderation of the differential is likely.

The second is that diminishing returns to incremental investment mean that extremely high rates of investment are wasteful, giving poorer and poorer returns for the sacrifice of current consumption that supports them. For this to become the basis for an argument that investment-led growth is unsustainable, the focus must be on the political unsustainability of the policies and governments that support it. The argument would be that sooner or later such a pattern of growth would become unacceptable to the polity, leading to policy change or more fundamental political instability. The former Soviet Union and its satellites in Eastern Europe provide models of unsustainable growth based on excessive rates of investment.

In contemporary China, however, while much investment is wastefully applied and generates meagre returns, most importantly in state-owned heavy industry, there are many areas in which returns to capital are high, especially within the rapidly growing domestic and foreign private sector. Total factor productivity growth is reasonably high, despite the wasteful allocation of some capital resources. A strong argument can be made for reform to remove remaining barriers to expansion of the private sector (Garnaut et al. 2001), and for financial reform to raise efficiency in the allocation of capital between competing uses. However, the contribution of incremental investment to growth remains positive, and there are no signs of the Chinese polity insisting on a rebalancing of resource allocation away from growth and towards consumption. Indeed, one would doubt the political feasibility of alternative development strategies that were premised on higher rates of current consumption and lower rates of investment and growth.

One variation on the theme of waste of economic resources through inefficient investment, is that distortions in Chinese financial markets, and in particular the underpricing of capital, are encouraging higher levels of investment than would be generated in an undistorted market economy. It is sometimes said that interest rates in China are uneconomically low, given China's developing country condition, the generally high returns on investment and the high rates of economic growth.

To the extent that this is the case, it is not easily corrected. Restrictions on international capital movements do tend to hold domestic real interest rates below what they would be in a smoothly functioning open economy. The attempts to raise interest rates in 2004 to ease rates of investment were offset to a considerable extent by capital inflow: the growth in China's foreign exchange reserves in 2004 of US$200 billion greatly exceeded the sum of the trade surplus and the inflow of direct foreign investment (together about US$90 billion).

The removal of exchange controls on capital movements would lead to somewhat higher real interest rates, at the margin encouraging savings and discouraging investment. (It would have the incidental effect of increasing China's trade and current account surpluses with the rest of the world, which is not an outcome that would be welcomed by many overseas advocates of foreign exchange liberalisation). This would only be feasible, however, in the context of more comprehensive market-oriented reforms in the financial sector. More efficient access to credit would be likely to encourage some forms of private consumption expenditure. But it would also support expansion of private business investment. The latter development would be large and beneficial for the economy, with an incidental effect of increasing investment and economic growth.

The third way in which it is argued that investment-led growth is unsustainable, is that it leads to excess productive capacity across the economy, which must be followed by deflation, financial instability and retrenchment. This argument is common in discussion of China today.

If there is truly excess capacity across the economy as a whole, however, it is evidence of inadequate rather than excessive aggregate demand. This would suggest the need for stimulation of demand in all its forms, including investment.

If, on the other hand, the excess capacity is confined to particular sectors, the problem is one of distortions in policy affecting resource allocation, or of errors in business sector decision-making. These are normal features of economic development in government-dominated as well as market economies, and not properly the concern of macroeconomic analysis or policy.

The presence in China of much excess capacity in the business sector, tendencies to deflation in many parts of the economy, and apparently huge underemployment of human resources suggests that the internal imbalance issue is one of inadequate rather than excessive final demand.

The other side of the coin of excess capacity and deflation, of course, is the presence of supply bottlenecks and inflationary pressures. Relative to historical and contemporary international experience, current inflationary tendencies are moderate (Figure 2.6). They are present most strongly in housing, but even here the nation-wide indexes suggest much lower average rates of increase in recent years than in most economies.

A fourth possible way in which growth based on high investment might be unsustainable would arise if it were generating such large deficits on the external current accounts that risks were emerging about whether the international markets would continue to finance them without destabilising increases in interest rates, or in the worst case, at any interest rates. This was the situation that triggered financial crisis in several East Asian economies in 1997–98 (Garnaut and McLeod

1998). China responded to financial crisis amongst its neighbours by expanding government expenditure and stimulating investment in a successful attempt to maintain reasonably strong growth. At this time there was some concern that China might also succumb to the doubts of international suppliers of capital.

But those times have passed. The recent experience is towards large surplus in trade and current payments. Both exports and imports have increased rapidly since China's entry into the WTO in 2001. From the beginning of 2004, however, the two growth rates began to diverge, with exports expanding twice as fast as imports. The trade surplus surged, amounting to US$32 billion in the 2004 and US$40 billion in the first half of 2005 (Figure 2.7). This is the analogue of the excess of savings over investment, even with current rates of investment, which was observed in Table 2.1. The growing trade and current account surpluses have generated tensions with the United States and some other Western countries. The recent textiles disputes with the United States and the European Union were special cases, as they were caused by removal of export quotas. But the protectionist responses to the expansion of Chinese trade do not depend on particular stimuli, and can be expected to survive resolution of the current textile disputes.

Any diminution of investment, domestic demand and growth could be expected to exacerbate the external imbalances.

A fifth possible way in which high rates of investment-led growth may be unsustainable is suggested by the experience of the East Asian financial crisis, by the Japanese investment boom of the late 1980s, and by the three inflationary Chinese expansions of the reform era. Growth led by high investment will not be sustained over long periods if it contains a high element of speculative activity, with investment commitments justified by expectations of continued increases in asset prices rather than by positive expectations of the present value of cash flows associated with the investment.

These are the circumstances of what in Japan became known as the 'bubble economy'. It is associated with asset price inflation, and often (although not in Japan in the late 1980s) with a combination of general inflation and deteriorating balances in external payments. It is more likely to be present and is more damaging when the financial sector of the economy is fragile.

China has weaknesses in the financial sector, but the state's capacity to support the weakest elements, the state-owned banks, limits fragility. None other of the typical symptoms of the bubble economy is prominent in contemporary China.

A sixth possible cause of unsustainability of rapid, investment-led growth is the difficulty of global economic adjustment to changes caused by the rapid growth of

Figure 2.6   **Inflation rates by product groups in China, January 2001–May 2004** (per cent)

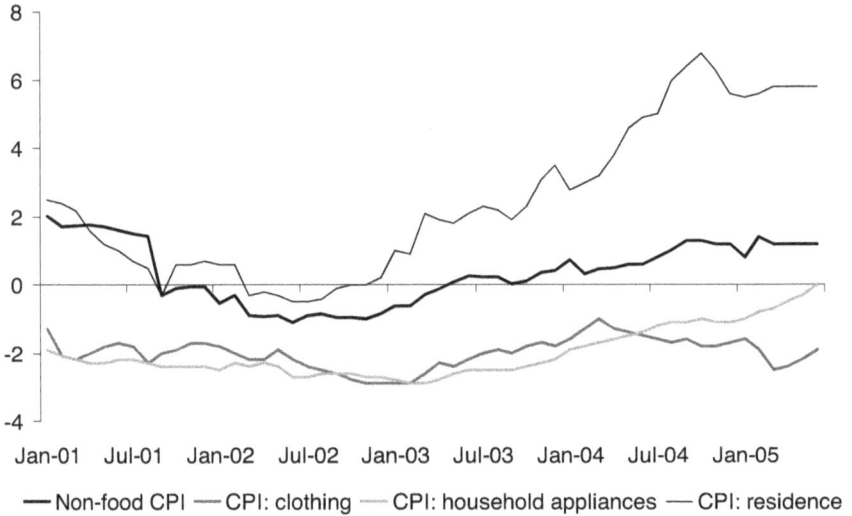

Jan-01   Jul-01   Jan-02   Jul-02   Jan-03   Jul-03   Jan-04   Jul-04   Jan-05

— Non-food CPI — CPI: clothing — CPI: household appliances — CPI: residence

Source: CEIC, 2005. *CEIC Database*, Hong Kong. Available online at http://www.ceicdata.com/.

Figure 2.7   **China's widening trade surplus** (per cent year-on-year, US$ billion)

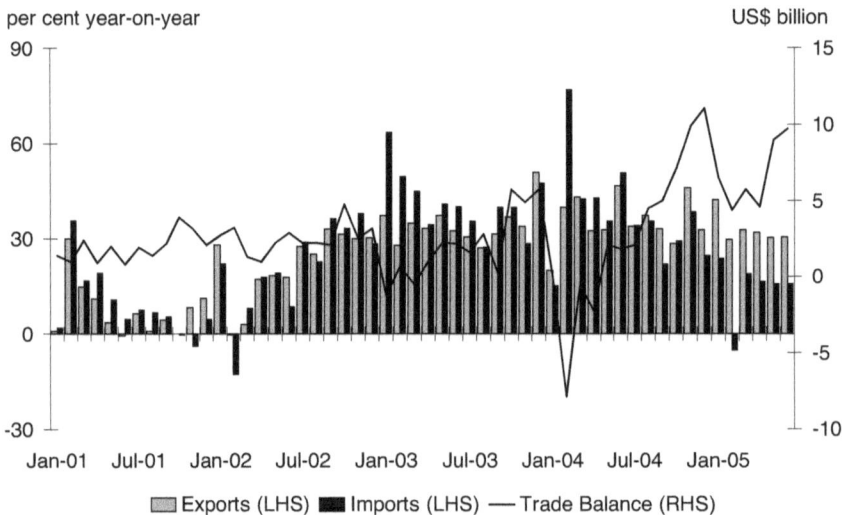

per cent year-on-year   US$ billion

Jan-01   Jul-01   Jan-02   Jul-02   Jan-03   Jul-03   Jan-04   Jul-04   Jan-05

Exports (LHS)   Imports (LHS)   — Trade Balance (RHS)

Source: Ministry of Commerce, China.

14

China, and tensions in international relations associated with those difficulties. This is important because China now bulks so large in the international economy, in a way that was not comparable in the newly industrialised economies in their periods of rapid growth, and present to much less degree in the earlier industrialisation of Japan. The more that is invested productively in the Chinese economy, and the greater the associated economic growth, the more that firms and workers in other economies will come under pressure to change their employment and modes of operation. This spurs demands increased protection of goods and services in industries in which China has comparative advantage. It generates increase in global and therefore Chinese import prices for goods and services. It exacerbates political tensions, as established powers react anxiously to the emergence of a competitor.

While each of these problems of international reaction is exacerbated by higher growth, each would be present at any conceivable rate of growth in China in the reform era. It is not clear that they would be much easier to manage if the rate of growth were moderately lower. And China earns some protection from negative international reaction to its growth from the increase in political weight that comes with a larger economy, and from the expanded opportunities that access to its growing markets provides.

There is no doubt that more rapid growth in China turns the terms of trade against itself. Prices for China's main manufactured export products have decreased at considerable rates over the past decade, and would over the immediate future fall more rapidly at higher rates of growth. But only for a while: rapid growth accelerates the change in Chinese comparative advantage into more capital-intensive and technologically sophisticated goods and services, in which global markets are much deeper and susceptibility to falling prices with increased Chinese supply correspondingly less. Incidentally, this same factor—rapid growth accelerating the transformation of comparative advantage into capital-intensive and more technologically sophisticated goods and services—provides some inoculation against international protectionist reactions to Chinese growth, since these products are subject to lower protection in advanced economies than are the main labour-intensive products.

The effect of Chinese import expansion on global prices for a wide range of natural resource-based products is substantial, and would seem to increase more or less in line with Chinese growth. As was evident with world prices for vegetable oils in 2003 and 2004, a powerful international supply response soon substantially offsets the price effects of rapidly expanding Chinese import demand for agricultural commodities. Metals and energy prices, on the other hand, are responsive to Chinese demand for many years, and for some energy minerals, perhaps indefinitely. The lead times are long for large increases in supply capacity. The income loss from the associated deterioration in the terms of trade, however, is small in comparison with the income gains from more rapid growth.

The future of investment-led growth in China

Doubts have been raised about the high rates of growth of investment and output in contemporary China, simply because the investment rates are beyond the range of experience in comparable countries. There are some circumstances in which such high rates of expansion might be unsustainable. But these do not seem to be present in significant degree in today's China.

Indeed, standard economic analysis suggests that rates of investment and output would rise to new heights in future, especially if commitment to productivity-raising reform remains strong, most importantly in the financial sector.

The Swan-Salter approach to macroeconomic policy analysis suggests that China—with its external payments surplus, underemployed human and in some sectors capital resources, and absence of inflation anxieties—requires upward adjustment in domestic expenditure. The efficient way to achieve this outcome would be through acceleration of financial sector reform, which would be likely to induce higher levels of consumption, but also of investment. Demand factors would lead this to generate higher rates of economic growth, as would the expansion of supply capacity with higher investment.

One theme that emerges from our discussion of investment-led growth, is that the acceleration of reform of the financial sector is pivotally important to expanding the benefits and minimising the risks of investment-led growth. One surprise about contemporary growth in China is that it is not even more rapid, given the prodigious savings and investment rates. The continuing biases, now unintended, against bank lending to the private sector, are a significant dampener to productivity improvement and investment. This is one of the several channels through which financial sector reform would contribute towards higher productivity growth—in effect, giving more growth bangs for the investment buck.

Acceleration of financial sector reform is also a promising path to moderation of external payments surpluses, through its impact on consumption and investment. This may not remove or even reduce tensions with the advanced industrial economies, because it would be associated with even more rapid rates of growth in China, with implications that pressures for structural change in the rest of the world would be even greater. Accleration of financial sector reform would also be good protection against financial fragility, so reducing the risks of financial crisis emerging from even higher rates of investment.

Domestic financial sector reform is also a necessary condition for the completion of the movement towards exchange rate flexibility that commenced in July 2005 (see Chapters 1 and 3). A freely floating exchange rate may be, eventually, a necessary element in the resistance to protectionist responses to China's growth. But as with the effects of banking reform on investment levels, the effects of reform may not be fully consistent with the prejudices and expectations of the reform promoters. A freely floating exchange rate accompanied by exchange control liberalisation would be helpful to stable economic growth in China, but may support higher capital outflow at least for a while, and an even stronger tendency to current account surplus.

The high rates of investment and growth in China seem to be so high that it is hard to believe that they could be sustained. In all likelihood, however, the maintenance of reform in the financial sector and elsewhere will lead to even higher rates. We are bound to be asking again and again whether the high levels to which growth rates of investment and output have risen are sustainable, as the data show these parameters rising continually to heights that would once have been beyond contemplation. And the answer for some time yet will be the conclusion of this chapter: if current high rates of Chinese investment and growth are a surprise, there are bigger surprises ahead.

Acknowledgments

Views expressed in this chapter are those of the authors and do not necessarily represent the views of the authors' affiliated organisations.

Notes

[1] Fixed asset investment here is a slightly different from the definition 'fixed investment' (or 'investment') used elsewhere in this chapter. In general, investment in this chapter refers to gross fixed capital formation, which is a part of the GDP by expenditure data. However, the Chinese statistics authorities only report annual data on fixed capital formation. During the year, they report fixed asset investment, which is total spending on fixed asset construction.

References

CEIC, 2005. *CEIC Database*, Hong Kong. Available online at http://www.ceicdata.com/.

Citigroup, 2005. *Global Economic Outlook and Strategy June*, Citigroup, Hong Kong.

Garnaut, R. and McLeod, R. (eds), 1998. *East Asia in Crisis: from being a miracle to needing one*, Routledge, London.

Garnaut, R., Song, L., Wang, X. and Yao, Y. (eds), 2001. *Private Enterprise in China*, Asia Pacific Press, The Australian National University, Canberra and China Centre for Economic Research, Peking University, Beijing.

Garnaut, R., Song, L., Tenev, S. and Yao, Y. (eds), 2005. *China's Ownership Transformation*, International Finance Corporation, Washington, DC.

International Monetary Fund (IMF), 2005. *International Financial Statistics*, IMF, Washington, DC.

Ministry of Commerce, 2003. Beijing. Available online at http://www.mofcom.gov.cn/article/200307/20030700112770_1.xml

National Bureau of Statistics (NBS), various issues. *China Population Statistic Yearbook*, China Statistics Press, Beijing.

3

Exchange rate flexibility

Jianping Ding and Ying Zheng

On 21 July 2005, China enlarged the renminbi's (RMB) band of fluctuation by 2 per cent, signalling a stage of exchange market reform. Rapid development of the Chinese economy, and recent political pressures from industrial economies, has prompted ever-stronger calls for the renminbi to be revalued. Different approaches to currency revaluation have been proposed. Goldstein (2005) argues that China should let its currency appreciate by 25–35 per cent and restore equilibrium to the balance of payments, using estimates about the sensitivity of trade flows to revise the exchange rate. Goldstein focuses on two approaches—the 'underlying balance' approach, determining which exchange rate will produce balance of payments equilibrium after adjustments for the economy's cyclical position and lagged effects from exchange movements, and the 'global payments imbalances' approach, examining imbalances between the currency and broader adjustments in global payments, particularly the US current account deficit. Balance of payments statistics from 2003 reveal China's current account surplus was equal to 4.5 per cent of GDP and 30–40 per cent of its total imports were inputs for assembly and finished-product exports. The combination of these trends means appreciation of the RMB would lead to a minimal increase in exports. Williamson (2004) concluded first that China is too large to make fixed exchange rates a sensible policy approach there, and, second, that the United States is not China's predominant trading partner, so pegging the RMB to the US dollar is even less sensible. He also argued that the Chinese government would also likely not accept the renunciation of monetary sovereignty that such a peg would imply. Williamson outlined a framework of exchange rate mechanisms, originally developed by Rudi Dornbusch—the 'BBC Rules'—which incorporates basket parity, a wide band and a 'crawling' exchange rate mechanisms.

A historical perspective of the RMB

The official exchange rate of the RMB has displayed 'crawling' characteristics since 1955 (Figure 3.1). The exceptions are the swap and black exchange markets when RMB rates were unified and the old unit 100 was converted into a new unit 1.

The RMB was allowed to appreciate against the US dollar after the collapse of the Bretton Woods system in 1971. This first period of 'crawling' maintained the RMB's stability for more than decade. The second period of 'crawling' occurred during the convergence of the swap and black rates and lasted for about five years. The third period of 'crawling' occurred in 1989, when the swap and black rates both returned to previous high levels. Rising black and swap rates were forerunners to a subsequent rise in the official rate, with the fourth period of 'crawling' in 1994. The black and swap rates vanished in 1994. The periods of currency 'crawling' all share the same characteristic—the official exchange rate eventually followed the market exchange rate and removed distortions between the official and market exchange rate. The RMB does not appear to be manipulated when the size of black market exchange is minimised.

Figure 3.1   **Historical 'crawling' of RMB**

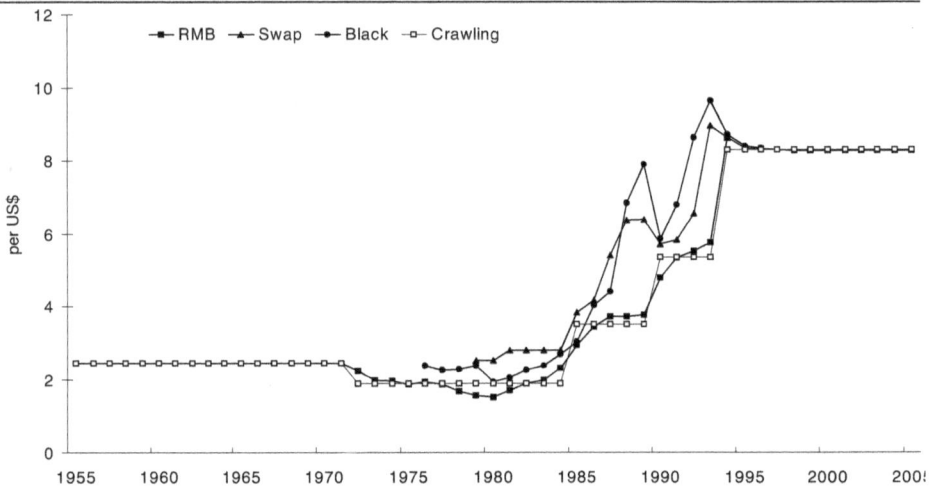

Source: International Monetary Fund, (various years). *International Financial Statistics*, National Administration of Foreign Exchange, International Monetary Fund, Shanghai. Cowitt, P.P. (ed), (various years). *World Currency Yearbook*, Pick's Currency Handbook Pick Publishing Corporation, New York.

Exchange rate reforms aimed at increasing the influence of market forces and transforming the exchange rate into a meaningful economic lever, by establishing realistic levels for the exchange rate (Zhang 2000). China currently adjusts the exchange rate on the basis of the national average per unit of foreign exchange rate earned through exports, with a mark-up of about 10 per cent to profit exporters (Zhang 2004). Empirical results reveal that exchange policies have followed the purchasing power parity rule and that adjustments to the nominal exchange rate will benefit relative tradable prices for Chinese exporters (Zhang 2004). This approach creates a mechanism that ensures the profitability of exports and allows China to pursue a policy of export-oriented development. Increases in the costs of inputs since 2003 have reduced the margins for Chinese exporters. Export costs of 8.3–8.4 yuan per dollar, after conversion from US dollars into RMB, already exceed the official exchange rate of 8.27 yuan per dollar.

'Crawling' with a basket exchange mechanism

Scholars have also discussed basket parity or 'crawling' rates using basket exchange mechanisms. This approach is not new and stresses the trade or investment weight of trading partners during the period of currency adjustment. Kawasaki and Ogawa (2003) studied Thailand, Indonesia and Korea under a currency-basket peg system, where the US dollar and the Japanese yen had equal weight in the currency-basket. The highly volatile dollar–yen exchange rate subjected East Asian economies to balance-of-payment crises. Kawasaki and Ogawa argue that a trade-weighted currency-basket should become the common currency of East Asia. The calculated weights of the US dollar, Japanese yen and the euro offer a useful insight. Singapore successfully 'basket-pegged' the Singaporean dollar with the US dollar representing 80 per cent of the weight. But the Singaporean economy, small and dominated by tertiary industrial sectors, differs significantly from China's strongly manufacturing-oriented economy. The Singapore currency administrators have also never made public its currency weightings. The behaviour of Singaporean currency administrators is consistent with that of a creditor economy with long-term, mature domestic capital markets. McKinnon and Schnabl (2003) argue that the East Asian financial crisis in 1997 did not significantly affect the dollar weights of the regional currency basket. Instead, East Asian economies gradually created a 'dollar bloc' with Japan as a dangerous outlier. China currently pegs its currency to a basket of other currencies, it has not made public the weighting of each currency in the basket, but, obviously, it should be appropriate to that currency's status in the Asian region.

China is clearly a member of the broader Asian 'dollar bloc' (see Tables 3.1 and 3.2). The ratio of Asian economies plus the United States overwhelms the currency demand for trade and investment from all other economies. Therefore, application of the 'basket-pegged' strategy would not significantly alter the *status quo*. McKinnon found 52.4 per cent and 70.7 per cent of Japanese exports and imports respectively were invoiced in US dollars in 2000. Williamson (2000) proposed a pegged weight of 33 per cent to the dollar, the yen and the euro in the aftermath of the East Asian financial crisis. While this weight would reduce variance in the Japanese yen, it may not be the best option for smaller East Asian economies. The spot exchange rate of the dollar against RMB for 60 days or 90 days would be more uncertain with a 'basket-pegged' weight.

The Chinese government uses the US dollar as an intervention currency and is obliged to continue to adjust the yuan/dollar rate in response to fluctuations in the dollar against the yen and euro. The timing is not yet right for a freely floating rate because China has not yet developed the necessary mature and long-term domestic capital markets, and domestic financial institutions still struggle with non-performing loans. Acceleration of exchange rate reform would only create further uncertainties in the financial system.

Table 3.1　**Trade weights of China's trading partners, 2003** (per cent)

	Asia	Japan[a]	Oceania	Europe	North America
Exports	0.51	0.14	0.02	0.20	0.22
Imports	0.66	0.18	0.02	0.17	0.09

Note: [a] Also included in calculations for Asia
Sources: International Monetary Fund, 2004. 'China customs statistics', *Direction of Trade Statistics,* International Monetary Fund, Washington, DC.

Table 3.2　**Ratio of foreign investment, 2002** (per cent)

East Asia[a]	Hong Kong	Japan	European Union	North America	United States
61.45	33.86	7.94	7.03	11.4	10.28

Note: [a] Hong Kong, Macao, Taiwan, Japan, Philippines, Thailand, Malaysia, SIngapore, Indonesia and Korea.
Source: Ministry of Commerce, 2003, Beijing. Available online at http://www.mofcom.gov.cn/article/200307/20030700112770_1.xml

Exchange parity

Historically, the RMB has 'crawled', with the official rate periodically falling to converge with the swap and black rate multilateral exchange rates (Ding Jianping 1998). Studies confirm that the Chinese administration has set the RMB exchange rate on the basis of the domestic cost per unit of foreign exchange earned through exporting since 1955. This strategy is a variant of adjusting the exchange rate in accordance with the purchasing power parity of tradable prices. Reforms have strengthened the relationship between the exchange rate and the purchasing power parity of tradable prices and increased the significance and size of the effects from shocks in relative tradable prices (Zhang 2000). Although many countries have 'crawling' pegs, exchange parities differ for targets such as inflation, foreign trade and economic growth. While each target is associated with some trade-offs, the external demand drivers are emphasised to avoid overvaluation of the currency and to make domestic currencies more competitive.

Three enterprises taken from a survey of the top 54 enterprises in Jiangsu province between 2001 and 2003 revealed that the domestic cost per unit of foreign exchange earned through exports was 7.732 yuan, 7.703 yuan and 7.685 yuan per US dollar respectively, with the profit margin of exports 6.96 per cent, 7.36 per cent and 7.61 per cent. This should be compared with the nominal exchange rate. The profit margin differs between industrial sectors. Profit margins tend to be high in the machinery-manufacturing sector but low for textile and apparel manufacturers due to the different investment intensity and recent price increases for input materials. In addition to inflation and trade variables, GDP and the value of economic growth play an increasingly important role in determining exchange parity. The asset and monetary approaches to exchange rates stress the effects of variable Y, being output or income, because economies must maintain both internal and external equilibrium. Exchange rates are calculated not only on the basis of bilateral inflation, productivity, trade and interest variables but also increasingly on multilateral variables. Therefore, China's economic growth with that of the rest of world is essential to determine exchange rate parity (Table 3.3).

If the rate of growth is sustained, the RMB will continue to appreciate. Ding (2003) correlated economic growth and the real (nominal) exchange rate in Asian economies during the period 1970–2000, finding that, in South Korea, Malaysia, Thailand, Philippines and Indonesia, appreciation of the nominal exchange rate was related to GDP growth. China, Taiwan and Thailand all currently link appreciation of the real exchange rate with economic growth. Although the correlation results are not significant, trends are evident. In addition, causality tests of some industrialised and emerging-market economies offer support for the trend (Table 3.4).

Table 3.3   **Comparison of GDP growth rates**

	Global GDP constant (2000,US$ trillion)	Growth rate of world economy (%)	China GDP constant (2000,US$bn)	Growth rate of Chinese economy (per cent)
1990	23.9	2.9	413	3.8
1991	24.3	1.6	451	9.2
1992	24.8	2.2	515	14.2
1993	25.3	1.7	584	13.5
1994	26.1	3.3	658	12.6
1995	26.9	2.8	727	10.5
1996	27.7	3.4	797	9.6
1997	28.8	3.7	867	8.8
1998	29.5	2.4	934	7.8
1999	30.4	3.1	1001	7.1
2000	31.6	4.0	1081	8.0
2001	32.0	1.4	1162	7.5
2002	32.6	1.8	1258	8.3
2003	33.5	2.8	1375	9.3

Source: The World Bank, 2005. *WDI Online*. Available online at http://devdata.worldbank.org/dataonline/.

Adjustment of exchange rates will not immediately reflect GDP growth rates. The timing of movements in 'crawling' exchange rates will relate to domestic and external government policies, with domestic issues usually outweighing external. Adjustments will not affect the exchange rate parity within the given time period (Figure 3.2).

Postponing or lengthening the duration of adjustment of the exchange rate will flatten the slope in a given time period, giving the economy a solid basis for development, but strong GDP growth will cause the currency to appreciate eventually.

A trade-off exists between the rate of 'crawling' and the width of the band of currencies included. Monetary administrators must choose between the margin of the band of currencies and the degree of the slope. Industralised economies have historically elected to widen the band of currencies, while developing economies prefer to 'jump' or abruptly alter the exchange rate parity. As an emerging market economy, China is more likely to take a gradual approach to altering the exchange rate and widening the band as the economy develops.

Table 3.4   **Granger test of nominal exchange rate**

	Thailand	Korea	Japan	Indonesia	UK
Trade account	-	-	**	-	-
GDP value	-	***	**	**	*
GDP growth	-	-	-	-	**

Notes: Trade accounts are calculated from exports minus imports; GDP is gross domestic product in value; GDP growth implies the growth rate of GDP. * = significant at the 0.10 level; ** = significant at 0.05 level; *** = significant at 0.01 level using a two-tailed test.
Source: The World Bank, 2005. *WDI Online.* Available online at http://devdata.worldbank.org/dataonline/.

The next step for exchange rate adjustment

Most developing economies have used the 'crawling' exchange rate mechanism and China is no exception. Exporters remain subject to foreign exchange rate surrender requirements, and the People's Bank of China has engaged in sterilisation operations to maintain the stability of the RMB and domestic prices. While this strategy has increased foreign exchange reserves, the economy is at risk of rising inflation. It is therefore expected that market mechanisms will be introduced into the existing 'crawling' regime to counterbalance inflationary pressures. Interest rates must be market-oriented to reflect market demand and supply, and to allow forward transactions and other exchange derivatives to cover exchange risks and the exposure of positions. Under the present arrangements, firms have no incentive because the RMB floating margin is too narrow to make forward transactions worthwhile. Nevertheless, international speculators still trade in 'non-deliverable forwards' on the RMB, betting on future depreciation or appreciation, because the RMB is a non-convertible currency (Figure 3.3).

Non-deliverable forwards are foreign exchange derivative products traded over-the-counter. Parties to a non-deliverable forward contract settle the transaction, not by delivering the underlying pair of currencies, but by making a net payment in a convertible currency, typically the US dollar. The net payment is proportional to the difference between the agreed forward exchange rate and the subsequently realised spot fixing. Non-deliverable forwards are distinct from deliverable forwards in that they trade outside the direct jurisdiction of the authorities of the corresponding currencies and pricing is not constrained by domestic interest rates (Ma 2004). The previous width of the band can be estimated using data from Figure 3.3 (Table 3.5).

If the non-deliverable forward rate for the RMB in 2002 is the standard parity, heavy depreciation pressures occurred in 1988–2001, while appreciation pressures

Figure 3.2   Timing options for the adjustment of parity in 'crawling' exchange regimes

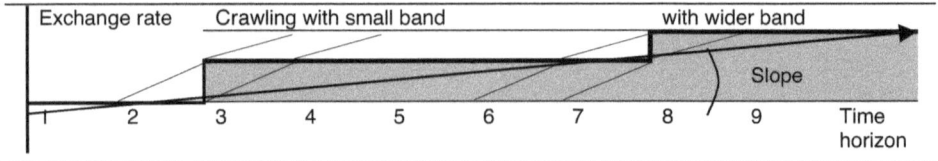

Source: Authors' calculations.

existed in 2003–05. The Chinese economy is not yet ready to cope with a wider band of currencies. The non-deliverable forward market offers an alternative hedging tool for foreign investors with RMB exposure or a speculative instrument to take positions offshore. The use of non-deliverable forwards by non-residents also reflects broader restrictions on access to the domestic forward market.

'Crawling' with a sustainable band width

As the slope of the exchange rate becomes steeper, the width of the band of exchange currencies will become narrower. The width of the band challenges the effectiveness of central bank intervention. Intervention by the People's Bank of China differs from most industrialised economies because China occupies a unique position in the Asian region. Most economies in the region peg their currencies to the US dollar, and Sino-US trade is the dominant trade flow in the region. Therefore, China must approach intervention in the exchange market with caution. The band of fluctuation in the RMB rate will widen in response to the approach used by neighbouring economies and the share of export trade (Table 3.6).

Reform of the exchange rate regime in China is a long-term process aimed at increasing the flexibility of engagement in international exchange markets. China occupies a difficult position between Japan, with its independently floating exchange rate, and other Asian economies, who are members in the 'dollar-pegged' group. There is scope for China to become jointly involved, but the People's Bank of China would need to carefully consider the level of market intervention undertaken by the Bank of Japan. The Chinese foreign exchange market is relatively small in comparison to Japan, so the People's Bank of China would need to be able to mobilise foreign exchange reserves to stabilise the market for a similar policy to be appropriate (Table 3.7). Large foreign exchange reserves and a willingness by central banks to defend currencies by selling reserves make East Asian economies unusual.

Figure 3.3   **Market speculations against RMB at NDF rates,1998–2004**

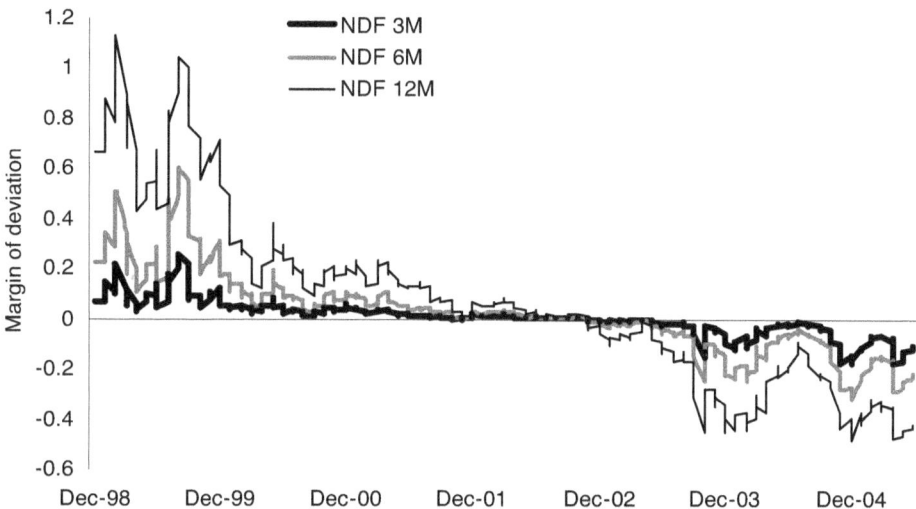

Note: The deviation implies the NDF rate minus the official rate
Source: Capital Market China, Calyon, Crédit Agricole Group's Corporate and Investment Bank, 2005.

Prerequisite to RMB flexibility

Restoring the market mechanism to the RMB exchange rate is not a straightforward task. So far, the RMB has no domestic forward market and its interest rates are separated from world interest rates (rates are not synchronised with those of the United States, although the RMB rate has been pegged on the US dollar in the past). Without the forward market, exchange derivatives of RMB cannot be formulated accordingly. However, its forward market rests on RMB interest rate movements reflecting market demand and supply. According to the interest rate parity, the flow of assets (money, capital and so on) from one economy to another will eventually be ironed out by changes in either interest or exchange rates. Chinese multinational corporations are able to cover exchange risks by using forward transactions. At present, China's interest rates and those of the rest of the world are not synchronised over time (Figure 3.4).

Since South Korea and Taiwan have their exchange market integrated into the world market, we compare the non-deliverable forward markets in order to discern market distortion or efficiency. Interest rates in Taiwan closely follow those of the

Table 3.5   **Estimated width of bands for the RMB, 1989–2005**

NDF rates	Depreciation	Appreciation	Band +, per cent	Band -, per cent
3 month	8.53	8.0924	3.1439	2.148
6 month	8.875	7.95	7.3156	3.869
12 month	9.3999	7.785	13.6626	5.865

Source: Authors' calculations

Table 3.6   **Uncertainty about the currency band width**

	Exchange regime	China's export share* (per cent)	US$ for exports (average, per cent)	Width of band to intervene
Hong Kong, Taiwan, Macao, South Korea, Thailand, Indonesia, India, Malaysia, Singapore	Pegged or semi-pegged exchange regimes	26	93	Will all Asian economies intervene jointly?
Japan	Floating regime	14	70	Unilaterally act to intervene?
United States	Floating regime	21	96	Unilaterally act to intervene?

Source: Adapted from International Monetary Fund, *China Customs Statistics*, Direction of Trade Statistics, International Monetary Fund, Washington, DC.

Table 3.7   **The Japanese and Chinese foreign exchange markets**
           (US$ billion)

	1998	1999	2000	2001	2002	2003
Japanese intervention	23.6	65.6	28.2	27.3	31.7	173.8
Chinese transactions	52.0	31.5	42.2	75.0	97.2	151.1

Note: Japanese intervention refers to the annual volume of absolute intervention. Chinese transactions refer to the annual volume of transactions in the Chinese foreign exchange market.
Source: Ministry of Finance, 2003. Tokyo. Available online at http://www.mofcom.gov.cn/article/200307/20030700112770_1.xml. State Foreign Exchange Administration and China Foreign Exchange Trading Center, 2003. *China Foreign Exchange Market Annual Report*, State Foreign Exchange Administration and China Foreign Exchange Trading Center, Beijing.

United States, as do those of South Korea. Chinese interest rates, however, do not seem to have any relationship to those of the United States (Figure 3.4). If the forward exchange rate is equal to the expected future spot rate, then the forward premium is also equal to the expected change in the exchange rate and uncovered interest rate parity will hold. The expected change in the exchange rate is equal to the interest differential. The foreign exchange market is in equilibrium when deposits of all currencies offer the same expected rate of return. With interest rate data of three economies, the forward exchange rate based on covered interest parity (CIP) can be derived according to the following formula.

$$S_{t+1} = \frac{(R_h - R_f)}{(1 + R_f)} \times S_t + S_t \tag{3.1}$$

S_{t+1} implies that the future covered rate (CIP) can be regarded as interest differential (or risk premium) plus spot rate S_t. R_h and R_f represent the home and foreign interest rates respectively. Although S_{t+1} can be calculated as long as the interest rates of relative economies are available, this calculation does not reflect reality in some cases. This is the condition of forward market efficiency where the forward rate equals the market's forecast rate. If forward rate (S_{t+1}, CIP) equals the forecast rate (here NDF is used as the proxy), there is no serious distortion in the exchange market—the market is efficient. The econometric estimation is carried out as follows. Data from three exchange markets are used to compare CIP and NDF.

$$NDF_{t+1,i} = \alpha + \beta CIP_i + \mu_{t+1,i} \quad (i=1, 2, 3) \tag{3.2}$$

Pairwise data with the Equation 3.2 are tested for stationary process and unit root. Many economic series are better characterised by unit roots, and an Augmented Dickey-Fuller Test is carried out.

All the data clearly indicate a stationary property and reject a hypothesis of a unit root at 1 per cent significance level. Therefore, it is necessary to identify whether two series (pairwise) have the same stochastic trend in common, and the regression analysis can reveal long-run relationships among time-series variables. Suppose CIP and NDF are integrated of order one, for some coefficient q, $NDF_t -$ $qCIP_t$ is integrated of order zero, then CIP_t and NDF_t are said to be cointegrated.

Tables 3.10 and 3.11 support the hypothesis that non-deliverable forward rates are based on covered interest parity in Taiwan and South Korea, bu not mainland China. The coefficients in the former are very high, with both reaching –0.999, and very weak in the latter, only reaching –0.295. The Granger causality tests cannot determine whether covered interest parity causes non-deliverable forwards or vice

Figure 3.4   **Comparison of interest rates across relative economies**

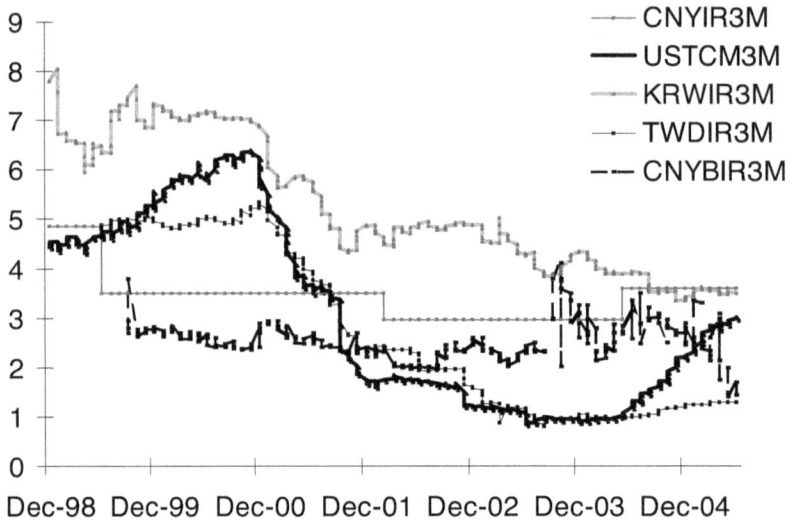

Notes: CNYIR3M: 3-month basic deposit rate (loan from the central bank to commercial bank) in China. USTCM3M: 3-month interest rate of Treasury Constant Maturities in the United States. KRWIR3M: 3-month Korean Interbank Offered Rates. TWDIR3M: 3-month Taiwan Interbank Offered Rates. CNYBIR3M: 3-month China's Interbank Bond Rates.
Source: Economagic.com, 2005. *Economic Time Series Page*. Available online from http://www.economagic.com/em-cgi/data.exe/fedstl/day-dexchus; http://www.pbc.gov.cn/detail.asp?col=462&ID=273. Capital Market China, Calyon, Crédit Agricole Group's Corporate and Investment Bank, 2005.

Table 3.8   **Augmented Dickey-Fuller test for the data**

Variable	Intercept	Lag	t-statistic
logNDF$_1$ (315 observations)	C	1	−1.248676
ΔlogNDF$_1$	C	1	−6.908235
logCIP$_1$ (315 observations)	C	1	−1.242992
ΔlogCIP$_1$	C	1	−6.264441
logNDF$_2$ (336 observations)	C	1	−0.717144
ΔlogNDF$_2$	C	1	−7.200970
logCIP$_2$ (336 observations)	C	1	−0.668972
ΔlogCIP$_2$	C	1	−7.082445
logNDF$_3$ (302 observations)	C	1	−2.062147
ΔlogNDF$_3$	C	1	−8.265479
logCIP$_3$ (302 observations)	C	1	−2.090392
ΔlogCIP$_3$	C	1	−12.02977

Notes: Taiwan=1, South Korea=2, and Mainland China=3; Δ=first difference
Source: Authors' calculations.

Table 3.9   **Johansen cointegration test**

Variables	Eigenvalue	Likelihood ratio	5 per cent critical value	1 per cent critical value	Hypothesised number of CEs[1]
NDF_1 CIP_1 lags 1-2	0.072817	23.67894	12.53	16.31	None ** [2]
	0.000289	0.090224	3.84	6.51	At most 1[3]
NDF_2 CIP_2 lags 1-3	0.047791	16.85180	12.53	16.31	None **
	0.001787	0.593671	3.84	6.51	At most 1
NDF_3 CIP_3 lags 1-5, with trend	0.074859	25.45596	25.32	30.45	None *
	0.008157	2.424406	12.25	16.26	At most 1

Notes: [1] CE is a abbreviation of cointegration equation. [2] *(**) denotes rejection of the hypothesis at 5 per cent (1 per cent). [3] Significance level L.R. test indicates 1 cointegrating equation at 5 per cent significance level.
Source: Authors' calculations.

Table 3.10   **Normalised cointegrating coefficients (with NDF_i coefficient as 1)**

	α	β	Trend	Log likelihood
CIP_1		−0.999892		2604.021
		(−4251.41)		
CIP_2		−0.999492		2487.757
		(−8866.99)		
CIP_3	−1.500058	−0.295160	7.94E-05	3119.100
		(−1.71779)		

Source: Authors' calculations.

Table 3.11   **Pairwise Granger causality tests**

Market	Hull hypothesis	Obs	F-statistic	Probability
Taiwan	CIP_1 does not Granger Cause NDF_1	312	7.31230	9.5E-05
	NDF_1 dose not Granger Cause CIP_1		0.76339	0.51533
South Korea	CIP_2 does not Granger Cause NDF_2	332	7.16285	1.5E-05
	NDF_2 dose not Granger Cause CIP_2		0.77521	0.54196
Mainland China	CIP_3 does not Granger Cause NDF_3	297	2.85747	0.01552
	NDF_3 dose not Granger Cause CIP_3		6.76865	5.5E-06

Source: Authors' calculations.

versa. The empirical results suggest that there is a long way to go for China to catch up to these emerging market economies, not to speak of industrialised economies. Without an RMB forward market, the establishment of a market mechanisms in China rings hollow. Further reform of RMB also rests on successful reform of the interest rate mechanism in the money market.

Conclusion

China will maintain some of the features of past regimes with an option to broaden the band of currencies gradually as the economy develops in the long term. The width of the band reflects market expectations, while restricting the flow of international 'hot money'. The fluctuation of non-deliverable forward rates reveals market expectations about the exchange forward market. Any gradual relaxation of exchange rate controls must be made with consideration of the actions of other Asian economies. Any unilateral actions would be ineffective. The 'crawling' feature will remain a key adjustment component of the exchange mechanism in China in the near future.

Acknowledgment

This study was financed by the project of National Natural Science Foundation of China.

References

Capital Market China, Calyon, Crédit Agricole Group's Corporate and Investment Bank, 2005.

Cowitt, P.P. (ed), various issues. *World Currency Yearbook*, Pick Publishing Corporation, New York.

Ding, J., 1998 'China's exchange black market and exchange flight–analysis on exchange policy', *The Developing Economies*, 36(1):24–44.

— —, 2003. 'Exchange rate volatility and economic growth in Asia', *World Economy*, 7:15–22 [in Chinese].

Dornbusch, R., and Park, Y.C., 1999. "Flexibility or Nominal Anchors?', in S. Collignon, J. Pisani-Ferry, and Y.C. Park (eds), Exchange Rate Policies in Emerging Asian Economies, Routledge, New York.

Goldstein, M., 2005. 'Renminbi appreciation seen in China's own best interest', *International Monetary Fund Survey*, 34(2):28–30.

International Monetary Fund, various issues. *International Financial Statistics*, International Monetary Fund, Washington, DC.

— —, various issues. 'China customs statistics', *Direction of Trade Statistics*, International Monetary Fund, Washington, DC.

Kawasaki, K. and Ogawa, E., 2003. What should be weights on the three major currencies for a common currency basket in East Asia?, Paper presented at Regimes and Surveillance in East Asia conference, Kuala Lumpur, 27–28 March.

Ma, G., 2004. 'Non-deliverable forward markets in Asian currencies', *China Money*, December, 38:4–11.

McKinnon, R. and Schnabl, G., 2003. The East Asian dollar standard, fear of floating, and original sin, Paper presented at Regimes and Surveillance in East Asia conference, Kuala Lumpur, 27–28 March.

Ministry of Commerce, 2003. Beijing. Available online at http://www.mofcom.gov.cn/article/200307/20030700112770_1.xml

Ministry of Finance, 2003. Tokyo. Available online at http://www.mof.go.jp/english/elc021.htm

State Foreign Exchange Administration and China Foreign Exchange Trading Center, 2003. *China Foreign Exchange Market Annual Report.*

Williamson, J., 2000. *Exchange Rate Regimes for Emerging Markets: reviving the intermediate option*, Institute for International Economics. Washington, DC

— —, 2004. 'The choice of exchange rate regime: the relevance of international experience to China's decision', paper presented at Reform of Exchange Rate Regime: international experience and China's selection conference, Beijing, 7–8 September.

World Bank, 2005. *WDI Online*, World Bank, Washington, DC. Available online at http://devdata.worldbank.org/dataonline/.

Zhang, Z., 2000. 'Exchange rate reform in China: an experiment in the real targets approach', *The World Economy*, 23(8):1057–81.

— —, 2004. When and how will China change its exchange rate policy? An historical perspective, Paper presented at Reform of Exchange Rate Regime: international experience and China's selection conference, Beijing, 7–8 September.

4

Demographic transition: implications for growth

Cai Fang and Dewen Wang

China will need to maintain an annual GDP growth rate of 7.2 per cent to meet official ambitions to raise the general prosperity of Chinese society, with GDP in 2020 predicted to be four times the level in 2000. Achievement of this goal would mean that China had sustained a high rate of annual economic growth for more than 40 years. This would not be unique. Economies in Asia, such as Korea, Malaysia, Singapore, Thailand and Hong Kong all sustained economic growth of more than 7 per cent per annum between 1960 and 2000 (Table 4.1). Growth patterns in the Japanese economy over the past 40 years, however, offer an alternative model. Between the early 1950s and mid 1970s, the Japanese economy grew quickly and overtook many industrial economies. High rates of economic growth in the 1980s were the product of an unsustainable 'bubble economy'; growth has stagnated since the bubble burst in the 1990s. The annual growth rate in Japan was 5.3 per cent between 1960 and 1990 but only 1.5 per cent during the 1990s.

What factors stimulate sustainable economic growth and what are the reasons for low growth rates? The literature is extensive. Growth economists consider a range of factors to explain economic growth, such as the domestic and international economic and political environment, improving education and public health standards, the implementation of family-planning and labour market policies, and policy support for greater international trade and savings (Barro 1997; Bloom et al. 2002). Demographic factors, especially the population and age structures, affect economic development. The reduction of high fertility rates creates opportunities for economic growth when accompanied by education, health and labour-market policies (Bloom et al. 2002). Sustained, rapid economic growth in East Asia demonstrates that developing economies can move swiftly to bridge the income gap with industrial economies. Recent studies indicate these successes can be attributed to a considerable extent to the demographic transition that occurred in East Asian economies (Bloom and Williamson 1997; Williamson 1997).

Demographic transitions in East Asian economies began in the 1940s and 1950s. Prior to 1970, economic growth potential was limited, income per capita was low and accompanied by a high child-dependence ratio. The average per capita GDP growth rate was estimated at only two per cent. As a result of the demographic transition, the proportion of the working population to the total population increased, while the population dependence ratios declined (Table 4.1). These population trends favoured the labour supply and savings rate and provided an additional source of economic growth—the demographic dividend. According to Williamson (1997), between 1970 and 1995, East Asian economies grew at average annual rate of 6.1 per cent, 4.1 percentage points above the steady state growth rate. Demographic transition contributed 1.5 to 2.0 percentage points to the steady state growth rate, accounting for one-quarter to one-third of the actual growth rate and one-third to one-half of the steady state growth rate during the period.

As the demographic transition progresses, the aging of the population reduces the productiveness of the population and reduces the demographic dividend. Japan completed the demographic transition first in East Asia and now has the most rapidly aging population among developed economies. Some researchers (Hewitt 2003) attribute the sustained stagnation of the Japanese economy to its rapidly

Table 4.1   Growth rates and dependence ratios in East Asia

	China	Japan	Korea	Hong Kong	Singapore	Thailand	Malaysia
GDP growth Rate (per cent)							
1960–70	2.7	9.4	7.4	8.9	8.5	7.0	5.9
1970–80	6.3	4.5	7.5	9.4	8.9	6.9	7.9
1980–90	9.4	4.1	8.7	6.5	7.4	7.9	6.0
1990–2000	10.1	1.5	6.3	4.6	7.7	4.6	7.2
1960–2000	7.8	5.3	7.9	7.8	8.7	7.1	7.1
Average dependence ratios (per cent)							
1960–70	79.2	49.1	84.7	75.3	81.8	95.1	95.4
1970–80	75.3	47.1	71.2	57.0	59.0	89.1	84.1
1980–90	56.9	46.3	52.4	44.8	41.9	66.1	72.3
1990–2000	53.3	49.0	45.5	45.1	43.6	54.9	71.7
1960–2000	65.0	46.8	62.4	54.6	55.8	74.9	79.3

Source: The World Bank, 2003. *World Bank Online Database*. Available online at http://devdata.worldbank.org/dataonline/.

aging population and inadequate pension system. The dependence ratio in Japan declined much earlier than in other East Asian economies and then rose again, suggesting that, as the population aged, Japan lost an additional source of economic growth (Table 4.1).

With the implementation of family-planning programs, China has undergone demographic transition more rapidly than most industrial economies. Challenging questions currently face Chinese scholars and policymakers. First, will China become an aging society before it becomes wealthy (Jackson and Howe 2004)? Second, how can China sustain the demographic dividend through policy adjustments? Third, through what other sources can China generate a demographic dividend? This chapter attempts to answer these questions by identifying the turning point where the demographic dividend becomes the demographic debt, analysing the mechanisms by which the demographic transition affects economic growth, and estimating the contribution of the population factor to economic growth.

Demographic transition, demographic dividend and sources of growth

A variety of theoretical models is used to illustrate the relationship between population and economic growth. These models also indirectly influence the orientation of policymakers. Prolonged debates have not produced a consensus.Observation reveals a conflict between the facts and theoretical assertions (Hodgson 1988). Population should be acknowledged as a factor affecting the conditions of economic growth, but the nature of population's impact on economic growth is uncertain, although its influence is certainly not independent (Kelley 1988). One shortcoming in conventional economic theories of growth is that theories consider population change as a steady process—that is, they only focus on the magnitude and growth of population, while neglecting changes in the age structure during the demographic transition (Williamson 1997).

The process of demographic transition is characterised by a time differential, as the decline of the birth rate and mortality moves through three phases, from a high dependence ratio of children to a high proportion of working population and finally a high dependence ratio of the aged. Different age groups within the population have different consumption patterns, savings behaviour and labour participation, and therefore different age groups will have specific effects on economic growth. A high proportion of aged population and/or children increases the burden on society of dependents and reduces productive, therefore negatively affecting

36

economic growth. Similarly, when the working population is relatively larger, the population structure is more productive because the labour supply and savings rates are larger. The demographic dividend is created in these circumstances (Bloom et al. 2002). A developing economy or region with a productive population structure can take full advantage of the potential demographic dividend. The demographic dividend provides an additional source of economic growth. Changes in the population structure during the demographic transition have both a direct and indirect impact on economic growth.

The first impact is through the effects of labour supply on growth. The growth of the working population may not keep pace with the growth of the total population during the process of demographic transition. The demographic transition changes particular segments of the population as it passes through the three phases. While the working population grows more slowly relative to the total population, the population must assume a greater economic burden for dependents. In contrast, faster growth of the working population relative to the total population is accompanied by a declining economic burden on the population. Without economies of scale, the production process and factors of production could be substituted for one another and changes in the labour supply would have little effect on long-run growth. However, the division of labour creates economies of scale and a decreasing labour supply will weaken the effects of the division of labour and reduce total output and income per capita. Even assuming the unchanged productivity of labour, any reduction in the magnitude of labour supply will cause a proportional reduction in total output.

The second effect is the impact of changes in the population structure on the relative shares of consumption and savings in national income (Kelly 1973). Demographic transition is a prolonged process, encompassing the full lifespan of individuals or even several generations. Over an individual's lifespan, savings will increase upon entering the workforce and decrease in retirement. Thus, the national savings rate and overall national capital formation will rise as the working population increases. As the population ages, public investment expenditure increases with the provision of pensions and medical care. As the proportion of non-productive expenses in total income increases, the proportion of public investment in productive investment declines. Decline in the levels of private savings and public investment reduces the growth of total output and income per capita. Peterson (1999) summarises six negative effects of an aging population for society. Feldstein (1995) finds an increase in social security expenses crowds out 60 per cent of private savings. Another study (Pench 2000) demonstrates that shocks from the labour supply and public finances will negatively affect economic growth rates in the European Union and Japan by 0.5 percentage points and the United States by 0.25 percentage points.

In China, the demographic transition began to occur as early as the 1950s. Its first effect was a dramatic decline in the mortality rate. In 1950, the mortality rate in China was 19 per 1,000, whereas the birth rate was 37 per 1,000. The natural rate of population growth was a high 19 per thousand. In the following two decades, with the exception of 1960, the mortality rate continued to decline and was accompanied with a more slowly declining birth rate. As a result, the natural rate of population growth increased, a trend which continued until its peak in the 1960s. The introduction of family-planning programs and the effects of socioeconomic factors combined to alter population trends, and the birth rate began to decline gradually in the 1970s. Since the 1980s, the birth rate and natural growth rate of population have declined significantly as a result of economic and social reforms and the adoption of strict state family-planning policies in urban and rural areas.

The structure of age within the population changes as the demographic transition moves through the three consecutive phases. The proportion of children in China's total population has declined and the proportion of working population increased, while the proportion of the aged population has not increased significantly. In the period between 1953, when first National Census was conducted, and 2000, when the fifth National Census was conducted, the proportion of children (0–14 years old) dropped from 36.3 per cent to 22.9 per cent, the proportion of working population (15–64 years old) increased from 59.3 per cent to 70.2 per cent, and the proportion of the aged population (65 years old and above) increased from 4.4 per cent to 7 per cent (National Bureau of Statistics 2001). Changes in the population structure have reduced population dependence, in terms of both child and overall dependence, and enhanced the productiveness of the population (Figure 4.1). The result has been strong labour supply and high savings rates, defined as the ratio of fixed asset value to total GDP, and potentially an additional source of economic growth — the so-called demographic dividend.

Given the potential economic advantages from the age structure of a population, high labour force participation and employment allow the productive use of human resources engendered by the population structure. In the period from 1978 to 2002, the size of the economically active population steadily increased and the labour force participation rate reached 70–86 per cent (Figure 4.2) — higher than

Figure 4.1   **Changes in the population dependence and savings rate**

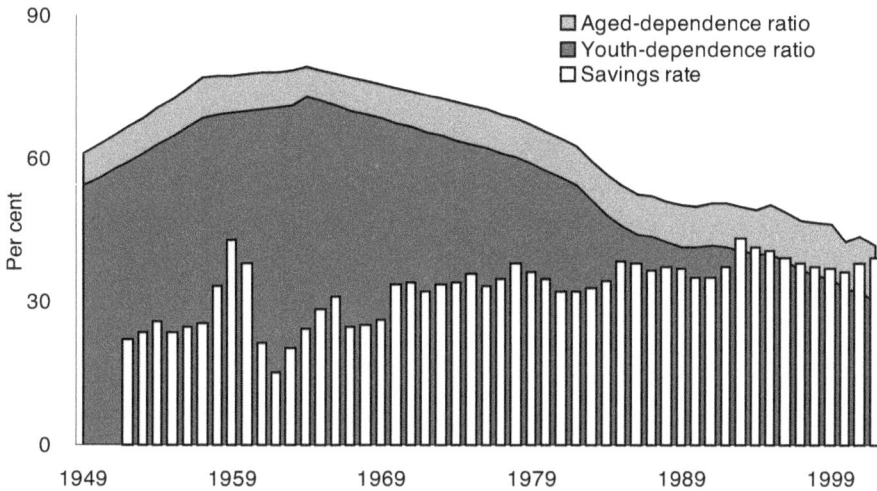

Source: National Bureau of Statistics (NBS), various issues. *China Population Statistic Yearbook*, China Statistics Press, Beijing.

most economies around the world. Despite changes in sectors of the economy and ownership structures, economic growth has driven employment growth in urban and rural areas. With favourable labour endowments and increasing expanded opportunities for employment, economic growth in China has been supported by an ample supply of low-cost labour, enabling the transformation of an advantageous population structure into a comparative advantage in labour-intensive industries.

The growth of the economically active population and employment has produced an economic surplus and helped China establish a high savings rate. The savings has remained more than 30 per cent and peaked at 44 per cent in 1993 (Figure 4.1), primarily because of the decline in the total dependence ratio under the development of markets for production factors, which has lessened the social burdens of dependents and enhanced the productiveness of the population.

The demographic transition and savings rate

Although there is little evidence of an absolute positive correlation between the savings rate and income levels, a critical minimum savings rate is an important

Figure 4.2   **Economically active population, employment, and labour force participation**

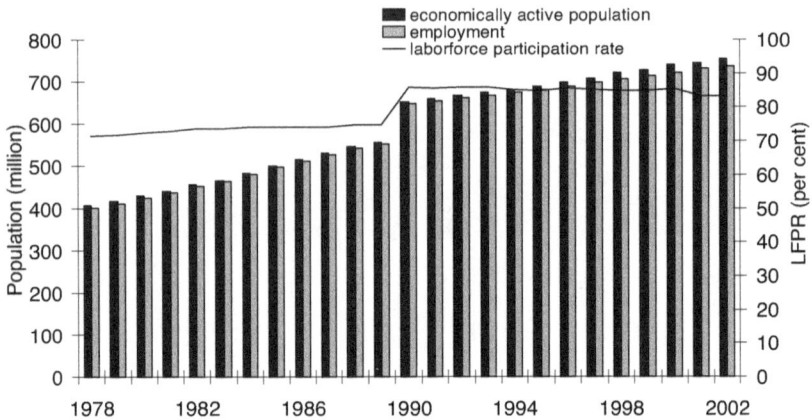

Note: Labour force participation rate is the ratio of economically active population to working population; working population is calculated based on *China Population Statistic Yearbook*.
Source: National Bureau of Statistics (NBS), various issues. *China Population Statistic Yearbook*, China Statistics Press, Beijing.

factor for developing economies to take off and a sustained high level of savings is necessary for long-term growth. The general level of income per capita and growth rate are preconditions to obtain the minimum savings rate. Savings rates in high and middle-income countries are generally greater than those in low-income countries (Table 4.2) because households at subsistence level have little surplus income for savings. Savings rates tend to be higher when incomes are rising. During their economic take-off, East Asian economies such as Japan, South Korea, Thailand, Malaysia, Singapore and Hong Kong had high savings rates, which offer a good explanation for their economic performance. Savings rates in East Asian economies were significantly higher than both the world and developed economy averages (Table 4.2). For example, the savings rate in Japan was more than 35 per cent in the 1960s, while savings rates in Hong Kong, Korea, Thailand and Malaysia were 20 to 30 per cent in the 1970s and continued to increase during the subsequent two decades. As the Japanese economy and population matured, the savings rate dropped gradually during the 1980s and economic growth slowed in the 1990s.

Table 4.2   **Comparison of international savings rate** (per cent)

	1960–69	1970–79	1980–89	1990–99	2000–02
World average	24.5	25.3	23.4	23.1	21.6
High-income countries	25.6	25.5	23.1	22.8	20.6
Middle-income countries	-	25.3	25.7	25.3	26.1
Low-income countries	11.3	17.3	19.6	20.7	20.0
OECD countries	12.9	25.4	22.9	22.6	20.4
United States	19.9	19.6	17.8	17.0	15.4
Japan	35.3	35.6	31.8	30.7	26.9
European Union	-	24.8	21.4	22.6	22.4
East Asia region	-	27.8	31.6	36.4	35.8
China	-	30.5	34.7	40.9	41.1
Hong Kong	22.5	30.8	33.5	32.4	31.0
Korea	8.7	22.3	31.0	35.1	29.3
Thailand	18.7	22.3	26.5	35.3	31.1
Malaysia	21.9	27.1	30.2	40.7	43.8
Singapore	-4.0	28.6	41.7	48.2	45.6

Sources: World Bank, 2003. World Bank Online Database. Available online at http://devdata.worldbank.org/dataonline/.

The savings rate in China has continued to rise since the 1950s, with the largest fluctuation in the period between the Great Leap Forward and the Cultural Revolution. With the initiation of economic reforms in the late 1970s, income per capita has substantially increased and the savings rate has also steadily risen (Figure 4.3). The high savings rate has been viewed as a key factor contributing to rapid economic growth since the reforms. While most debates about the savings rate focus on government efforts to mobilise savings and capital market development, whether household savings and consumption behaviour has an impact on national savings and the extent of the impact has not been extensively discussed in the existing literature. As the Chinese economy continues to undertake market liberalisation and the structure of the population changes, the effects of the demographic transition on individual saving behaviour will have important implications for policymakers.

In addition to factors such as income level, the real interest rate, resident location in rural or urban areas, the mobility and maturity of the capital market and macroeconomic policies, demographic characteristics such as household size, household savings, consumption behaviour and population dependence have recently been included in models to explain the savings rate in the Chinese economy. Shi et al. (2002) constructed a model that explains the impact of the demographic

Figure 4.3   **Trends of savings rate and per capita GDP**

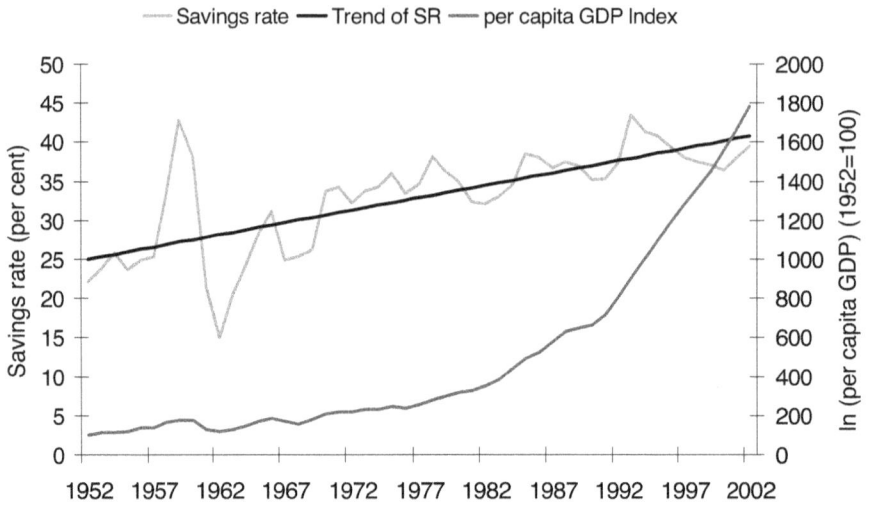

Source: National Bureau of Statistics (NBS), various issues. *China Population Statistic Yearbook*, China Statistics Press, Beijing.

transition on China's savings rate by employing variables such as the real interest rate, child-dependence ratio, aged-dependence ratio, and economic growth rate and time trends. Using a time-series dataset from 1958 to 1998, a cointegration regression was run, which showed that both the child and aged-dependence ratios were negatively correlated with the savings rate. However, the results are sensitive to the dataset. Leff (1969, 1971) ran a cross-section regression using data from 74 countries in 1964 and found variables such as per capita income, economic growth rate, child-dependence ratio, aged-dependence ratio and total dependence ratio have a significant effect on the national savings rate. Ram's (1982) further study used cross-section data of 128 countries in 1977 with similar findings.

Following Leff's (1969, 1971) model, this paper examines the impact of the Chinese demographic transition on the savings rate using a provincial panel data set. The data was collected in China's population censuses in 1982, 1990 and 2000, population sampling over 13 years (1987, 1989, 1991–99, 2001 and 2002), comprehensive statistical data and The Provincial Data in 50 years of People's Republic of China (1999) and *China Statistical Yearbooks* (2000–03) (all published by the National Bureau of Statistics). The variables are defined and generated as follows—the savings rate is the share of gross capital formation in GDP; per capita income equates to per capita GDP at 1952 constant prices; the economic growth rate is a five-year arithmetic average to eliminate the influence of annual economic fluctuations; the child-dependence ratio is the percentage of population-aged 0–14 years to population aged 15–64 years; the aged-dependence ratio is the percentage of population aged 65 years and above to population aged 15–64 years; the total dependence ratio is the summation of child-dependence ratio and aged-dependence ratio.

The regression results of equations (1) and (2) in Table 4.3 are based on the Ordinary Least Square method (OLS). Except for the variable of per capita income, the coefficients for other variables including economic growth, the child-dependence ratio, the aged-dependence ratio and total dependence ratio, are all significant at the statistical level of 1 per cent or 5 per cent, and directions are consistent with theoretical expectation. Heteroscedastic tests of regression equations (1) and (2) show the values of χ^2 are 7.01 and 3.74 respectively; p-values for rejecting constant variances are 0.008 and 0.05 respectively, indicating the existence of heteroscasticity.

When a regression equation has a heteroscedastic issue, the estimated coefficients are unbiased and consistent, but the statistical values of the regression equation, like the t-value and F-value, are inefficient. To overcome the problem, the Feasible Generalised Least Square method (FGLS) was run to generate equations (3) and (4). The significant difference between the results from the two methods is that the coefficients for variables of per capita income in the new equations reached the one per cent significance level, and the direction is consistent with theoretical expectations. The coefficients for variables of economic growth and dependence ratio are also significant, but the absolute values are less than equations (1) and (2).

The eastern region of China was chosen as a reference group. In all regression equations, coefficients for the central region dummy variable reached the one per cent significance level, but coefficients for the western region dummy variable were insignificant. Earlier economic reforms and liberalisation in the eastern region attracted a greater inflow of foreign capital and investment, which quickened economic growth there relative to other regions. Financial transfers from the central government contributed to savings and investment in the western region, but the absence of preferential policies has led to a low savings rate in the central region when other variables are held constant.

Apart from the regional dummy variables, the coefficient for other variables in Table 4.3 is values for the elasticity of savings rate. Absolute values for the elasticity of the child-dependence ratio, aged-dependence ratio and total dependence ratio are greater than for per capita income and economic growth, indicating the demographic age structure has an important effect on the savings rate.

Table 4.3   **Regression results of the demographic transition on savings rate**

Variables	OLS Method		FGLS Method	
	(1)	(2)	(3)	(4)
ln(per capita GDP)	0.013	0.015	0.044	0.040
	(0.89)	(1.05)	(3.44)**	(3.52)**
ln(average growth rate of				
GDP in the previous five years)	0.127	0.092	0.058	0.054
	(3.03)**	(2.23)*	(2.41)*	(2.53)*
ln(child-dependence ratio)	−0.186		−0.109	
	(3.25)**		(2.48)*	
ln(aged-dependence ratio)	−0.216		−0.113	
	(3.74)**		(2.59)**	
ln(total dependence ratio)		−0.225		−0.154
		(2.99)**		(2.97)**
Central region dummy	−0.216	−0.186	−0.178	−0.159
	(7.25)**	(6.64)**	(9.90)**	(10.73)**
Western region dummy	−0.035	0.009	−0.037	−0.006
	(1.02)	(0.28)	(1.50)	(0.33)
Intercept	4.622	4.377	3.749	3.734
	(15.21)**	(13.24)**	(16.57)**	(15.70)**
R^2	0.38	0.36		
Observations	426	426	426	426

Note: (1) Variables of year dummy are deleted for simplicity; (2) Absolute values of t-statistics in parentheses in equations (1) and (2); Absolute values of z-statistics in parentheses in equations (3) and (4); * significant at 5 per cent level; ** significant at 1 per cent level.
Source: Authors' calculations.

These results support Leff's (1969) findings. Although the coefficients for all variables are significant and the directions consistent with theoretical expectations, the absolute values for coefficients differ in magnitude with Leff's results. Based on cross-country data, Leff (1969) reported the values of the elasticity of savings rate of per capita income, economic growth rates, child-dependence ratio, aged-dependence ratio and total dependence ratio were 0.160, 0.025, −1.352, −0.399, and −1.489 respectively. The absolute values of coefficients for China are less than Leff's results. The greater variability in the cross-country dataset is the main reason for the difference between the magnitudes of the coefficients in Leff's results and this study. However, the provincial dataset used in this study has an advantage in that it effectively eliminates the unobserved effects of policies and institutions. These possible effects cannot be eliminated from a cross-country dataset. Another possible reason for the difference is the introduction of a year dummy variable into regression equations to control for temporary shocks on the savings rate. The coefficients of year dummy are significant with a range from 0.13 to 0.39, which may absorb some effects of other variables.

Based on the values of elasticity in equation (3), the average contribution of explanatory variables to the savings rate was calculated. The contribution of per capita income is 17 per cent. Of that, economic growth rates comprise 0.3 per cent, the child-dependence ratio 4.9 per cent, the aged-dependence ratio –5.1 per cent and total dependence ratio 5.1 per cent. There is a mutually opposing trend between the child-dependence ratio and aged-dependence ratio; the effects of each ratio counteract the other.

In assuming the child-dependence ratio and aged-dependence ratio affect the savings rate in the same way, equation (4) defines the relationships appropriately for further discussion. The contribution of total dependence ratio to savings rate was calculated as approximately 5.0 per cent. Dividing the contribution of the total dependence ratio into two components—namely, the contribution of child-dependence ratio and aged-dependence ratio—allows the relative changes to be examined. From 1982 to 2002, the total dependence ratio dropped by 33.3 per cent, of which –17.2 percentage points can be attributed to the decrease of child-dependence ratio and 017.2 percentage points to the increase of aged-dependence ratio. Therefore, the contribution of the child-dependence ratio to the savings rate is 6.0 per cent and the contribution of the aged-dependence ratio to the savings rate is –0.9 per cent.

From the discussion of the results summarised in Table 4.3, we can draw some conclusions. First, per capita income and economic growth rates are two important determinants of the savings rate. Second, the demographic transition has a significant impact on the savings rate. The decrease of child-dependence ratio reflects the reduction of both the economic burden on the working-age population and consumption expenditures for the national income, contributing to an increase in the savings rate. However, this effect is offset by the increase in the aged-dependence ratio as the population ages. Finally, dummy variables denoting regional policies and institutions have a significant role in explaining the savings rate.

Effects of demographic transition on growth

The steady-state growth of income per labour is theoretically determined by a series of variables that includes physical and human capital, technological advances, natural resources endowment, policies and institutions. This is illustrated as $y^* = X\beta$. Where y^* is the steady-state growth of income per unit of labour; X is a vector representing the initial conditional and structural variables, and β represents the marginal effects of the variables. In this standardised conditional convergence model, the factor of demographic transition is often excluded. However, if the variable of demographic transition is incorporated into the above steady-state growth equation, the following mathematical equation reveals that the demographic structure variable does have an impact on economic growth.

$$\tilde{y} = \frac{Y}{N} = \frac{Y}{L} * \frac{L}{N} = y\frac{L}{N} = y\frac{1}{(L+L*D)/L} = y\frac{1}{1+D}$$

Where Y is Gross Domestic Product (GDP), L is the number of labour force, N is the number of total population, D is the total dependence ratio, y is GDP per labour using the number of labour force as denominator and $\tilde{y}$ is per capita GDP. Applying logarithm manipulation to both sides of the formula, the growth rate of per capita GDP equals the growth rate of GDP per labour minus the logarithmic value of total dependence plus one, expressed as

The formula introduces the variable of demographic transition, demonstrating that the increase (decrease) of total dependence ratio has a negative (positive) impact on the growth of per capita income. The conditional convergence theory asserts that the growth of per capita GDP is a function of initial conditional variables and economic, policy and institutional structural variables. The demographic structure should be included as one of the structural variables determining long-run growth of per capita income. The regression equation can be expressed as

$$g_{\tilde{y}} = \beta_0 + \beta_1 \ln GDP78 + \beta_2 \ln Life82 + \beta_3 Invest + \beta_4 Open + \beta_5 Gov + \beta_6 D + e$$

where GDP78 represents the initial per capita GDP, Life82 represents the initial life expectancy, Invest represents the investment rate, Open represents the share of trade in GDP, Gov represents the share of government consumption in GDP, D represents the total dependence ratio, β_i represents parameters and e is the error term.

According to these theoretical assumptions, $\beta_2, \beta_3, \beta_4$ are positive, while $\beta_1, \beta_5, \beta_6$ are negative. After controlling for structural variables, the growth of per capita GDP is negatively correlated with the initial level of per capita GDP, which implies that it is possible for low-income regions to catch up with more advanced regions. Life expectancy is a proxy for the human capital stock variable. A longer life expectancy equates with a high stock of human capital, and is expected to have a positive effect on economic growth.[1] Investment is the sole means to increase physical capital stock. A higher investment rate can induce more rapid economic growth. Trade has been viewed as an important engine of economic growth. The share of trade in GDP was selected as an indicator of economic openness that indicates the level of regional market development and integration into the international market. Government intervention is generally assumed to have a negative impact on long-run economic growth. The share of government consumption in GDP is used as a proxy variable for government intervention. The total dependence ratio represents changes in the demographic structure, which can affect economic growth through the labour supply, savings rate and technological advances. These are negatively correlated with economic growth.

The dataset is from the same source used in in the previous section. Assuming that the long-run economic growth rate is the same as the steady-state economic growth rate is the most common method used. The effects of initial conditional variables and structural variables (Barro 1997, Bloom and Williamson 1997, Demerger et al 2002) on the long-run economic growth rate are examined. Given data availability, two periods of time were selected—1982 to 1990 and 1990 to 2000 for the regressions. There were two considerations; first, three population censuses conducted in 1982, 1990 and 2000 can provide the necessary detailed information about total population and age structure at a provincial level, and, second, the two periods of time have a close interval, 8 years and 10 years. Pooled data on a provincial level from the two time periods can substantially increase the sample observations and thus improve the efficiency and precision of regression estimation.

Dependent and explanatory variables are defined as follows. Per capita GDP growth rates are the provincial arithmetic average in each period of time. Initial per capita GDP is the logarithmic value of provincial per capita GDP in 1978. Investment, share of government consumption and openness ratios are also the provincial average values in each time period. The total dependence ratios are the average of provincial ratios in the same period of time. Because of the unavailability of data for Tibet, Hainan, Chongqing and Ningxia before 1990, there are 27 sample observations in the period between 1982 and 1990, while there are 28 in the period between 1990 and 2000.

Equations (1) and (2) are derived from regressions from the data from each period, while equations (3) and (4) are from regressions from the pooled data (Table 4.4). Equations (3) and (4) are more significant. In equation (4), equation (3) was expanded by introducing a time period dummy variable, but the coefficient was insignificant. Therefore the results from equation (3) are used for further analysis. The good fit (R^2) of the equation (3) indicates the regression equation can explain about 57 per cent of the variation in the economic growth rate. The coefficients for variables of the initial per capita GDP, investment ratio, openness, and total dependence ratio are all significant at the 5 per cent or 1 per cent levels. The coefficient for the variable of life expectancy is close to the 10 per cent significant level, but the share of government consumption is insignificant. The coefficients for all variables have the expected signs.

This study also focuses on the impact of the demographic transition on economic growth. In equation (3), the marginal effect of total dependence ratio is −0.115, implying an increase in the total dependence ratio of 1 percentage point will cause a decrease in economic growth of 0.115 percentage points. From 1982 to 2000, China's total dependence ratio dropped by 20.1 percentage points, contributing the equivalent of 2.3 percentage points to the growth rate. The average growth rate during the same period was 8.6 per cent. That is, about one-quarter of the growth rate in per capita GDP can be attributed to the decline in the total dependence ratio during the period.

Table 4.4   **Regression results of economic growth versus demographic transition (OLS)**

	1982–90	1990–2000	1982–2000	1982–2000
ln (per capita GDP in 1978)	−3.239	−2.933	−3.234	−2.801
	(3.53)**	(3.20)**	(5.64)**	(4.09)**
ln(Life expectancy in 1982)	−7.01	25.87	10.783	13.004
	(0.84)	(3.25)**	(1.84)	(2.11)*
Investment ratio	0.065	0.086	0.077	0.079
	(1.62)	(2.38)*	(2.63)*	(2.71)**
Share of government consumption	0.059	−0.272	−0.067	−0.114
	(0.55)	(2.15)*	(0.85)	(1.29)
Openness	0.088	0.021	0.039	0.033
	(3.29)**	(1.89)	(4.03)**	(3.12)**
Total dependence rate	−0.158	−0.031	−0.115	−0.072
	(2.25)*	(0.41)	(2.87)**	(1.33)
Time period dummy				0.745
				(1.15)
Intercept	61.629	−80.654	−14.126	−28.075
	(1.55)	(2.22)*	(0.54)	(0.98)
R²	0.48	0.69	0.57	0.58
Observations	27	28	55	55

Note: Absolute values of t statistics are in parentheses; * represents significance at 5 per cent; ** represents significance at 1 per cent.
Source: Authors' calculations.

Figure 4.4   **Predicted child-dependence ratio, aged population-dependence ratio and rate of population ageing**

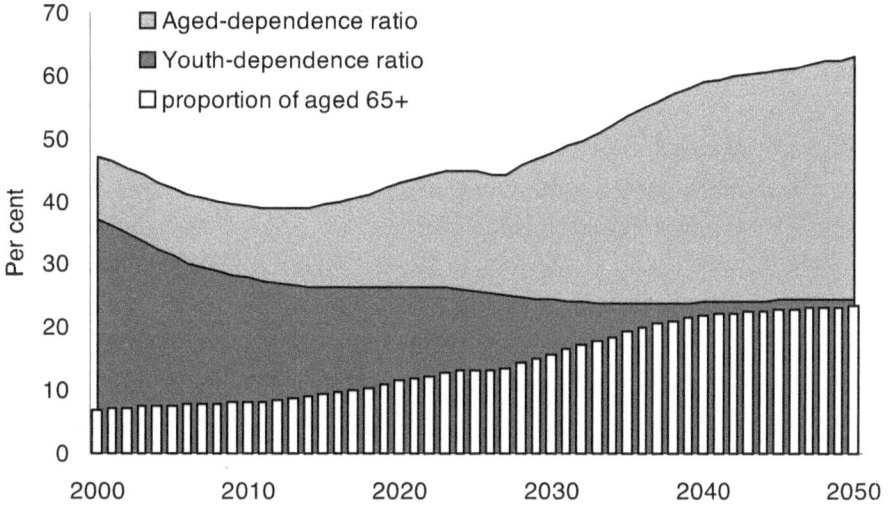

Source: Authors' own calculations, as based on data provided by China Center for Population and Development Studies.

Conclusion and policy implications

China has had the potential to take advantage of the demographic dividend since the mid 1960s, but reforms were necessary to take advantage of the potential sources of economic growth. Since the reforms, the decline of the total dependence rate has contributed 5 per cent to the increase in the savings rate and one-quarter of GDP growth. However, the increase in the working population will slow by about 2015, and the size of the aging population will increase (Figure 4.4). Recent predictions suggest the total dependence rate in China will further decline from 42.6 per cent in 2000 to 39.4 per cent in 2015, and the 3.2 percentage point drop in total dependence rate will add 0.4 percentage points to annual GDP growth. The demographic dividend will have contributed one-third of the annual economic growth rate before the turning point is reached in 2015, when the demographic dividend becomes a demographic debt. Most industrial countries have benefited from the demographic dividend, but this extra source of growth eventually ceases as the demographic transition is completed.

Fulling using the economic potential of its advantageous population structure will not only sustain economic growth, but also enable China to prepare for a rapidly aging population. The next 10 years are a critical period for China, to simultaneously reap the demographic dividend and promote alternative sources of economic growth. China has undertaken a demographic transition quickly—experience with unprecedented fast growth suggests the pace and direction of the demographic transition can be guided by appropriate government policies. The adjustment of population policies is needed to prevent the Chinese population from aging too rapidly. Industrial economy experience suggests the use of a favourable population structure as an extra source of growth can be replaced by other factors, such as fuller employment, improved education and health levels and more efficient institutional environments for economic activities.

Models of long-term economic growth assume the work-age population will remain fully employed and unemployment is only a phenomenon of the short-term business cycle. That is, stable labour force participation rates and full employment of the work-age population are assumed for regression analysis. If unemployment becomes a long-term problem for a high proportion of the economically active population, the total dependence rate will not reflect the actual population burden and the contribution of the potential demographic dividend will be less than the regression results would indicate. Since the late 1990s, radical reform of state-owned enterprises has caused massive unemployment and a fall in labour force participation in China. Increasingly, levels of employment and the economically active population have lagged behind increases in the size of the working population. Therefore a demographic dividend still exists. While economic growth is a precondition for full employment, maximum employment *per se* is a source of economic growth. The more effectively labour resources are utilised, the longer the demographic dividend is maintained and the advantageous development conditions, from low labour costs and high savings rates, can be maintained. These conditions will require further reforms in a variety of areas, including the elimination of institutional barriers that deter labour mobility and the market-based determination of wages.

While the greatest advantage of the demographic dividend in China has been the size of the labour force, this advantage will soon be lost. The accumulation of human capital through increasing returns has been fuelled by the enormous size of the labour force until now. The Chinese government faces two contemporary challenges. First, the reallocation of public investment in education is critical for improving education levels throughout the country. Second, it must promote the development of a more efficient labour market that encourages individuals and families to accumulate human capital through investment in education because returns to human capital can only be generated in the labour market.

The population structure will continue to age on average in the coming decades. China will need to establish a sustainable pension system and make some critical policy adjustments to safeguard society in this process. First, the transition from the pay-as-you-go system to a fully funded pension system must be immediately implemented. This transition will require setting up individual accounts for workers who entered the labour market after 1997, the year in which pension system reform began. Second, the government needs to undertake a variety of policy adjustments and public education programs to make society better informed and prepared for an aging population. Third, improving labour market efficiency is a critical condition for transformation of the pension system. Creating more work opportunities in the labour market and raising the retirement age will reduce the dependence of older people on social pensions by prolonging the number of years in the workforce. Including rural-to-urban migrant workers in the pension system will also enhance the total premium and financially support the transformation of the pension system.

Note

[1] The number of years of schooling was included in the regression, but the coefficient was insignificant.

References

Barro, R.J., 1997. *Determinants of Economic Growth: a cross-country empirical study*, MIT Press, Cambridge.

Bloom, D.E. and Williamson, J.G., 1997. *Demographic transitions and economic miracles in emerging Asia*, NBER Working Paper No.6268, National Bureau Economic Research, Massachusetts.

——, Canning, D. and Sevilla, J., 2002. *The Demographic Dividend: a new perspective on the economic consequences of population change*, RAND, California..

Demurger, S., Sachs, J.D., Woo, W.T., Bao, S., Chang, G. and Mellinger, A., 2002. 'Geography, economic policy and regional development in China', *Asian Economic Papers*, 1(1):146–97.

Feldstein, M., 1995. *Social security and saving: new time series evidence*, Working Paper No. 5054, National Bureau of Economic Research, Massachusetts.

Hewitt, P.S., 2003. *The gray roots of Japan's crisis*, Asia Program Special Report, No.107, Woodrow Wilson International Center for Scholars, Washington, DC.

Hodgson, D., 1988. 'Orthodoxy and revisionism in American demography', *Population and Development Review*, 14(4):541–69.

Jackson, R. and Howe, N., 2004. *The Graying of the Middle Kingdom: the demographics and economics of retired policy in China*, Center for Strategic and International Studies, Washington DC.

Kelly, A.C., 1973. 'Population growth, the dependence rate, and the pace of economic development', *Population Studies*, 27(3):405–14.

Leff, N. H., 1969. 'Dependence rates and savings rate', *American Economic Review*, 59(5):886–96.

——,1971. 'Dependence rates and savings rate: reply', *American Economic Review*, 61(3):476–80.

——, 1984. 'Dependence rates and savings rate: another look', *American Economic Review*, 74(1):231–33.

National Bureau of Statistics (NBS), 1999. *The Provincial Data in 50 Years of People's Republic of China*, China Statistic Publishing House, Beijing.

——, 2001. *Tabulation on the National Census in 2000*, China Statistic Publishing House, Beijing.

——, (various years). *China Population Statistical Yearbook*, China Statistic Publishing House, Beijing.

Pench, L., 2000. Ageing and economic growth in Europe, Paper presented at The Graying of the Industrial World: a policy conference on global ageing, Washington, DC, 25–26 January.

Peterson, P.G., 1999. *Gray Dawn: how the coming age wave will transfer America and the world*, Random House, New York.

Population Division of the Department of Economic and Social Affairs of the United Nations Secretariat, 2002. *World Population Prospects: the 2002 Revision and world urbanisation prospects—The 2001 Revision*, United Nations Secretariat, New York.

Ram, R., 1982. 'Dependence rates and aggregate savings: a new international cross-section study', *American Economic Review*, 72(3):537–44.

Shi, Y., Reza, S. and Zhu, L., 2002. The impact of changes in China's population-age structure on its national saving behavior: an empirical analysis, Department of Economics, National University of Singapore, Singapore (unpublished).

Williamson, J., 1997. *Growth, distribution and demography: some lessons from history*, NBER Working Paper No. 6244, National Bureau of Economic Research, Massachusetts.

World Bank, 2003, *World Bank Online Database*. World Bank, Washington, DC. Available online at http://devdata.worldbank.org/dataonline/.

Yang, Z., 1996. *Historical Population Data in China*, Reform Publishing House, Beijing.

5

Political institutions and economic growth

Tao Kong

Why have some economies grown and developed, while others have not? Why have some countries experienced rapid economic growth for extended periods, whereas growth in others halted after a relatively short phase? Explaining the erratic and uneven economic growth across countries and over time has been one of the most important and fascinating quests among economists and other social scientists.

Economic theory has indicated a series of determinants likely to affect economic growth significantly. Among these factors, some are immediate variables that explain economic growth in a direct growth accounting fashion, such as physical and human capital accumulation, population growth, technological progress or total factor productivity growth. However, reference to changes in factor endowments and productivity does not explain the ultimate causes of economic growth and development. Rather, it leads to another set of determinants, which fundamentally shape the proximate factors, and often include geographical factors, international integration, and institutions.

While acknowledging that a wide range of factors may significantly affect economic performance, this study focuses on the critical role of institutions in the process of economic growth. Institutions often refer to the quality of formal and informal sociopolitical arrangements (Matthews 1986; North 1990; Greif 1998; Hodgson 1988, 1998; Eggertsson 1990; Acemoglu et al. 2001). Amongst the various institutional variables, political institutions will be brought to the forefront due to the interrelated nature of political and economic decisions and outcomes. Major economic decisions based purely on economic logic are rare. The process of economic growth is always intertwined with political decision-making.

The main issues considered in this chapter concern the determinants of growth, the importance of institutional factors in shaping alternative feasible growth paths, and their implications. Specifically, it looks into the characteristics of political institutions and the incentive structures relating to various organisational forms, and examines their consequent economic growth effects. Specifically, by distinguishing institutional designs and outcomes, it suggests that governance quality is an important channel through which the growth effects of political institutions operate.

The search for the general pattern of economic performance based on aggregate political institutional characteristics does not necessarily (and presumably should not) suggest a unique economic outcome for a certain political institutional structure, regardless of the socioeconomic environment with which it is associated. This study acknowledges that 'economic behaviour is "embedded" in institutions and practices' (Radice 2000:722). Therefore, even if there is a general pattern as to how political institutions affect growth, the optimum implied by the general pattern may differ when applied to different countries.

The focal point of this study is the growth effects of political institutions, but in exploring these effects in reality it is impossible to escape too far from their context. It explores the political institutional characteristics that contributed to the growth path and overall economic performance of China in an international context. In addition, it looks at the implication of the statement that the optimal institutional structure for economic growth varies for countries at different levels of development.

Theoretical analysis

The literature puzzles

Economic growth is an immediate outcome of accumulation of various factors and productivity improvement, each of which is a function of underlying incentive structures. As North (1989, 1990) and many others have argued, such incentive structures—or, more fundamentally, the institutions that shape such incentive structures—are the deeper determinants of economic growth. Furthermore, since the Second World War a great deal of empirical work based on the varied experiences of myriad developing countries has provided a fairly robust foundation for analysis of the impact of institutional factors (including political institutions) on economic growth. Broadly speaking, there are emerging well-accepted statements on the merits of political institutions that engender a high quality of governance.

The established political science, political economy and economics literatures have acknowledged the important implications of political institutional factors on economic growth (Elster 1994; Engerman and Sokoloff 1994; Weingast 1995). The political institutional factors being widely discussed in both theoretical and empirical studies include regime types (Przeworski and Limongi 1993), electoral systems (Persson and Tabellini 2000), and legislative structures (Persson and Tabellini 2000). Many open questions related to the growth effects of political institutions remain, however, such as: what is the overall impact on growth of different political institutions?

Previous studies, which investigated the likely relationship between the patterns of governance and the aggregate characteristics of political institutional arrangements, are mainly theories from political science and political economy. The central theme in the related literature is that political institutional structure entails a trade-off between the credibility of the government's policy commitments and its flexibility of policymaking and implementation (Cox and McCubbins 2000, MacIntyre 2003). However, contingent on the relative risks argued by various researchers, the established literature forcefully pulls in opposite directions.

One school of thought stresses the risk of arbitrary government action and advocates political institutional structures that disperse power, thereby increasing the credibility of government policy commitments (Kydland and Prescott 1977, Clague 1997). A separation-of-power type of regime also tends to reduce the risk of discretionary government behaviour such as expropriation of private properties, thereby positively affecting economic performance (Henisz 2000a, 2000b, Clague 1998, Persson and Tabellini 1990, 2000). The other strand of thought, albeit with diverse reasoning, stresses the importance of flexibility and autonomy in the process of government policymaking and implementation—features often characterised by a centralised-power type of regime. It is argued that, with such political architecture, government is more likely to be able to act swiftly in response to external situations (Haggard 1990; MacIntyre 1994; Woo-Cumming 1999). The division in the literature presents a theoretical puzzle concerning the basic relationship between political institutional structures and their impact on governance quality.

Even more controversially, at the empirical front, existing studies have reached little consensus on whether a particular regime type is associated with a positive or negative overall impact. Or, as much research has concluded, perhaps the link between political institutions and growth, or economic performance in general, is insignificant (Przeworski and Limongi 1993; Benabou 1996; Brunetti 1997). Such inconclusiveness has led to calls for efforts to understand better the impact of political institutions on economic growth.

Key variables

Before elaborating the theoretical arguments, the key variables used in this chapter are introduced.

- With respect to the concept of institutions, while there are ideas of all kinds throughout the literature defining various notions of institutions, what they claim and imply often differs.[1] Following Lin and Nugent (1995), institutions are considered broadly as a set of human-devised constraints that structure human interaction, in part by aiding in forming expectations of what other people will do. Institutions are considered the elements that define the 'rules of the game'. They form the incentive structure of a society, and the political and economic institutions shape economic agents' behaviour.[2] In consequence, institutions are one of the underlying determinants of economic performance (Coase 1960, North 1989, 1994, 1999).

- Throughout this chapter, the phrases 'economic outcomes', 'economic growth' and the 'level of economic development' are used in precise ways. 'Economic outcomes' is used as the higher order descriptor and 'economic growth' is the indicator or dependent variable selected to study. 'Level of economic development' is used as a static descriptive term and income per capita is used as a proxy for it.

- The structure of political institutions is defined as how governmental decision-making powers are shared at the aggregate level among veto players. Such rules are usually granted by constitutions and other key laws (MacIntyre 2003).[3] This is a relatively generalised approach, which does not apply restrictively to modern western-style democracies, but includes a broader and continuous spectrum of the configuration of aggregate decision-making power among veto players. Political institutional structures shape the capacity and opportunity to exercise discretion over the rules that organise social life.

- Governance quality is a complex notion. It can take many forms and there may be tradeoffs between different dimensions of governance quality.[4] I define governance quality as the capacity of a government to internalise externalities. It particularly concerns the externalities that drive a wedge between the individual and social costs and benefits, where individuals do not fully recognise the positive or negative social effects in the process of individual optimisation. Essentially, the quality of governance is reflected in the capacity of a government to align the interests of self-seeking individuals with that of the society as a whole. In concrete terms, good governance results from government adjustment of incentives through means such as laws, regulatory policies, and the provision of other goods and services. With good governance, individual actors' optimising decisions on issues such as investment, education and environment will not deviate too much from the optimal choices for the society.

Importantly, good governance does not necessarily refer to a minimal level of interference by the state in economic affairs. Rather, with good governance, a state seeks to intervene in the economy in ways that internalise the external economic costs of private decisions. Equally important, good governance is not equivalent to good economic performance. If it were, the relationship between good governance and good economic performance would be tautological. Given the current definition, a certain level of governance quality may have very different implications for economic growth depending not only on other determinants of growth, but also the nature or characteristics of the governance itself.

Central arguments

To answer the question of 'how political institutional configurations affect governance quality' in the light of the diverging literature, this paper builds upon the arguments of political scientist MacIntyre (2003) and reconciles the two somewhat contradictory ideas by arguing that political institutional arrangements affect governance quality in a non-monotonic fashion.

Political institutions affect economic growth through the channel of governance quality characterised by two important desirable features, credibility and flexibility. Credibility particularly implies control of predatory and arbitrary government behaviour. Flexibility is about government enjoying a degree of insulation in the decision-making process and being able to respond to various circumstances decisively and in a timely manner. In terms of institutional structure, credibility is often achieved by separation of powers, whilst a relatively concentrated power-sharing structure is often endowed with flexibility and decisiveness. As a result, a balanced political institutional configuration is likely to deliver a higher quality of governance than political institutional configurations close to either extreme of the power-sharing spectrum. Because governance quality directly affects the underlying incentive structure of various immediate determinants of economic growth, a balanced political power-sharing structure is also conducive to favourable growth and economic performance in general.

Using economic development levels as a proxy for the different prevailing conditions and challenges of different countries, the present study also highlights the contingent nature of the optimality of political institutions. The differences inherent in various countries encompass a host of factors, including history, culture, demographic composition as well as prevailing political systems and social-economic conditions. These differences are crucial in determining the feasible set of choices of political institutional arrangements and their subsequent impact on growth. Specifically, depending on the different developmental paths various countries have taken, different arrangements of political institutions to optimise economic performance are often required. Consequently, countries at different levels of economic development may have different optimal structures of political institutions. This implies that a political institutional order that is favourable for economic growth at one time may hinder the sustainability of growth at a later time. In summary, there is no unique optimal political institutional configuration that can fit different countries across development stages. Rather, the compatibility of political orders with the underlying socioeconomic conditions holds the key for sustained economic growth.

Empirical investigation

I employ quantitative analysis to explore the implications of the theoretical arguments. Data and econometric strategies are introduced before estimation results are discussed.

Political institutional structures

Most of the institutional-related indicators are proxies for the quality or performance of institutions, rather than the institution itself (Aron 2000). In other words, while these indicators are outcomes instead of attributes of institutions, this important distinction is often not made explicit. In this study, political institutional structures focus on the fundamental configuration of political power, data on which are obtained from the Database of Political Institutions 2000 (Keefer et al. 2002) (hereafter DPI 2000).[5] This dataset provides particularly useful information on many aspects of political institutions across 177 countries and over 26 years, 1975–2000. The particular variable used is *CHECKS*, which provides information on numbers and preferences of veto players in countries' political systems. Higher values of *CHECKS* indicate higher degrees of checks and balances and lower levels of power concentration.

Governance quality

Despite a number of measures that have been used in previous studies, institutional quality, as it is typically measured, remains a nebulous concept (Rodrik 2004).[6] In addition, there has been no consensus on which variable(s) should be used.

Consequently, different mixes of indicators as well as various weightings of a similar group of variables may have been used to address particular aspects of a research question, not surprisingly leading to conflicting conclusions.

The source of data for governance quality is the governance indicators in Kaufmann et al. (2003),[7] one of the most comprehensive evaluations of governance quality. Covering 199 countries in 2002, Kaufmann et al. (2003) captures six dimensions, including voice and accountability, political stability, government effectiveness, regulatory quality, rule of law, and control of corruption. The values of these indicators are derived from several hundred variables measuring perceptions of governance drawn from 25 separate data sources constructed by 18 different organisations.[8] Using an unobserved components model, individual measures of governance perceptions are assigned to the above six categories to capture the key dimensions of governance.

Growth data

Data on economic growth, initial levels of income per capita and other widely used economic variables such as openness, education attainment, and trade, and so on are obtained from various sources, including the Penn World Table Database 6.1 (Heston and Summers 2002), World Development Indicators (WDI) of the World Bank Data series, Barro and Lee's (1996) international measures of schooling, and so on.

Econometric strategy

A general observation across countries seems to suggest that countries with relatively more fragmented power-sharing structures (many of which are characterised by modern democratic regimes) arguably exhibit better economic performance than countries with more concentrated structures. It is not at all obvious, however, that fragmented political institutional structures universally lead to more favourable economic performance. It has been emphasised by various researchers, such as Barro (1996), Przeworski and Limongi (1993), and Alesina (1996), that the variance of economic performance of countries with a relatively concentrated power-sharing structure is larger than that of countries with a more fragmented power-sharing structure.[9] Consequently, if data for all economies are pooled together with a linear specification between political institutional structures and economic performance, regardless of stages of economic development, results are likely to be inconclusive. Relevant to this assertion, Bardhan (2004) examined the multi-dimensional process through which democracy tends to affect the pace and pattern of development. He found that not all of the impact is desirable.[10]

Derived from the theoretical arguments, the following hypotheses are tested.

1 Political institutional configuration affects governance quality in a non-monotonic fashion.

2 Countries at different levels of economic development have different optimal power-sharing structures. The power concentration of the optimal structure decreases, becoming less concentrated with the progress of economic development.

3 Governance quality positively affects economic growth.

4 The impact of political institutional configuration on economic growth is non-monotonic.

5 The partial effect of institutional configuration on economic growth will depend on the distance between actual structure and optimal structure at the corresponding level of development.

To test the first hypothesis, mean values of *CHECKS* over the years for every country and the Kaufmann et al. (2003) indicators of governance quality are used. Averaging the values of the relevant variables for a relatively long period of time is a main characteristic shared by many studies, including Scully (1988), Levine and Renelt (1992), Persson and Tabellini (1994), and Helliwell (1994).

One of the methods to examine the existence of a non-monotonic relationship is to test a quadratic specification between the indicators of governance quality and the power concentration index. Henderson (2003) provides some useful econometric strategies, particularly on testing for optimal degree of a variable impact on a dependent variable. The basic model hypothesises that governance quality is a function of political institutional structure and an unobserved variable, included as an intercept.

$$\pi_i = \beta_0 + \beta_1 CHECKS + \beta_2 CHECKS^2_i + \varepsilon_i \tag{3.1}$$

where, $CHECKS_i$ denotes the degree of political power dispersal of country i, with higher values of $CHECKS_i$ indicating greater fragmentation of power and more checks and balances, π denotes levels of governance quality, and ε_i is assumed to be a contemporaneous error term. The working hypothesis for Equation 3.1 is that $\beta_1 > 0$ and $\beta_0 < 0$, and consequently it implies the optimal degree of power-sharing is the point $-\beta_1/2\beta_2$, where π is maximised.

To test the second hypothesis, the econometric model is similar to Henderson's (2003) approach, in the following form

$$\pi_i = \beta_0 + (\alpha_0 + \alpha_1 \ln(\frac{Y_i}{N_i}))CHECKS_i + \beta_1 CHECKS_i^2 + \varepsilon_i \tag{3.2}$$

The working hypothesis is that the collection of terms multiplying power-concentration is positive, that is, $(\alpha_0 + \alpha_1 \ln(\frac{Y_i}{N_i})) > 0$, while $\beta_1 < 0$; and $\alpha_1 > 0$ so that the best structure of political institutions becomes more fragmented as output per worker (or income per capita) increases. The optimal power concentration is given by

$$-\frac{\alpha_0 + \alpha_1 \ln(\frac{Y}{N})}{2\beta_1} \qquad (3.3)$$

An alternative method to test the above hypothesis is to include dummy variables that characterise differences in levels of economic development in the regression. Specifically, countries can be divided into groups according to various income levels. If the estimates of these income dummy variables turn out to have a statistically significant impact on the relationship between governance quality and the configuration of political institutions, it implies various income levels captured by such dummy variables affect the optimal political power concentration levels. Furthermore, with division of the sample countries according to their income groups, the hypothesis is that the benefit of power separation is smaller in low-income countries than in rich countries. Finally, it is worth noting that this exercise implicitly assumes the actual degrees of power concentration, z, are randomly distributed. A normality test based on the Jarque-Bera statistic for skewness and excess kurtosis on *CHECKS* shows this assumption is not unrealistic with an overall test statistic (chi squared) of 18.56 and p-value of 0.0001.

Hypotheses 3–5 essentially concern growth regressions. Empirical studies on economic growth have nearly reached a consensus on a set of key explanatory variables for growth, including initial level of development, level of investment in physical capital, level of investment in human capital, population growth and openness to world trade. However, enquiries for fundamental determinants of economic growth cry out for a comprehensive growth model that captures various specific considerations. Notably, Bleaney and Nishiyama (2002) investigated a number of influential growth regression specifications, including those of Barro (1997), Easterly and Levine (1997) and Sachs and Warner (1997). They derived a useful encompassing model against which additional explanatory variables can be tested. Specifically, if including untried variables improves the fit of this 'benchmark model', it indicates that additional explanatory power is present or that the new variables have an indirect impact on growth.

The focus of the following growth regression is to explore the core question: does political institutional structure affect growth in a non-monotonic fashion?

Given the research focus, unlike Bleaney and Nishiyama's (2002) encompassing model where institutional quality (a democracy index) is included as an independent variable, quality of governance is considered an outcome of political institutional structures. In addition, Bleaney and Nishiyama (2002) considered all the regressors effectively independent variables. Consequently, the complex question of endogeneity is not clearly discussed. In the following growth regressions, a two-stage least square approach is adopted to help reduce the endogeneity problem. Given that the data on political institutions are independent from economic performance measurements and relate to the quality of governance, DPI can be used as instruments for governance quality measurements in the growth regression.

Results

Table 5.1 shows that the estimates uniformly rejected a monotonic relationship between political institutional structure and the quality of governance. In the meantime, variation in the results probably reflects the various aspects of governance quality captured by different indicators. For example, the Voice and Accountability indicator captures the degree of transparency. Transparency, as a means to encourage political competition and regulate power, is about the feedback mechanism that rewards good policies and punishes bad ones. In Figure 5.1, fitted values of governance quality (Voice and Accountability) based on the above estimation are demonstrated. In the background, original values of Voice and Accountability are plotted against the proxy of political power structures (CHECKS). The non-monotonic relationship between political institutional structure and governance quality is apparent.

Regression results of estimating Equation 3.2 using six governance quality indicators from Kaufmann et al. (2003) are reported in Table 5.2. In comparison to the results reported in Table 5.1, the econometric model retains a quadratic term to the basic structures of political institutions. In addition, an interaction term of the power-sharing structure (CHECKS) and the log of GDP per capita are included. As expected, the coefficient estimates of CHECKS have positive sign, indicating that the more fragmented the power, the higher the quality of governance. Consistent with the estimates reported in Table 5.1, the set of results in Table 5.2 continues to reject the hypothesis of a monotonic relationship between political institutional structure and governance quality at an overall level.

In particular, the quadratic terms all have opposite signs to the first order terms, despite the finding that, after taking the levels of development into consideration, for some indicators the quadratic term becomes statistically insignificant. The

Table 5.1   **Basic relationship between political institutional structure and governance quality**

Dependent variable various governance quality indicator	Government effectiveness	Regulatory quality	Voice and accountability	Control of corruption	Rule of law	Political stability
Structure						
CHECKS	0.87***	0.85***	1.13***	0.83***	1.01***	0.78***
	(6.17)	(6.12)	(9.71)	(5.68)	(7.67)	(5.09)
Structure-squared						
(CHECKS²)	−0.07***	−0.07***	−0.09***	−0.07***	−0.09***	−0.08***
	(-3.70)	(-3.59)	(-5.81)	(-3.45)	(-4.87)	(-3.51)
Constant	−1.50***	−1.50***	−2.00***	−1.43***	−1.68***	−1.26***
	(−7.64)	(−7.74)	(−12.36)	(−7.02)	(−9.17)	(−5.91)
N [countries]	171	171	171	171	171	168
Adjusted R²	0.32	0.32	0.54	0.27	0.39	0.19
Implied optimal power structure						
(CHECKS*)	6	6	6	6	6	5

Note: t-ratios are in parentheses. ***, **, * Indicates estimates are significant at 1 per cent level, 5 per cent and 10 per cent levels, respectively.
Source: Author's calculations.

negative signs of structure-squared indicate the positive impact of fragmented power diminishes as the degree of dispersal increases. Whilst the power structure gets less concentrated, the negative effect of fragmentation dominates.

Regardless of the governance indicators employed, the estimate coefficient of the interaction terms (Structure*GDP per capita) is statistically significant and has a positive sign. Corresponding optimal structures of political institutions (*CHECKS**) implied by regressions using each of the indicators are calculated. The estimations are generally supportive to the hypothesis that optimal dispersal of political power is positively correlated with income level. Prior research, such as Barro (1997), Helliwell (1994) and Burkhart and Lewis-Beck (1994), has found that the positive relation between income levels and democracy is mostly attributable to the former's impact on the latter rather than the other way around. These results are consistent with the above cited conclusions as well as Lipset's (1959) earlier interpretation of the correlation between income and democracy.

Figure 5.1   **Illustration of the regression results on the relationship between political institutional structure and governance quality**

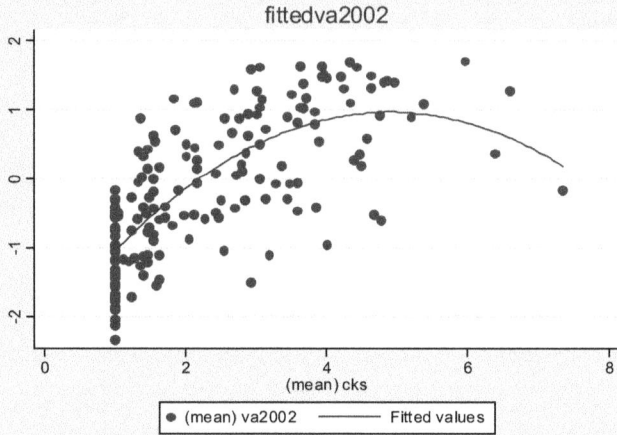

fittedva2002

(mean) cks

● (mean) va2002 ——— Fitted values

Source: Author's calculations.

Table 5.3 presents the results of a series of growth regressions, including all the key variables identified in Bleaney and Nishiyama (2002). Column (1) shows the specification used as a benchmark in this study, which is built upon the encompassing model of Bleaney and Nishiyama (2002) and extracted institutional quality variables and the squared term of initial income level.[11] Even though male schooling and terms of trade growth turn out to be statistically insignificant, the overall statistics are satisfactory with adjusted R-squared of 0.80 and pass all diagnostic tests.

Using the results obtained in Column (1) as a basis, the subsequent regressions include additional institutional variables in various specifications. Column (2) shows that the fit improved when predicted values of governance quality are added to the regression. The governance quality indicator presented in Table 5.3 is Control of corruption,[12] and the predicated values are obtained from estimating Equation 3.2. Indicators of governance quality are treated as outcomes of political institutional structure, and results of this first stage estimation have been reported in Table 5.2. In summary, whilst it passes all the diagnostic tests, the two-stage least-square (2SLS) approach improves the adjusted R-squared and reduces the standard deviation of residuals. Thus, the above results provide evidence to support the

Table 5.2   **Estimation results of the relationship between optimal political institutional structure and levels of economic development**

Dependent variables	Control of corruption	Government effectiveness	Rule of law	Political stability	Regulatory quality	Voice and accountability
α_0	−1.56***	−1.37***	−1.31***	−0.57*	−0.76***	0.19
	(−5.80)	(−5.26)	(−4.96)	(−1.61)	(−2.97)	(0.76)
α_1 (Coefficient of CHECKS *lnGDP p.c.)	0.22***	0.21***	0.20***	0.13***	0.16***	0.09***
	(10.35)	(9.98)	(9.51)	(5.17)	(7.85)	(4.32)
$(\alpha_0 + \alpha_1 \ln(\frac{Y_i}{N_i}))$ (Coefficient of CHECKS)	0.18	0.25	0.28	0.45	0.5	0.86
Structure-squared (CHECK^2)	−0.02*	-0.02	−0.02	−0.05**	−0.05***	−0.07***
	(−1.11)	(−1.41)	(−1.35)	(−2.24)	(−2.89)	(−4.54)
Number of observations	144	144	144	141	144	144
Adjusted R^2	0.59	0.61	0.60	0.33	0.59	0.61
Implied optimal power structure (CHECKS*)	5	6	7	5	5	6

Note: t-ratios are in the parentheses.
***, **, * Indicates estimates are significant at 1 per cent level, 5 per cent level and 10 per cent level, respectively.
Source: Author's calculations.

theoretical argument that political institutional structures affect long-run economic growth through the channel of governance quality. Moreover, governance quality has a positive impact on economic growth.

Columns (3) and (4) present the estimation results when political institutional structures (*CHECKS*) as well as a quadratic specification are included in the growth regression. The null hypothesis is that the relationship between growth and configuration of political institutions (*CHECKS*) is monotonic. Results show that the inclusion of *CHECKS* and *CHECKS-squared* strengthens the results not only by improving the degree of fit and reducing the standard deviation of residuals but also by increasing the significance of the coefficient estimate of the governance quality indicator. Interestingly, in the meantime, the estimate of openness falls from being significant at the 5 per cent level to statistically insignificant. A close look at the openness variable given by Sachs and Warner (1997) suggests that openness is defined in such a way that, apart from meeting a series of economic criteria, a country also has to be non-socialist. The inclusion of political institutional structure variables has perhaps picked up some impact of political systems, and therefore weakens the explanatory power of openness.

Column (5) provides the testing results of the hypothesis that long-run growth is negatively affected by distance. The variable distance is the absolute value of the difference between a country's actual political institutional structure (*CHECKS*) and its optimal structure (*CHECKS* *) implied by Equation 3.3. The coefficient estimate of distance is negative and statistically significant at the 10 per cent level. These results suggest the data do not reject the hypothesis that such distance is a determinant that helps explain long-run economic growth.

In summary, across the results presented in Columns (3)–(5), the initial state of economic development (log 1965 income per capita), is always statistically significant and negative. Life expectancy (log 1965 life expectancy), ratio of central government saving with respect to GDP (central government saving/GDP), and the ratio of primary products with respect to GDP (primary products/GDP) are significant in all specifications, at least at 5 per cent significance level. The geographical factor, location in tropics (tropical climate), reduces growth, whilst the difference between the growth rates of economically active and total population growth (economically active minus total population growth) increases economic growth. In addition, Columns (4) and (5) present the estimation results when a number of regional dummy variables are included. Similar to Bleaney and Nishiyama's (2002) findings, regional dummies are generally statistically insignificant (p>0.10) except for the East Asian dummy. With respect to the diagnostic tests results, none of the above specifications exhibits significant non-normality of residuals, misspecification or heteroscedasticity. In particular, when the channel of governance quality and the non-monotonic impact of the political institutional structures on growth are considered in Column (4) the adjusted R-squared rises from 0.80 to 0.85, and the standard deviation of the residuals falls from 0.723 to 0.597.

Case study of China

Despite a generally unenthusiastic attitude among economists towards case-study research, case studies have played a broad and versatile role in shaping of economics and political science.[13] For the purpose of this chapter, the case study mainly focuses on the general economic development of China and the broad direction of changes in the political institutional arrangements.

China's top leadership includes at least the Politburo and Secretariat of the Chinese Communist Party, the Standing Committee of the State Council, and the top commanders of the military. Within this group, a pre-eminent leader often has the highest decision-making power in the realm of the state, the Party and the military. The precise role of the pre-eminent leader has varied considerably over time, but the core tasks have included personnel appointments at the highest levels, enunciation of ideological principles and—usually after extensive discussion with colleagues—identification of the primary tasks confronting the nation (Riskin 1987). Mao Zedong was the pre-eminent leader until 1976 and, after a brief interregnum, Deng Xiaoping from 1978 till 1990. Even after he officially retired from the political scene in the early 1990s, Deng's direction, development strategy and methods were still continuously implemented in China's reform. Jiang Zemin was designated by Deng as the third pre-eminent leader under Communist Party rule, and assumed leadership, albeit without authority comparable to that of Mao or Deng. Hu Jintao has now moved into the similar posts in the Communist Party (General Secretary), State (President) and military (Chairman of the Central Military Commission). As a result, Hu Jintao has established himself as the fourth pre-eminent leader.

In the past 50 years, China has experienced rapid political and economic change. From the establishment of the People's Republic of China to the mid 1970s, China experienced a series of political movements and mass campaigns. Throughout most of this period, the capital-scarce economy followed a Soviet-type economic planning system which essentially promoted a capital-intensive heavy industry development strategy.[14] Politically, the leadership of Mao tolerated little opposition and concentrated power within the Chinese Communist Party (hereafter CCP) for a considerable length of the period. By the end of the Cultural Revolution in 1976, the Chinese economy faced the formidable task of recovery and reconstruction of a vast nation in ruins. In dramatic contrast, since the late 1970s, the Chinese economy led by Deng has been undergoing a fundamental transition from a planned economy to a market economy and has experienced extraordinary growth for a sustained period.

On the other hand, the Party's control of the nation's political, military and economic power remained unchallenged throughout the period. The major economic transition seems to have been accompanied with a relatively modest change in the aggregate political institutional structure. The conventional wisdom that has emerged from the experiences of various developing countries suggests that successful economic performance often requires a list of pre-requisites to be

Table 5.3   Growth regressions: growth effects of political institutional structures

	(1) Coefficients (t-statistic)	(2) Coefficients (t-statistic)	(3) Coefficients (t-statistic)	(4) Coefficients (t-statistic)	(5) Coefficients (t-statistic)
Constant	-2.65 (-0.80)	0.19 (0.05)	-0.24 (-0.07)	-1.75 (-0.48)	1.12 (0.28)
Log initial income per capita (Y)	-1.63*** (-6.90)	-1.87*** (-6.93)	-2.40*** (-6.92)	-2.30*** (-6.81)	-2.05*** (-6.06)
Openness	6.76** (2.70)	5.80** (2.30)	1.80 (0.61)	0.58 (0.19)	3.23 (1.11)
Openness times Y	-0.48* (-1.86)	-0.48 (-1.51)	0.02 (0.05)	0.09 (0.24)	-0.22 (-0.60)
Log 1965 life expectancy	4.14*** (4.32)	3.84*** (4.02)	4.05*** (4.36)	4.13*** (4.52)	4.27*** (4.41)
Male schooling	0.17 (1.13)	0.16 (1.13)	0.14 (1.03)	0.11 (0.77)	0.09 (0.62)
Central government saving/GDP	0.098*** (3.32)	0.093*** (3.97)	0.080*** (3.42)	0.059** (2.57)	0.079*** (3.52)
Primary product export/GDP	-3.40*** (-2.63)	-2.72** (-2.17)	-2.55** (-2.10)	-3.06** (-2.63)	-2.52** (-2.03)
Terms of trade growth	-4.09 (-0.42)	-3.42 (-0.44)	-3.10 (-0.41)	-2.66 (-0.38)	0.79 (0.10)
Tropical climate	-1.40*** (-4.31)	-1.31*** (-4.08)	-0.82** (-2.18)	-0.78* (-1.98)	-1.18*** (-3.15)
Economically active minus total population growth	1.69*** (4.26)	1.43*** (3.41)	0.97** (2.17)	0.98** (2.21)	1.17** (2.58)

Predicted governance quality	0.56* (1.72)		2.65*** (2.88)	3.23*** (3.50)	1.84** (2.56)
Political institutional structure (CHECKS)		(2.12)		10.14**	11.44**
CHECKS^2		−5.59* (−1.83)		−6.12** (−2.13)	
Distance (CHECKS - CHECKS*)					−3.45* (−1.81)
Sub-Saharan Africa dummy				0.69 (1.52)	0.20 (0.46)
Latin America and Caribbean dummy				−0.13 (−0.34)	−0.35 (−0.95)
East Asian dummy				1.19** (2.46)	0.94* (1.93)
Europe dummy				0.28 (0.68)	0.03 (0.06)
Number of observations	71	71	71	71	71
Adjusted R^2	0.80	0.81	0.82	0.85	0.84
F-statistic(p-value)	F(10,60)=29.94 (0.00)	F(11,59)=28.39 (0.00)	F(13,57)=26.09 (0.00)	F(17,53)=24.24 (0.00)	F(16,54)=23.61 (0.00)
Standard deviation of residuals	0.723	0.705	0.671	0.597	0.625
Heteroskedasticity (χ^2)(p-value)	0.00 (0.98)	0.12 (0.72)	0.02 (0.88)	0.51 (0.47)	0.13 (0.72)
Normality (χ^2)(p-value)	0.03 (0.99)	0.93 (0.63)	2.67 (0.26)	4.35 (0.11)	0.15 (0.93)
RESET (p-value)	F(3,57)=0.55 (0.65)	F(3,56)=0.23 (0.88)	F(3,54)=1.11 (0.35)	F(3,50)=0.38 (0.77)	F(3,51)=0.41 (0.75)

Notes: The dependent variable is per capital average annual growth of PPP-adjusted GDP, 1965–1990.
'Normality' presents an overall test statistic for normality based on skewness and kurtosis.
'RESET' is the Ramsey test for omitted variable.
'Heteroscedasticity' is the Breusch-Pagan/Cook-Weisberg test for heteroscedasticity.
***, **, * Indicatse estimates are significant at 1 per cent, 5 per cent and 10 per cent levels, respectively.
Source: Author's calculations.

met, which typically include clearly defined and well enforced property rights, effective rule of law, accountable government and so on. Most importantly, it requires restraint on political predation and the uncertainties associated with it.[15] However, the potential political discretion in China and the absence of a system of private property rights and other conditions for a successful market economy have presented a puzzle and challenged the conventional wisdom in relation to the political basis of economic success.

From a political institutional perspective, the analysis of the impact of political institutions on economic performance postulated in the early sections can assist greatly in understanding the evolution of the political institutional factors and corresponding development path of the Chinese economy.

Political institutional development in the Mao and post-Mao era

The history of China over the past fifty years can be divided into two periods marked by a political as well as an economic turning point in 1978. The Third Plenum of the Eleventh Party Congress in December 1978 was not only the starting point of new political leadership under Deng Xiaoping, replacing Mao Zedong, but also led to the subsequent reform and economic take-off. A quick glance at Chinese political history may suggest that the political institutional arrangements have not changed a great deal, in the sense that the CCP has always been the only authority over high-level policy since the People's Republic of China was established. However, close examination indicates critical transition has been proceeding throughout the period.

Upon assuming power in 1949, the CCP faced the daunting task of governing a vast nation after a century of foreign invasions, civil warfare, exploitation and natural calamities. In the subsequent several decades, China recorded a series of social campaigns launched by Mao at great cost, including notably the mass campaigns of the Three Antis Campaign, the Five Antis Campaign of the early 1950s[16], the Great Leap Forward in 1958 and the Cultural Revolution of 1966–76.

After the People's Republic of China was established in 1949, the CCP was led by the People's Central Committee, a group that holds all major civil and military positions. The main decision-making of the Central Committee fell to a smaller Politburo headed by Chairman Mao. In spite of the continuing importance of military power, with cadre advisors attached to military contingents at all levels, the army remained clearly subordinate to the Party. Before the Great Leap Forward of 1958, China followed Mao's strategy of the Soviet model of communist development. During this period, internal to the CCP, the central government was under the leadership of Mao and his supporters, with all political and economic decision-making power extremely concentrated and unchecked. Externally, criticisms were discouraged and sometimes severely punished. For example, in the mid 1950s, punishment of those who openly criticised the policies, the Party, and, explicitly or implicitly, the leadership under the 'Two Hundred' Scheme clearly demonstrated the intolerance of the political regime in Mao's era.[17]

The Great Leap Forward was initiated with the rationale that an economic miracle of 'super-industrialisation' could be achieved through collectivisation and the use of massive amounts of cheap labour. Contrary to the bold slogan of 'surpassing Great Britain and the United States', the 'great leap' turned into a major economic disaster. Politically, this event also marked the emergence of factional strife within the CCP between bureaucrats led by Deng Xiaoping and Liu Shaoqi and the anti-bureaucrats faction of Mao (Riskin 1987). In the aftermath of the Great Leap Forward, Mao stepped to the sidelines of leadership and Liu and Deng were left in charge of the economic recovery. However, soon after this power shift, Mao regained power and restructured the political architecture so as to eliminate the power base of his rivals and grant his loyalists more power (Shirk 1993). The strife between the two major political factions escalated and became increasingly hostile during the 1960s, the first half of the 1970s and throughout the Cultural Revolution (1966–76).[18] The constellation of the top political leadership changed dramatically during the turbulent years, and the violent and intensified factional struggle eventually led to the critical transition of political institutional structures in the late 1970s.

In the wake of the traumatic Cultural Revolution and with the reestablishment of order and stability, it became clear to the leaders of the CCP that to restore prestige and popular trust, it was necessary to demonstrate they could deliver the goods (Shirk 1993). As a result, the members of China's political elite decided to shift the base of party legitimacy from virtue to competence (Shirk 1993). By then, the political struggle was between the dogmatists and anti-dogmatists (Baum 1994). In the second half of 1978, Deng launched an anti-dogmatic campaign under the slogan 'Seek Truth from Facts' as opposed to the dogmatic ideology 'Two Whatevers'.[19] In a couple of months, the anti-dogmatic faction of Deng gained control over the media, obtained the support of the majority of regional leaders and subsequently established a new era.

Immediately after the anti-dogmatic faction won the battle, the Chinese government set about solidifying political power by implementing new policies, many of which were intended to break the political influence of the dogmatic loyalists in the central bureaucracy and to decentralise decision-making power to the more 'loyal' provincial leaders. More fundamentally, Deng's extension of his power base relied on his ability to solve the severe economic problems China faced. Chen Yun's retrenchment strategy suggested the economic problems inherent in the planning and management system would have to be solved through a decentralisation of decision-making (Baum 1994). The political decentralisation has put considerable limits on the central government's discretionary action, which, in turn, provides the beginning of a strong and credible political foundation for market-oriented reform (Montinola et al. 1995).

Importantly, the incentive structures within the government and the Party changed considerably after the first decade of the reform. In the past, central authorities retained a variety of incentives to control the behaviour of lower officials: fiscal control of local government operations allowed them to manipulate local decision-making. These incentives have been weakened under the decentralised arrangements. Although the central government retains control over the army and the appointment and dismissal of high-level personnel, the power of these tools is weaker than when they were combined with the more micro-level incentives employed during previous eras. This transformation engendered a significant degree of checks and balances within the central government, while the Party's authoritative position was retained and so was the associated political stability and insulation of the central government. As a result, in comparison to Mao's radicalisation of politics in the 1950s, the aggregate power-sharing structure of the post-Mao era was less concentrated, in spite of the fact that power was reserved within the CCP.

Economic development in the pre-reform and reform periods

As far as economic development is concerned, from the early 1950s, inspired by the Soviet Union's exceptional economic expansion in the 1930s, Mao applied the 1930s Soviet model to China. Throughout the pre-reform period, the Chinese economy had a Soviet-type planning economic system, which is perhaps best described as an endogenous choice of a comparative-advantage-defying (hereafter CAD) heavy-industry-oriented development strategy (Lin et al. 2003). In accordance with such a development strategy, China's economic structure of China consisted of three integrated components concerning macro-policy, micro-management and a resource allocation mechanism. As Lin et al. (2003) articulated, the macro-policy environment was distorted and characterised by artificially depressed interest rates, over-valued exchange rates and low nominal wages, as well as low prices for living necessities and raw materials. At the micro level, the state-owned enterprises (hereafter SOEs) had no autonomy over management or flexibility in the marketplace. In the case of collective agriculture in the countryside,[20] distorted low prices for agricultural products and a compulsory procurement policy left farmers with neither income that reflected the value of their economic contribution nor any incentive to improve output or productivity. In addition, a centrally-planned administrative system controlled resource allocation.[21]

Under such a development strategy and the resulting economic structure, an overall assessment of the economy during the pre-reform period suggested both allocative and technical inefficiency, as well as appallingly low growth rates. Average annual economic growth rates between 1952 and 1981 were as modest as 0.5 per cent, far below the average growth rates of 19 developing countries in the same period (World Bank 1985). Furthermore, total factor productivity (TFP) growth during the same period was either stagnant or negative depending on the calculation method (Wang and Yao 2001).

Having experienced the major economic setback of Mao's era, the reform leadership concluded that society should be a richer one and that socialism must make considerable use of market forces to provide incentives and signal relative scarcities (Riskin 1987). The economic transition from 1978 began in rural economic management. Replacing collective farming with the Household Responsibility System (hereafter HRS) and revising the compulsory procurement system significantly improved farmers' incentives to enhance productivity and output. Statistical analysis shows that, between 1978 and 1994, the average annual growth of gross agricultural output was 5.1 per cent (Maddison 1998). Furthermore, half of the growth in the agricultural output of 1978–84 could be attributed to growth in productivity, mainly due to the implementation of the HRS (Lin 1992).

Another growth engine in rural China was the non state-owned enterprises, in particular township and village enterprises (TVEs), which flourished from the 1980s (Garnaut 1996). Operating with hard budget constraint and market mechanisms, non state-owned enterprises are significantly more productive than SOEs in terms of both resource allocation and technical productivity. Specifically, non state-owned enterprises typically operate in labour-intensive industries, which are consistent with the comparative advantage of the Chinese economy. Moreover, operating in a competitive environment, non state-owned enterprises are required to have considerable adaptability for a timely response to price signals. Reflecting its fast expansion, by 1999, the non state-owned enterprise share of gross industrial output had increased to 72 per cent from 24 per cent in 1980 (SSB 1994, 2000).

At the macro-level, the 'open door' symbolises China's sharp turn towards participation in the world market to speed up economic growth and technological modernisation. The reform process involved a massive expansion of the productive forces accomplished by means of quasi-capitalist institutions (commodities, markets, corporations, material incentives, 'scientific management', and the like) and the attitudes concomitant to them (Riskin 1987). In the meantime, government was to be divested of its economic management role, enterprises given decision-making autonomy, the scope of mandatory planning sharply reduced, that of the market correspondingly increased, and price reform finally undertaken. As China increasingly participated in the international division of labour and took advantage of its comparative advantage, economic reform greatly improved China's economic power and its people's welfare.

Implications

China has been largely categorised with other highly centralised regimes. Mao was dominant in China during the pre reform period and the political system was formally organised on Marxist-Leninist principles with a socialist or Soviet-type economy. Compared to most other countries, the top leaders wielded enormous power and few if any institutional checks existed to guard against the exercise and abuse of this power (Lieberthal and Oksenberg 1988:4).

With an extremely high degree of central planning, virtually all enterprises were either state-owned or treated as though they were. The central government not only set the priorities, but carried them out administratively by distributing materials and finance to, and ordering output from, the various enterprises (Riskin 1987). However, it was unable to provide the organising principles for a non-bureaucratic socialism that could survive the great prestige of its founder and unite the Chinese people. Instead, it gave rise in the end to a violent and repressive episode in which heady idealism degenerated into warfare between dogmas and factions (Riskin 1987).

From an institutional perspective, the political architecture of the pre-reform period represented Mao's tight grip on political life and policymaking in general. Overly concentrated power often implies lack of checks and balances and carries a major risk of arbitrary and discretionary action. These all contribute to poor governance, which in turn is detrimental to economic development. An unchecked and extremely concentrated political institutional structure explained, at least partly, the catastrophic outcome of the pre-reform period.

In contrast to Mao's era, the political architecture of the reform period has experienced profound change. While the central government and the CCP retained strong leadership at the national level, it has substantially departed from Mao's system, particularly in terms of allocation of power. This is primarily because, from the beginning of the post-Mao period, the base of legitimacy of the CCP has fundamentally shifted from political ideology to competence. The means to realise this was by improving economic performance and raising living standards (Shirk 1993). Mao's bias against foreign technology and foreign products had severely hurt China's modernisation. Where Deng Xiaoping differed from his predecessors was in the strength of his desire to turn China into a wealthy and powerful state and his lack of interest in Maoist ideas of a new kind of society where such things as material incentives would play little or no role (Perkins 1994). The shift in the base of legitimacy of the CCP led to a new development strategy characterised by decentralisation of decision-making. In the meantime, this effectively moved the power-sharing structure away from an individual dominating within the Party and introduced a critical degree of checks and balances within the political system.

Moreover, the significant change of the national political architecture during the transition can be viewed in terms of the power of the central government to influence decision-making at the micro-level. In the pre-reform period, state planning and centralisation were stressed and the Party had absolute power and influence. Through bureaucratic and Party channels, the central government was politically capable of implementing village-level programs nationwide (Perkins and Yusuf 1984:4). Such substantial control has fundamentally changed due to the division of authority between central and local governments during the reform. As a result, local governments have primary control over economic matters within their jurisdictions (Montinola et al. 1995).[22] Specifically, the provincial governments do not serve merely as administrative units of the central government, but have a significant degree of autonomy within their own jurisdiction in terms of economic decision-making. This creates limits on the national government's discretionary control.

While this decentralisation of power took place, the central government did not excessively compromise its overall authority. The division of power between national government and subnational government was not operated in an overly fragmented form to the extent that provincial governments behaved like de facto national government in their own jurisdiction. To a large extent, the tendency for excessive fragmentation of power was balanced by the authoritative role of central government over subnational governments within an institutionally durable framework (Montinola et al. 1995; Weingast 1995). For instance, although the most important source of rural economic reform initiatives was perhaps not the central government, as the two major drivers of the growth of rural economy, HRS and TVEs were not central government innovations, the market-oriented reform initiatives were soon embraced and reinforced by the central government on a national scale. The central government had the commanding capability to implement reform policies when they were considered appropriate. Similar determination and flexibility to execute the reform initiatives were demonstrated in the SOEs and macro environment reform, from a dual-track price system,[23] to gradual changes made in interest rate policies, foreign exchange policies and the banking sector.

The relationship between the centre and the provinces was the object of continual reform, as China's leaders sought an appropriate blend of national uniformity and provincial authority (Lieberthal and Oksenberg 1988). Budgetary and other changes enhanced the ability of various provincial and lower level units to make their own decisions. Central-provincial relations were characterised by intense bargaining, with neither capable of totally disregarding the interests and needs of the other (Weingast 1995).

While policies resulted from the initiative of top leaders, they were formulated by the top leaders among contending and powerful bureaucracies with diverse purposes, experience, and resources (Lieberthal and Oksenberg 1988). The Party will rule as trustee of the workers' objective interest in the now distant goal of communism. State enterprises were allowed to keep a share of profits and their managements were permitted more autonomy in production and supply decisions.

In summary, the gradual decline of the personal authority of national leaders and the rise of local governments led to a more balanced political institutional structure in China. The stratified structure of the state promotes a system of negotiations, bargaining, and the seeking of consensus among affected bureaucracies. The policy process in this sphere is disjointed, protracted, and incremental (Lieberthal and Oksenberg 1988). Stronger provincial governments have increasingly modified the political equation, and occupied significant roles in shaping the direction of economic development.[24]

Importantly, the political transition created a more balanced configuration of political institutions, which, in contrast to Mao's regime, do not function within the paradigm of personality-oriented politics. Rather, they retain the authority of central government over the regions whilst institutionalising sufficient autonomy of subnational governments over issues of economic development within their own jurisdictions. At local levels, this led to competition among the provinces, mainly in the form of providing positive incentives to attract investment. At an aggregate level, such competition served as experiments in exploring the most effective ways to achieve faster growth. Thus, without compromising the decisiveness associated with the Party's authoritative role, a natural limit on the misuse of power for self interest, favouritism and other discretionary behaviour was created within the authority. As such, a more balanced political institutional structure greatly improved governance quality.

As economic development continues, questions have been raised regarding China's future development. Many observers both within and outside China question the degree to which a one-party system can indefinitely maintain control over an increasingly dynamic and prosperous Chinese society. Will China's current political architecture keep the promise of sustaining rapid economic growth?

It is important to note that the favourable institutional arrangements at a certain period of time do not necessarily translate to arrangements conducive to economic growth all the time. A concentrated power structure may provide the necessary conditions for growth to take place, but the potential perils associated with such a structure can manifest themselves through poor governance, failure to sustain growth or even economic devastation. Garnaut (1999:23) emphasised, 'rapid economic growth is a stressful process…it can destabilise the political order that is responsible for the policies that sustain it, unless the political order itself evolves with the economic structure'. Will the political institutions that have exerted a positive impact on economic performance in the past always be conducive to future economic growth? Economic growth can always end with political convulsion that removes the primacy of the growth objective.

The optimal configuration of political institutions is determined by a wide range of factors, among which the level of development is a crucial one. A failure of political institutions to adjust to the changing conditions and aspirations of the community can undermine social and political cohesion around the objective of growth. This proposition suggests a favourable structure, which has fostered growth for a certain period of time, can gradually become less pertinent due to changes in the broad socio-economic conditions, which can be approximated by levels of development.

The risk of deviation from a balanced structure of political power can eventually constitute an obstacle for future development. This is not to say that a framework that severely concentrates decision-making power does in fact behave in a volatile fashion at any given moment. This will always depend on a complex totality of factors shaping individual decisions that, in an important sense, may not ultimately be knowable. What is emphasised is that the potential for such an outcome was embedded in the political architecture of these countries, and that, as economic and then political pressure mounted, the full potential for policy volatility was laid bare for all to see, with very costly consequences (MacIntyre 2003).

More generally, perfect policy is not a necessary condition for rapid economic growth. Policies that reduce the gains from trade, market imperfections that keep some resources in relatively unproductive uses, periods of economic instability that inhibit the accumulation of capital, inadequate public investment in education and infrastructure — all hold growth back from attainable levels, and at the same time, depending on their extent, may not be inconsistent with rapid growth. As growth proceeds and the frontiers of world technology and living standards are approached, the tolerance of growth to weaknesses in policy and institutions declines. Poor policy — resulting from professional weakness or political manifestations of resistance to change — can block the continual re-allocation of resources to more productive uses (Garnaut 1993, 1999).

Where Mao kept alive Utopian principles to light the distant goals but failed to consistently chart the way there, his successors focused on the immediate path ahead. In so doing, they have moved into new ideological territory. The earlier reform leadership, Hu Yaobang and Zhao Ziyang, was led by experience to the view that successful economic reform and development would require a widening of the scope for open discussion of policy, for dissent within limits set by the imperatives of continued Communist Party rule, and for reform of the political system to make policy somewhat more open to pressures from a rapidly changing society beyond the central leadership (Garnaut 1999). As economic progress continues, China needs to modify further its political institutional structure so as to be compatible with the evolving status of broad social and economic conditions. Although the seemingly unchanged political structure has in fact undergone critical transition during the reform period, the question is whether such political transition is sufficient to be compatible with China's improved level of development? Economic reform and change had its own momentum that carried along continued social and political change in the local sphere (Garnaut 1999). Having moved quite a few rungs upwards on the economic development ladder, China risks creating institutional impediments to further growth if it does not undertake further institutional reform.

Conclusion

This chapter argues that a balanced configuration of political power, rather than overly concentrated or excessively fragmented structures, is optimal in terms of maximising economic growth.

The political institutional arrangements in China can be characterised as a relatively concentrated structure over a period of the past fifty years. The excessively concentrated political institutional structure constituted a major cause of the crisis that ended the Mao era. Since the reform period, however, continuous efforts have been made to alter some aspects of the basic political rules in ways that reshape the national political architecture. As a result, unchallenged authority at the national level gives the government sufficient insulation to make decisive choices, whereas the division of power within the CCP as well as between the various levels of governments provides the political system with a degree of credibility and commitment. With a favourable degree of decisiveness and credibility, the political institutions provided a strong foundation for economic reform and have contributed to the rapid economic growth over the past two and half decades.

The process of economic development is complex and it is imperative to note the fundamental contingency. The influences of political institutions on economic growth are associated with their multifaceted interaction with other institutional and non-institutional variables. An institutional arrangement that has delivered good economic performance at one time may become inappropriate at another time if the level of economic development has significantly changed. As Jones (1988) argued, growth can occur, only within an 'optimality band', where 'factor and commodity markets are freed and the government is neither too grasping nor too weak', but, for growth to be sustained, government has to provide the institutions that were necessary to the effective operation of the market itself: enforcement of the rights to property and contract; freedom of secure movement and exchange over large areas; the personal security that makes long-term investment in education feasible and worthwhile; and much else.[25] China has so far demonstrated a unique path in transforming from a central-planned economy to an increasingly market-oriented economy. This chapter suggests that the prospect of China's economic future hinges, to a significant degree, on the compatibility of its institutional environment.

Notes

[1] In general, the definition of institutions is at least twofold. First, an institution is an organised pattern of roles, often enforced with positive and negative sanctions. This strand of the definition is particularly related to firm organisation and governance. Williamson (1975, 1985) in particular, has emphasised institutions as a 'governing structure'. As such, the concept of institutions would seem quite compatible with designation of governing structures other than firms (Nelson

and Sampat 2001). Second, it is considered to be the patterned habits of thought learned by individuals performing those roles.

[2] Specifically, well-understood rules establish baseline conditions for human interaction, and give certain predictability as to what other people will do in a particular context (Nelson and Sampat 2001). As such, institutions permit individual decision-making and multi-party negotiation to proceed with some extent of certainty.

[3] Veto players refer to those whose consent is necessary for any policy reform and legislative changes (Tsebelis 2000). In this study, political institutional structure, political institutional configuration and political institutional arrangements will be used interchangeably. Fragmentation of power in this study primarily focuses on the horizontal separation of power at the aggregate level rather than vertical decentralisation that disperses state responsibilities to regional branch offices (Oates 1972; Gordon 1983; Sinn 1990). In many previous studies, the term 'separation of power' has often referred to Locke and Montesquieu's concept of the need for separation of the legislative, executive, and judicial branches of government. The main purpose is to avoid usurpation and tyranny by the holder of these powers.

[4] For example, World Bank defines governance as the traditions and institutions by which authority in a country is exercised for the common good. This includes (i) the process by which those in authority are selected, monitored and replaced, (ii) the capacity of the government to manage its resources effectively and implement sound policies, and (iii) the respect of citizens and the state for the institutions that govern economic and social interactions (Kaufmann et al. 1999, 2002, 2003).

[5] This is the latest version after a series of revision and updates. Earlier versions of DPI include DPI (Beck et al. 2000) and DPI Version 3 (Beck et al. 2001).

[6] More specifically, Aron (2000) has pointed out that, in the empirical literature, the terms politics and institutions encompass a wide range of indicators, including institutional quality (often in terms of enforcement of property rights), political instability (riots, coups, civil wars), characteristics of political regimes (election, constitutions, executive power), social capital (the extent of civic activity and organisations), and social characteristics (differences in income and in ethnic, religious, and historical background).

[7] Kaufmann, Kraay and Mastruzzi (2003) are an update and expansion of the previous work by Kaufmann, Kraay and Zoido-Lobaton (1999. 2002), for simplicity, therefore, the dataset is referred as KKZ.

[8] Details of these 25 sources are listed in Kaufmann et al. (1999, 2002) and Kaufmann et al. (2003).

[9] For example, Barro writes that 'the theory that determines which kind of dictatorship will prevail is missing' (1996:2). Przeworski and Limongi (1993) cite that economic performance varies

more dramatically among dictatorships than among democracies, largely because some dictators are constructively 'developmentalist', while others are simply 'thieves'.

[10] In particular, Bardhan (2004) pointed out the rewards and punishments by a politician's local constituency need not be consistent with the development goals of the economy as a whole, as in the case of the durable politician who regularly brings the 'pork' home.

[11] The inverted U-shape relationship between growth and initial per capita income is not explored in these models because an inclusion of a second-order term of initial income level not only makes the specification unnecessarily more complicated, but also drives down the significance of the first-order term of the initial income level.

[12] Using any of the other governance indicators in Kaufmann and Keefer (2003) leads to statistically equivalent results.

[13] For related references to the literature on the methodological issues, see Blaug (1980), and Hausman (1989, 1992).

[14] Lin et al. (2003) include an eloquent analysis on the Chinese economy for the pre-reform period.

[15] See North (1989, 1994) for the fundamental role of institutions, particularly property rights.

[16] The Three Antis Campaign was against corruption, waste, and excessive bureaucracy. The Five Antis Campaign was against bribery, tax evasion, theft of state property, cheating on government contracts, and stealing economic information.

[17] The 'Two Hundred' Scheme was the campaign to 'Let a hundred flowers bloom and let a hundred schools of thought contend'. At the beginning of the campaign, it was encouraged by Mao for mainly intellectuals to speak out freely. But as critics flushed into the society, Mao abruptly shifted gears and denounced the criticisms as 'poisonous weeds'. Many of those who had criticised openly were struck with demotions, prison sentences and other forms of punishment.

[18] See Chan (1985) and Meisner (1986) for detailed accounts of the Cultural Revolution.

[19] The 'Two Whatevers' refers to the statement that 'we must resolutely uphold whatever policy decisions Chairman Mao made, and must unswervingly follow whatever instructions Chairman Mao gave'. This statement was contained in a joint editorial, entitled 'Study the Documents Well and Grasp the Key Link' of 7 February 1977 in the People's Daily, Hongqi Journal and Liberation Army Daily.

[20] Mao and his supporters introduced the Mass Line approach, and the subsequent formation of the agricultural cooperatives began in 1955. In the following year, cooperatives became farming collectives and soon accounted for more than 90 per cent of the peasant population.

[21] Lin et al. (2003) provide a persuasive analysis of the economic rationale behind the joint presence of these three components in light of the CAD strategy.

[22] Montinola et al. (1995) summarised that the political institutional structure of China, which they term as 'market preserving federalism', encompasses a set of conditions that governs the

allocation of authorities and responsibility among different levels of government. In the case of China, its political institutional structure shares, to some degree, each of the important features of market-preserving federalism. Such an assertion is primarily based on the balance of power between the central government and local provincial governments.

[23] A dual-track price system was introduced in 1984. It allowed the SOEs to sell their output in excess of quotas at market prices and plan their production accordingly.

[24] Examples of provincial governments as an influential part of economic policy decision-making include the endorsement of market-oriented reform, open-door policy and opposing the reversal of decentralisation.

References

Acemoglu, D., Johnson, S. and Robinson, J.A. 2001. 'Colonial origins of comparative development: an emprical investigation', *American Economic Review*, 91(5):1369–1401.

Alesina, A., Ozler, S., Roubini, N. and Swagel, P., 1996. 'Political instability and economic growth', *Journal of Economic Growth*, 1(2):189–213.

Aron, J., 2000. 'Growth and institutions: a review of the evidence', *World Bank Research Observer*, 15(1):99–135.

Bardhan, P., 1999. *Democracy and Development: a complex relationship*, in I. Shapiro and C. Hacker-Cordon (eds), *Democracy's Value*, Cambridge University Press, Cambridge.

Barro, R. 1996. 'Democracy and growth', *Journal of Economic Growth*, 1(1):1–28.

— —, and Lee, J., 1996. 'International measures of schooling years and schooling quality', *American Economic Review*, 86(2):218–23.

— —, 1997. *Determinants of Economic Growth: a cross-country empirical study*. MIT Press, Massachusetts.

Baum, R., 1994. *Burying Mao: Chinese politics in the age of Deng Xiaoping*, Princeton University Press, Princeton.

Beck, T., Clarke, G., Groff, A., Keefer, P. and Walsh, P., 2001. 'New tools and new tests in comparative political economy: the database of political institutions', *World Bank Economic Review*, 15(1):165–76.

Benabou, R., 1996. 'Inequality and growth', *NBER Macroeconomics Annual*, MIT Press, Cambridge:11–76.

Bleaney, M. and Nishiyama, A., 2002. 'Explaining growth: a contest between models', *Journal of Economic Growth*, 7(1):43–56.

Brunetti, A., 1997. *Politics and Economic Growth: a cross-country data perspective*, Development Centre of the Organisation for Economic Cooperation and

Development, Paris.

Burkhart, R.E., and Lewis-Beck, M.S., 1994. 'Comparative democracy: the economic development thesis', *American Political Science Review*, 88(4):903–10.

Chan, A., 1985. *Children of Mao: personality development and political activism in the red guard generation*. University of Washington Press, Seattle.

Clague, C. (ed.), 1997. *Institutions and Economic Development: growth and governance in less-developed and post-socialist countries*, Johns Hopkins University Press, Baltimore.

— —, 1998. 'Economics, institutions, and economic development', in E.M.U. Karol Soltan and V. Haufler (eds), *Institutions and Social Order*, University of Michigan Press, Michigan:201–29.

Coase, R., 1960. 'The problem of social cost', *Journal of Law and Economics*, 3:1–31.

Cox, G.W. and McCubbins, M., 2000. 'The institutional determinants of economic policy outcomes', in S. Haggard and M.D. McCubbins (eds), *Presidents, Parliaments, and Policy*, Cambridge University Press, New York.

Easterly, W., and R. Levine. 1997. 'Africa's growth tragedy: policies and ethnic divisions', *Quarterly Journal of Economics*, 112(4):1203–50.

Eggertsson, T., 1990. *Economic Behaviour and Institutions*, Cambridge University Press, Massachusetts.

Elster, J. 1995. 'The impact of constitutions on economic performance', *Proceedings of the World Bank Annual Conference on Development Economics 1994*, World Bank, Washington, DC:209–226.

Engerman, L. and Sokoloff, K.L., 1994. *Factor endowments: institutions and differential paths of growth among new world economies: a view from economic historians of the United States*, NBER Working Paper No. H0066, National Bureau of Economic Research, Massachusetts.

Garnaut, R., 1993. 'The market and the state in economic development: some questions from East Asia and Australia', in M.A.B. Siddique (ed.), *A Decade of Shann Memorial Lectures 1981-90 and the Australian Economy*, Academic Press International, Nedlands:303–23.

— —, Kuo, S. and Ma, G. (eds), 1996. *The Third Revolution in the Chinese Countryside*, Cambridge University Press, New York.

— —, 1999. 'Twenty years of economic reform and structural change in the Chinese economy', in R. Garnaut and L. Song (eds), *China: twenty years of reform*, Asia Pacific Press, Canberra:1–26.

Gordon, R.. 1983. 'An optimal tax approach to fiscal federalism', *Quarterly Journal of Economics*, 98(4):567–86.

Greif, A. 1998. 'Historical and comparative institutional analysis', *American Economic Review*, 88(2):80–84.

Haggard, S., 1990. *Pathways from the Periphery: The politics of growth in the newly industralizing countries*, Cornell University Press, Ithaca.

Helliwell, J. 1994. 'Empirical linkages between democracy and economic growth', *British Journal of Political Science*, 24(2):225–48.

Henderson, V., 2003. 'The urbanization process and economic growth: the so-what question', *Journal of Economic Growth*, 8(1):47–71.

Henisz, W.J., 2000a. 'The institutional environment for economic growth', *Economics and Politics*, 12(1):1–31.

— —, 2000b. 'The institutional environment for multinational investment', *Journal of Law, Economics and Organization*, 16(2):334–64.

Heston, A. and Summers, R., 2002. *Penn World Table Version 6.1*, Center for International Comparisons at the University of Pennsylvania, Pennsylvania. Available online at http://pwt.econ.upenn.edu/.

Hodgson, G., 1988. *Economics and Institutions*. Polity Press, Cambridge.

— —, 1998. 'The approach of institutional economics', *Journal of Economic Literature*, 36(1):166–92.

Jones, E.L. 1988. *Growth Recurring: economic change in world history*, Clarendon Press, New York.

Kaufmann, D., Kraay, A. and Zoido-Lobaton, P., 1999. Governance matters, World Bank, Washington, DC (unpublished).

— —, 2002. Governance matters II: updated indicators for 2000/01, World Bank, Washington, DC (unpublished).

Kaufmann, D. and Kraay, A., Governance Matters III: governance indicators for 1996–2002 and 2003, World Bank, Washington, DC (unpublished).

Keefer, P., 2002. *Database of political institutions: changes and variable definitions*, Development Research Group, World Bank, Washington, DC.

Kydland, F.E., and Prescott, E.C., 1977. 'Rules rather than discretion: the inconsistency of optimal plans', *Journal of Political Economy*, 85(3):473–91.

Levine, R. and Renelt, D., 1992. 'A sensitivity analysis of cross-country growth regression, *American Economic Review*, 82(4):942–63.

Lieberthal, K., and Oksenberg, M., 1988. *Policy Making in China Leaders, Structures, and Processes*, Princeton University Press, Princeton.

Lin, J.Y., 1992. 'Rural reforms and agricultural growth in China', *American Economic Review*, 82(1):34–51.

— —, and Nugent, J.B., 1995. 'Institutions and economic development', in J. Behrman and T.N. Srinivasan (eds), *Handbook of Development Economics*, Volume 3A, North Holland, Amsterdam:2301–70.

— —, Cai, F. and Li, Z., 2003. *The China Miracle: development strategy and economic reform*, The Chinese University Press, Hong Kong.

Lipset, S.M., 1959. 'Some social requisites of democracy: economic development and political legitimacy', *American Political Science Review*, 53(1):69–105.

MacIntyre, A. (ed.), 1994. *Business and Government in Industralising Asia*, Cornell University Press, Ithaca.

— —, 2003. 'The power of institutions: political architecture and governance', in P.J. Katzenstein (ed.), *Cornell Studies in Political Economy*. Cornell University Press, Ithaca.

Maddison, A., 1998. *Chinese Economic Performance in the Long Run*, Organization for Economic Cooperation and Development (OECD), Paris.

Matthews, R.C.O., 1986. 'The economics of institutions and the sources of growth', *Economic Journal*, 96(384):903–18.

Meisner, M.J., 1986. *Mao's China and After: a history of the People's Republic*, Free Press, Collier Macmillan, New York.

Montinola, G., Qian, Y. and Weingast, B.R., 1995. 'Federalism, Chinese style: the political basis for economic success', *World Politics*, 48(1):50–81.

Nelson, R.R. and Sampat, B.N., 2001. 'Making sense of institutions as a factor shaping economic performance', *Journal of Economic Behavior and Organization*, 44:31–54.

North, D.C., 1989. 'Institutions and economic growth: an historical introduction', *World Development*, 17(9):1319–32.

— —, 1990. *Institutions, Institutional Change, and Economic Performance*, Cambridge University Press, Massachusetts.

— —, 1994. 'Economic performance through time', *American Economic Review*, 84(3):359–68.

— —, 1999. *Understanding the Process of Economic Change*, Institute of Economic Affairs, London.

Oates, W.E., 1972. *Fiscal Federalism*, Harcourt Brace Jovanovich, New York.

Perkins, D.H. and Yusuf, S., 1984. *Rural Development in China*, John Hopkins Press, Baltimore.

Perkins, D.H., 1994. 'Completing China's move to the market', *Journal of Economic Perspectives*, 8(2):23–46.

Persson, T. and Tabellini, G., 1990. *Macroeconomic Policy, Credibility and Politics*, Harwood Academic Publishers, Chru.

— —, 1994. 'Does centralization increase the size of government?', *European Economic Review*, 38(3–4):765–73.

— — (eds), 2000. *Political Economics: explaining economic policy*, Zeuthen Lecture Book Series, MIT Press, London.

Przeworski, A. and Limongi, F., 1993. 'Political regimes and economic growth', *Journal of Economic Perspectives*, 7(3):51–69.

Radice, H., 2000. 'Globalization and national capitalisms: theoreizing convergence and differentiation', *Review of International Political Economy*, 7(4):719–42.

Riskin, C., 1987. *China's Political Economy: the quest for development since 1949*, Oxford University Press, Oxford.

Rodrik, D., 2004. 'Getting institutions right', *CESifo DICE*, Report 2:10–15.

Sachs, J.D. and Warner, A., 1997. 'Fundamental sources of long-run growth', *American Economic Review, Papers and Proceedings*, 87(2):184–88.

Scully, G.W., 1988. 'The institutional framework and economic development', *Journal of Political Economy*, 96(3):652–62.

Shirk, S., 1993. *The Political Logic of Economic Reform in China*, University of California Press, Berkeley.

Sinn, H., 1990. *Taxation and the birth of foreign subsidiaries*, NBER Working Paper 3519, National Bureau of Economic Research, Massachusetts.

State Statistics Bureau (SSB), various years. *China Statistical Yearbook*, China Statistics Press, Beijing.

Tsebelis, G., 2000. 'Veto players and institutional analysis', *Governance*, 13(4):441–74.

Wang, Y. and Yao, Y., 2001. 'Sources of China's economic growth, 1952–99: incorporating human capital accumulation', *China Economic Review*, 14(1):32–52.

Weingast, B.R., 1995. 'The economic role of political institutions: market-preserving federalism and economic development', *Journal of Law, Economics and Organization*, 11:1–31.

Williamson, O.E., 1975. *Markets and Hierarchies, Analysis and Anti-Trust Implications: a study in the economics of international organization*, Free Press, New York.

— —, 1985. *The Economic Institutions of Capitalism*, Free Press, New York.

Woo-Cummings, M. (ed.), 1999. *The Developmental State*, Cornell University Press, Ithaca.

World Bank. 1985. *China, Economic Structure in International Perspective*, World Bank, Washington, DC.

— —, 2003. *World Development Indicators*, World Bank, Washington, DC.

6

Rural-urban labour migration and regional income disparity

Xiaolu Wang

Economic growth has varied considerably across China's regions since economic reforms began. The more developed east coast provinces have always experienced higher growth rates than the central or western regions. According to the National Bureau of Statistics (National Bureau of Statistics 1999, 2001, 2002, 2004, 2005), GDP growth rates in the central and western provinces, including minority autonomous regions and municipalities under the direct administration of the central government, were lower than the eastern provinces by approximately one percentage point during the 1980s and by 2–3 percentage points in the 1990s.[1] As a result, inter-region income disparity has increased, especially during the 1990s (Wang and Fan 2004).

In 1980, the less developed central and western regions achieved 65 per cent and 47 per cent of the eastern region's GDP per capita respectively. By 2004, these ratios had dropped to 48 per cent and 38 per cent, respectively. The east–west regional gap continued to increase even after the implementation of the West Development Strategy in the late 1990s (Table 6.1). The gap reduced slightly in 2004 by 0.3 percentage points compared to 2003.

Inter-regional differences in income levels were not quite as severe for rural as for urban areas, but widened more rapidly for rural areas. They have been greater in rural than in urban areas in recent years (Tables 6.2 and 6.3). From 1980 to 2004, the urban disposable income per capita in the western relative to the eastern region dropped from 78 to 69 per cent. In the same period, rural net income per capita dropped from 83 to 53 per cent in the western region relative to the eastern region.

Table 6.1   **Changes in regional GDP per capita**

	1980	1990	2000	2004
GDP per capita (yuan person)				
East	602	2,232	11,680	19,351
Centre	391	1,338	5,895	9,376
West	284	1,065	4,602	7,430
Ratios (per cent) (East as 100 per cent)				
Centre	64.9	60.0	50.5	48.4
West	47.1	47.7	39.4	38.4

Sources: National Bureau of Statistics,1999. *Comprehensive Statistical Data and Materials on 50 Years of New China*, China Statistics Press, Beijing. National Bureau of Statistics, 2001, 2005. *China Statistical Yearbook*, China Statistics Press, Beijing.

These statistics indicate that slower rural development in the western region is largely responsible for the widening of the regional income gap (Tables 6.2 and 6.3).

Cross-regional and rural-urban income disparities have resulted in population and labour migration between the rural and urban areas and among regions since the mid 1980s, which has been associated with the relaxation of administrative restrictions on labour migration. 'Floating labour' has grown every year and has totalled nearly 100 million people in recent years. Close to half of all migration is cross-provincial, mainly from the less developed central and western rural areas to urban areas in the east. These migration patterns have provided a huge supply of cheap labour to the export-oriented industries in coastal areas. Population density in the coastal areas and the level of urbanisation has consequently increased, particularly in the Zhujiang River Delta, Yangzi River Delta and Bejing–Tianjin mega-city areas.

The Fifth National Census in 2000 indicated that 42.4 million people were living in provinces other than their registered residential province. Of this total, 78 per cent were residing in the eastern region having moved from the central and western regions. The 'floating population' accounts for 6.8 per cent of the total population of the eastern region, but only 0.8 per cent and 1.6 per cent of the central and western regional populations, respectively (Table 6.4). The migration outflow represented 4.7 per cent and 3.9 per cent respectively of the central and western regional populations.

These statistics do not accurately reflect the full size of the floating population for several reasons. First, cross-provincial migration accounts for only part of the total floating population, which totalled 153 million in 2000 (National Bureau of Statistics

Table 6.2   **Regional disparity in urban disposable income per capita**
(yuan person)

	1980	1990	2000	2004
Urban disposable income per capita				
East	458	1,628	7,692	9,327
Centre	386	1,175	5,181	6,395
West	357	1,268	5,622	6,647
Ratios (per cent) (East as 100 per cent)				
Centre	84.3	72.2	67.4	67.9
West	77.9	77.9	73.1	69.2

Sources: National Bureau of Statistics,1999. *Comprehensive Statistical Data and Materials on 50 Years of New China*, China Statistics Press, Beijing. National Bureau of Statistics, various years. *China Statistical Yearbook*, China Statistics Press, Beijing.

Table 6.3   **Regional disparity in rural net annual income** (yuan person)

	1980	1990	2000	2004
Rural net income per capita				
East	150	862	3,187	3,463
Centre	128	621	2,073	2,280
West	124	550	1,690	1,842
Ratios (per cent) (East as 100 per cent)				
Centre	85.3	72.0	65.0	66.6
West	82.8	63.8	53.0	53.4

Sources: National Bureau of Statistics,1999. *Comprehensive Statistical Data and Materials on 50 Years of New China*, China Statistics Press, Beijing. National Bureau of Statistics, various years. *China Statistical Yearbook*, China Statistics Press, Beijing.

2003). Second, the statistics do not include migrants who have already changed their official household registration status, although this is a relatively small proportion. Third, census data was incomplete where migrant workers living in their places of work, such as construction sites, factories, shops or restaurants, were overlooked.

The pattern of cross-regional floating labour is consistent with overall trends in population movements, which have tended to be from the central and western regions to the east (Figures 6.1a and 6.1b). This data is extrapolated from a nationwide survey of 60,000 rural households in 2002 by the Employment and Social Security Department of the Ministry of Labour and Social Security.[2]

Table 6.4   **Cross provincial 'floating population' by region, 2000**
(million persons)

Current residence	Total number of 'floating' immigrants	Share of local population (per cent)	Originally from the east	Originally from the centre	Originally from the west
East	33.2	6.8	5.3	17.4	10.4
Centre	3.3	0.8	1.1	1.2	0.9
West	6.0	1.6	1.1	1.6	3.2
Total	42.4	3.3	7.6	20.3	14.6

Source: National Bureau of Statistics, 2003. *Fifth National* Census, China Statistical Press, Beijing.

Table 6.5   **Cross-provincial 'floating rural labour' by region, 2000**
(million persons)

Current residence	Total number of 'floating' immigrants	Share of local larbour force (per cent)	Originally from the east	Originally from the centre	Originally from the west
East	23.2	9.8	2.1	13.7	7.3
Centre	2.9	1.4	0.5	1.7	0.7
West	2.1	1.2	0.2	0.4	1.5
Total	28.2	4.5	2.8	15.8	9.6

Source: Employment and Social Security Department of the Ministry of Labour and Social Security, 2002. *The Situation of Employment and Flow of China's Rural Labour*, China Labour Market Web. Available online at www.lm.gov.cn.

The total number of cross-provincial migrant workers in 2000 was 28.2 million (Table 6.5). Another 33 million rural workers migrated within provinces between counties and cities.

This data indicates that outgoing floating labour across provinces accounts for 9.7 per cent and 6.5 per cent, respectively, of the local rural labour force in the central and western regions.

Comparison of the floating rural labour and floating population data between the central, western and eastern regions indicates that the central and western regions account for 70 per cent of the total floating population living in the eastern region. An unpublished survey carried out by the National Economic Research Institute in 2004 indicated that more than 80 per cent of the randomly selected 3,200 'floating' rural workers were aged 40 or below, and 72 per cent of those surveyed were male (National Economic Research Institute 2004).

Figure 6.1a **Distribution and origin of 'floating population'**

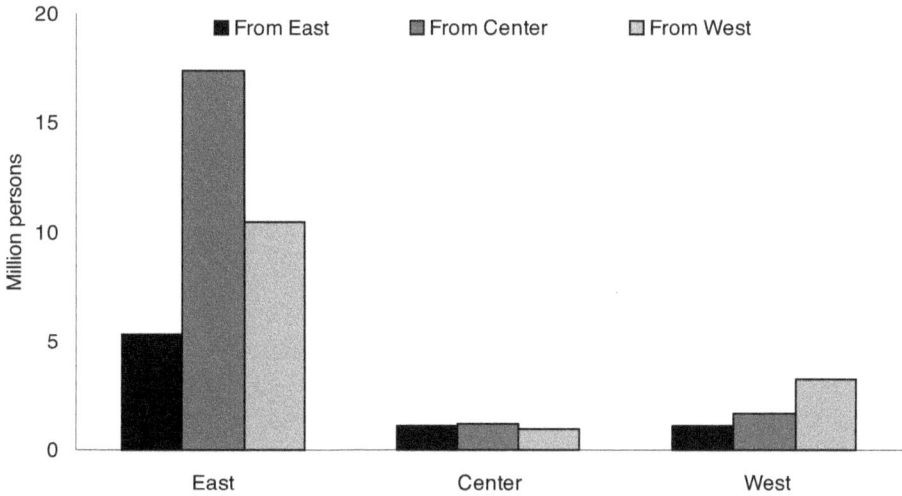

Source: National Bureau of Statistics, 2003, *Fifth National* Census, China Statistical Press, Beijing.

Figure 6.1b **Distribution and origin of 'floating labour'**

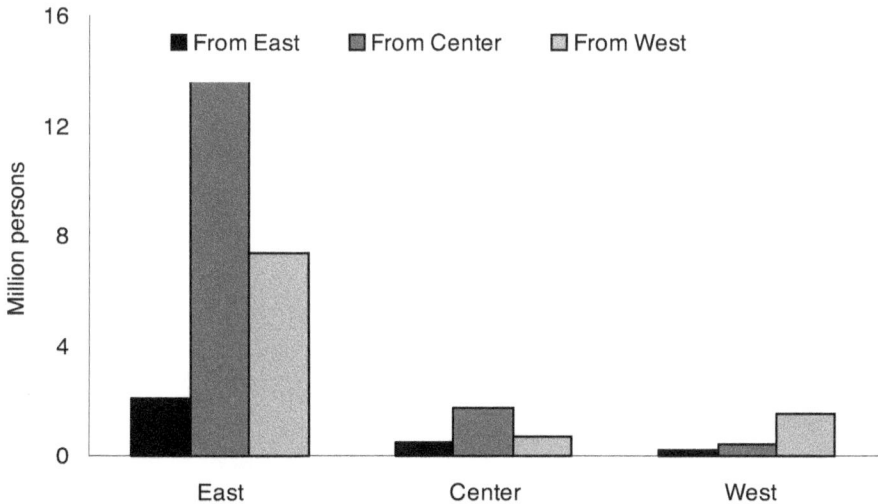

Source: Employment and Social Security Department of the Ministry of Labour and Social Security, 2002. *The Situation of Employment and Flow of China's Rural Labour*, China Labour Market Web. Available online at www.lm.gov.cn.

The impact of labour flow on regional income disparity

There is a large theoretical and empirical literature on the economic effects of labour transfer, either cross-region, rural–urban, or between sectors (Beladi and Naqvi 1987; Harris and Todaro 1970; Lewis 1954; World Bank 1996). Labour migration from low-income to high-income areas is unavoidable in a market economy when institutional, policy, geographic or other barriers are removed or reduced. Labour migration improves resource allocation, increases economic efficiency and eliminates or reduces regional income disparities. Both the destination and source regions can benefit (Figure 6.2).

The horizontal axis represents the total rural labour force, L, in two regions 1 and 2, which have the different levels of development. L is divided into L_1L' and $L'L_2$. The vertical axis represents the value of the marginal product of labour, and wage rates, in the two regions. The two VMPL curves are in opposite directions. With institutional and policy restrictions or high costs on transportation and information transmission, there are differentials between the two VMPL curves. Wages are determined by the VMPL in each region, and the wage gap between the two regions, depicted as the distance between points a and b, is due to institutional or physical barriers that hinder labour reallocation from region 2 to 1. This is equivalent to a tax (t) on the wages, resulting in $\frac{w_1}{1+t} = w_2$.

When the barriers are removed, labour force $L'L'$ reallocates from region 2 to 1. This makes the two VMPL converge to point c, driving up incomes in region 2, and increasing economic efficiencies through the elimination of previous deadweight losses. Losses are indicated by the triangle abc. Both regions benefit from the Pareto improvement.

It is expected in practice that reallocation would be achieved in the long term and would not cause the wage rate in region 1 to decrease. Instead it would restrain increases and simultaneously accelerate income growth in region 2. These two trends would establish equilibrium in the labour market. When equilibrium is achieved, labour flow towards a particular direction will cease.

In some countries population migration towards urban centres has led to underpopulation and economic decline in rural areas. Migration from rural regions to state capitals in the twentieth century in Australia is one prominent example. This is an unlikely scenario for China because of its high population density— population per square kilometre in China is 50 times that of Australia. However, China will need to undertake land reforms in response to the large-scale migration of rural populations in the future.

The effect of cross-region labour migration on regional income disparity can be calculated. In 2004, the average urban disposable income was 11,550 yuan per

Figure 6.2   **Effects of cross-regional labour flow on income disparity**

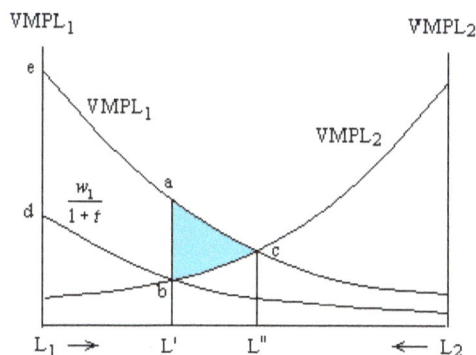

Source: Author's calculations.

person in the eastern region and the ratio of total employment to population was 52.3 per cent. The average rural net income in the central and western regions was 2,454 yuan per person and the ratio of total rural labour to rural population was 52.7 per cent. It is assumed that returns to labour contribute 50 per cent of total household income (with the remainder being returns to capital, human capital and land) and is determined by the marginal product of labour. The derived marginal product of labour in the eastern urban areas and western rural areas is 11,042 yuan and 2,328 yuan, respectively. The marginal product of labour in the eastern region is 4.7 times that of the western region. A migrant worker from the western rural region to the eastern urban region can create greater economic value. It is assumed that the total number of floating labourers from the central and western rural areas to eastern urban areas was 26.5 million in 2004, or an annual 6 per cent per annum higher than the 21 million in 2000. As a result, the migration of workers created at least 293 billion yuan of value-added in 2004. Had workers remained in the central and western rural areas, the total value of their economic activities would have been only 62 billion yuan. The additional 231 billion yuan contributed to national GDP can be attributed to efficient labour reallocation. It is equal to 19 per cent of the total agricultural value-added in the central and west regions or 1.7 per cent of China's total GDP.

Labour outflows from underdeveloped rural areas do not cause a decrease in agricultural output because of the labour surplus in these areas. In fact, growth rates of gross agricultural output in central and western provinces are not significantly lower than the eastern provinces over the past five years. It is reasonable to assume that an important effect of labour outflows has been the distribution of agricultural income in the central and western regions among fewer people. In 2004, total rural population in these two regions was approximately 534 million. The total rural population in the central and western regions decreased by 6.1 per cent, as 34.5 million workers and some of their non-working family members (assuming that these family members accounted for 30 per cent of the migrant workers) migrated to the eastern provinces. These statistics indicate that migration contributed to a 6.5 per cent increase in rural per capita income in their hometown, above levels had they remained in their rural hometowns.

In addition, migrant workers' remittances to their hometowns have become one of the most important sources of income in the labour-exporting regions. According to a National Economic Research Institute survey of 3,200 rural migrant workers in 2004, each cross-province migrant rural worker remitted on average 5,808 yuan to their hometown, accounting for 57 per cent of their total income. Using these numbers, one can derive that a total 153 billion yuan of remittance was sent to the central and west rural areas in 2004, raising rural per capita income in the regions by 11.5 per cent.

In summary, rural–urban labour migration from less developed central and western regions to the more developed eastern provinces has raised rural incomes in the central and western rural areas by 18 per cent, when compared to expected incomes had workers remained in rural regions. These calculations do not incorporate the income effects of labour migration within provinces and regions.

Labour migration has also slowed the growth rates of wage incomes in the eastern region, although this effect is difficult to quantify. As a result, the manufacturing sector in the eastern region has been able to retain its competitive advantage in world markets with the continued low labour costs.

Why regional incomes are diverging

Statistics demonstrate that labour migration has contributed to the reduction of regional income disparities. However, regional incomes remain divergent (Tables 6.1, 6.2 and 6.3). The following discussion offers some reasons for this divergence.

Higher population growth in the western region

Despite the high levels of labour migration across regions during the past two decades, the relative size of the population in the three regions has not changed significantly. In 1980, the distribution of China's total population across the eastern, central and western regions was 37.4 per cent, 33.9 per cent, and 28.7 per cent, respectively. In 2003, population distribution was 37.9 per cent, 33.4 per cent and 28.8 per cent, respectively. This represents only a minor 0.5 percentage point increase in the eastern regions and 0.5 percentage point decrease in the central regions, and no change in the western region.

The lack of change in the distribution of China's population is the result of faster population growth in the central and western regions, particularly the western region. The regional aggregate of natural population growth rates, calculated by the author from National Bureau of Statistics data (1991, 1995, 2000, 2004) at a provincial level, averaged 0.6 per cent in the eastern region, 0.8 per cent in the central region and 1.0 per cent in the western region from 1990 to 2003. Without labour migration, the population of the eastern region would have increased by only 8.4 per cent during this period, compared with 11.1 per cent and 13.4 per cent in the central and western regions. The faster population growth in the western provinces resulted in an additional 5 per cent, or 18 million people, compared to the eastern region. The difference is the result of higher birth rates in the central and western regions. In 2004, the provincial birth rate was 1.0 per cent, 1.05 per cent and 1.34 per cent, respectively in the eastern, central and western regions. As a result, the differences in natural population growth rates between regions cancelled out the effects of migration.

Regional differences in natural population growth and regional income disparities are reciprocally causative, and neither can be eliminated in the short run. However, regional differences in the natural population growth may also be affected by policies, the effectiveness of the social security system, and by popular opinion. Improved implementation of family planning policies and completion of the social security system is expected to moderate population growth in less developed regions, contributing to a reduction in regional income disparities.

Regional disparities in capital inflow

If the high-income region receives a continued capital inflow, the marginal product of capital diminishes and the marginal product of labour increases. There is an upward shift of the VMPL1 curve, and regional income disparities increase (Figure 6.2). These effects can be shown through conventional production function analysis.

Such effects occurred in the eastern coastal region. From 1979 to 2004, a total of US$560 billion of foreign direct investment, including investment from Chinese Hong Kong, Macao and Taiwan, flowed into mainland China. At least 85 per cent of investment was located in the eastern region. Net capital inflow to the eastern region, including both foreign and domestic capital, totalled RMB 100–300 billion per year during the 1990s, compared to only tens of billions per year into the central and western provinces. The inflow of investment capital has raised the VMPL in the eastern regions faster than in other regions. The western region has received RMB 100 billion of new capital inflow annually, but only after 1999 when the West Development Strategy was established (Wang and Fan 2004). The convergence of marginal product of capital and divergence of marginal product of labour between the eastern and western regions has been observed over a long period (Cai and Wang 2004).

The large capital inflow into the eastern region has sought the higher returns to capital within this region, mainly from higher productivity. Preferential government policies in the eastern region (such as tax holidays and deductions, exemption from import duties and reduced land prices) also attracted foreign direct investment by increasing the actual return to capital. This changed the overall pattern of capital allocation.

Policy differentials between the regions are a historical legacy of the initial stages of economic openness and reforms. However, the continuation of these policy distortions has created negative effects, such as low effiency in resource allocation, expansion of the regional development gap and income disparity. Some policy adjustments have been made for more equal treatment for investment across regions, but policy differentials are retained to prevent sudden shocks. The swifter removal of regional policy differentials will reduce regional income disparities and simultaneously increase efficiencies.

Education and vocational training

Although the floating rural labour across provinces totals more than 30 million, it equals only 8 per cent of total agricultural employment, and barriers still prevent the transfer of employment to different sectors. The NERI survey indicated 54 per cent of the total 3,200 migrant rural workers interviewed experienced difficulties due to a 'low level of education' and 38 per cent believed the 'lack of professional skills' was the main obstacle to job seeking.

A calculation by the author based on the NBS population survey in 2003, indicated the average year of schooling in the eastern region above 6 years old was 8.4 years, whereas it was only 7 years in the western region. The regional education gap is even more significant in rural areas. The difference in the level of education between regions accounts for reduced job-seeking opportunities for populations in the central and western regions and the lack of potential for technological progress and long-run development in the region.

For underdeveloped rural areas, a lack of financial resources for education and a dearth of qualified teachers are serious constraints. Compulsory primary education has not been fully achieved in some regions. At the same time, massive funds have been allocated for higher education in recent years, particularly to 'keystone' universities. The rationality behind the fiscal distribution of education funds needs to be re-examined.

The education system also lacks vocational education, with government educational departments emphasising the progression of students from secondary education to higher education, while ignoring vocational secondary education. Tertiary education enrolments have increased over recent years, and in 2004 totalled 4.5 million students. The current number of tertiary enrolments is double those of 2000, and 7 times 1990 levels. This is a significant achievement, but only a small proportion of students have the opportunity for higher education and this situation is unlikely to change in the forseeable future.

The total number of young job seekers entering the labour market is 17–18 million annually, including workers both with and without a secondary education; this number is several times higher that the annual level of tertiary enrolments. The major role of the secondary education system is to provide candidates for universities; vocational training for occupational skills is not catered for. From 1995 to 2003, the annual enrolment in the regular senior high schools increased from 2.74 to 7.52 million, an increase of 175 per cent. Enrolments in technical and vocational schools increased from 3.28 to 4.06 million, an increase of only 24 per cent. In the western region, vocational education is even less developed. The proportion of vocational school students to secondary school students in the western region is usually only half that in the eastern region.

The small size and slow growth of vocational education is not a result of weak demand. After completing even short-term vocational training, rural migrant workers are likely to find work much more easily. Most young migrant workers do not have the opportunity to enrol in vocational schools as local government-financed schools in urban areas are not open to migrant workers without the payment of a large additional fee.

This problem is the result of the current allocation of government education funding. Funding is distributed through administrative districts for local residents, thus discriminating against migrant workers. Clearly, education-funding policy must be reformed. The 'education voucher' system, proposed by some scholars, enabling all young residents to receive education regardless of where their official residence is registered, should be given attention.

Compulsory education in rural areas and underdeveloped regions must also be strengthened. China needs a larger secondary vocational education system to train young job seekers for employment, rather than exclusively concentrating on educating candidates for university. Vocational education and training will have a strong positive effect on reducing regional disparities and increase the long-term return on human capital.

Rapid change to the high level of urbanisation across China is a critical factor affecting the extent of rural labour migration. The urbanisation ratio, the proportion of urban residents to total population, increased from 28.5 per cent to 41.8 per cent from 1994 to 2004. The rural population has experienced a general decline since 1995. However, urbanisation has occurred in the eastern region faster than in other areas and this is likely to continue in the near future. Further urbanisation provides scope for continued labour migration (Wang and Xia 1999).

In summary, the current income disparity between regions might be averted in the foreseeable future with the appropriate adjustment of social policies.

Potential for future labour migration

Labour migration has important effects in reducing income disparity between regions in China. But what is the probability of the source areas continuing to export labour without hindering their own economic development in the long term? What is the population-carrying capacity of the destination areas? These questions will be discussed in the following section.

Origin of rural migrant workers

The MLSS survey (2002) indicated that six provinces—Jiangxi, Sichuan, Hunan, Anhui, Hubei and Henan—out of a total 20 central and western provinces, have each exported more than 2 million floating labourers. The total labour outflow from these six provinces is 18 million, accounting for two-thirds of the total cross-provincial labour outflow (Figure 6.3). Jiangxi has experienced the greatest outflow—25 per cent of its rural labour force resides in other provinces. Among the five other provinces, 10–15 per cent of the rural labour force resides in other provinces. In eight of the total twelve western provinces the total labour outflow is about 4 per cent or less.

The structure of labour outflows between provinces is unbalanced (Figure 6.3). This may be the result of customs between different provinces. For example, in northwestern China, the rural population strongly prefers to remain in the local area, despite the opportunity to earn much higher incomes elsewhere. The unbalanced structure of labour outflows is also the result of insufficient employment information in some areas. Labour outflows were observed to have a 'chain reaction' where one outgoing worker can prompt family members, relatives, friends, neighbours and villagers also to leave. This occurs when rural populations become aware of the job opportunities in urban areas.

The potential for labour outflows remains in most underdeveloped provinces. Where labour outflows are already significant, further outflow may have a temporary negative effect on agricultural production. Potential negative effects can be balanced through scale-economy effects from land transfer in the longer term. This process is a necessary precondition for modernisation of the agricultural sector. To achieve a comparable rural labour–land ratio to Japan, high compared to other developed countries, 80 per cent of current agricultural workers in China will need to transfer to non-agricultural sectors.

Capacity of destination areas

In 2000, five of the eleven east coastal provinces absorbed 75 per cent of the cross-province migrant rural labour. Guangdong province absorbed 14.5 million workers, accounting for half the total cross-province migrant workers. Zhejiang, Shanghai, Beijing and Fujian provinces absorbed 23 per cent of the total migration, and the other six coastal provinces received 11 per cent (Figure 6.4). In these six provinces, migrant workers only accounted for around 10 per cent of total urban employment.[3]

The distribution of migrant workers across the provinces is also unbalanced. Given the ability of Guangdong province to absorb large labour inflows, there appears to be potential for other eastern provinces to continue to absorb migrant workers. This ability will depend on the level and rate of economic development, urbanisation and the labour intensity of the industries at a provincial level.

Only Shanghai has reached a high population density of 2,600 persons per square kilometre. The population density of Beijing, Tianjin and Jiangsu is approximately 700–800 persons per square kilometre, while other coastal regions range from 200–500 people per square kilometre.[4]

In comparison several large cities around the world have a higher population density than Shanghai or Beijing. Tokyo has a population density approximately 13 000 persons per square kilometre, and the greater Tokyo area which includes Saitama, Chiba and Kanagawa prefectures is 2,400 people per square kilometre. Chinese Hong Kong had a population density of 6,163 persons per square kilometre in 2002, twice the density of Shanghai. Although the average population density in the United States, United Kingdom and France is significantly less than China, population densities in New York, London and Paris are equal to or higher than Beijing (Table 6.6). Potential exists for labour migration to provinces with lower

Figure 6.3   **Provincial comparison of emigration and total rural labour**

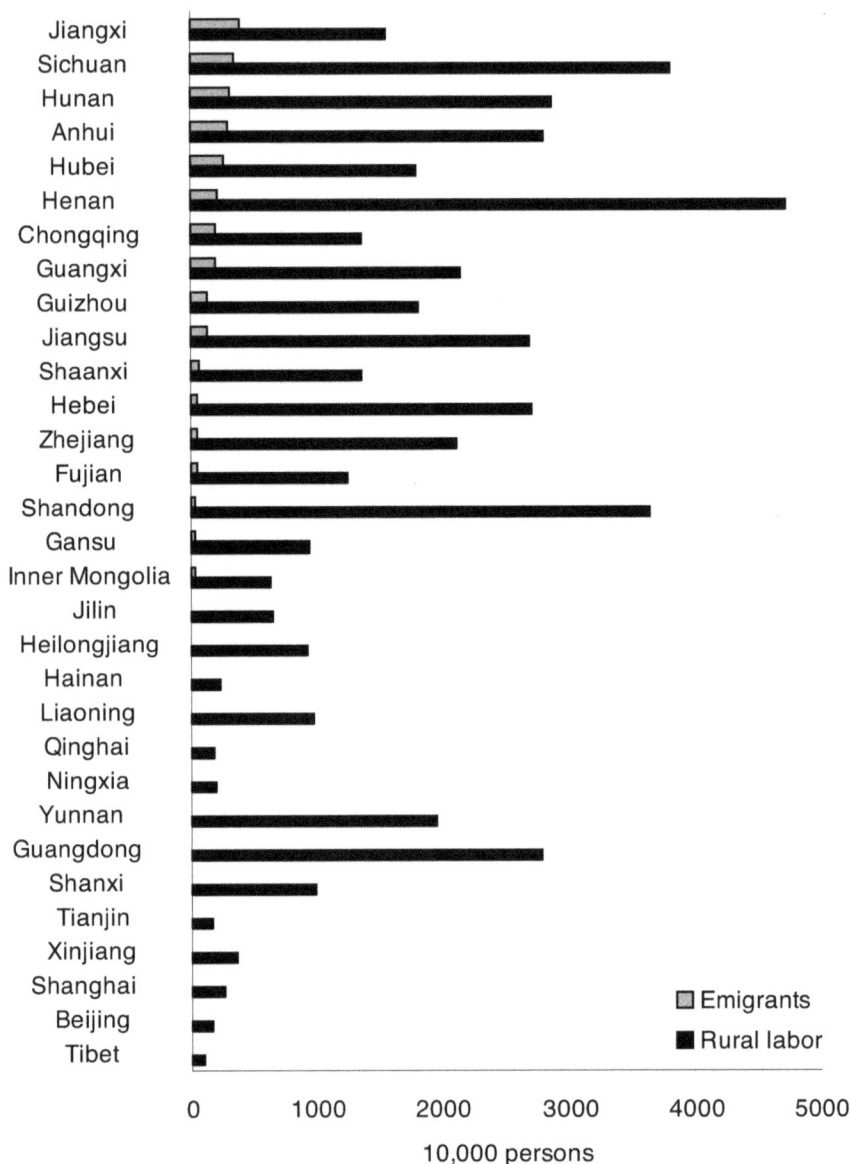

Source: National Bureau of Statistics, 2003. *Fifth National* Census, China Statistical Press, Beijing. Employment and Social Security Department of the Ministry of Labour and Social Security, 2002. *The Situation of Employment and Flow of China's Rural Labour*, China Labour Market Web. Available online at www.lm.gov.cn.

Figure 6.4   **Provincial comparison between the number of immigrants and total urban employment**

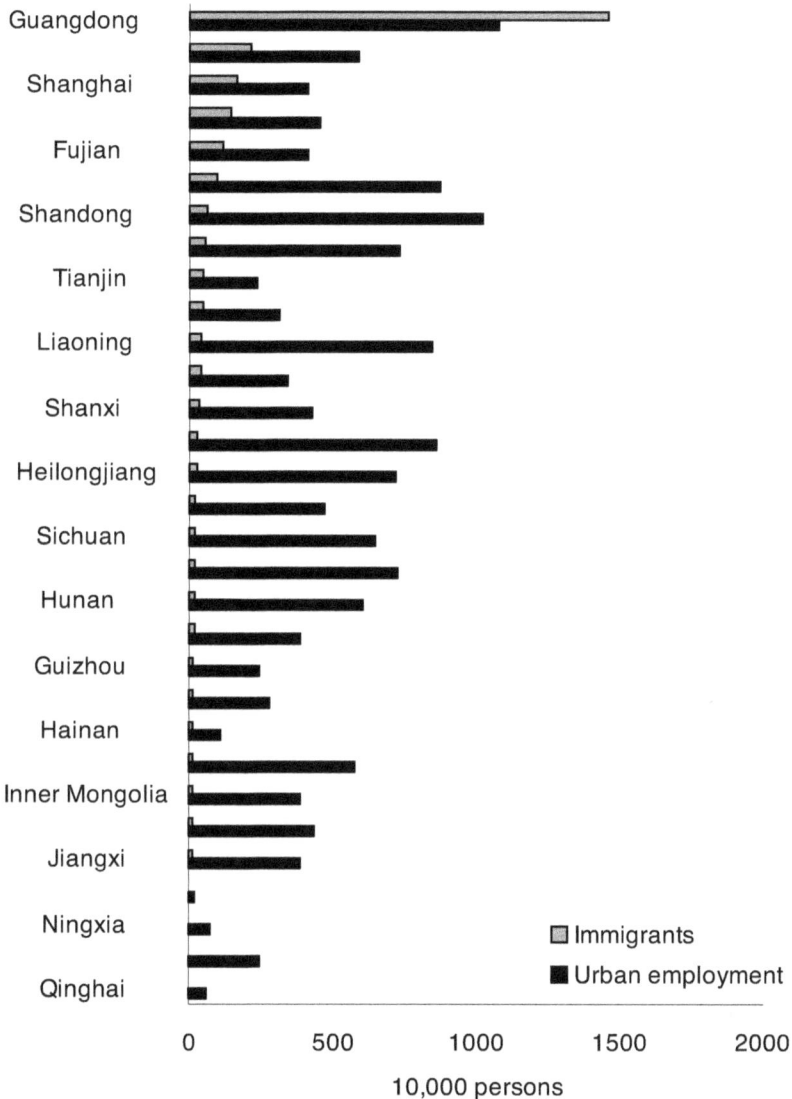

Note: Urban employment statistics in some provinces may be underreported. As a result, urban employment appears to be less than the number of immigrants.
Source: National Bureau of Statistics, 2003. *Fifth National* Census, China Statistical Press, Beijing. Employment and Social Security Department of the Ministry of Labour and Social Security, 2002. *The Situation of Employment and Flow of China's Rural Labour*, China Labour Market Web. Available online at www.lm.gov.cn.

population densities. Common problems in urban centres, such as traffic and air pollution can be resolved through the improvement of urban planning, municipal administration and environment controls.

'Floating workers' and 'floating' employment

Most floating workers are insecurely employed, their continued residence in urban centres uncertain. Migrant workers face difficulties in bringing their families to urban areas and most workers leave family in the countryside, regularly remitting money and returning for periods of time. As a result, trends in urbanisation are unstable, which has caused problems for the redistribution of unused land in the agricultural sector. To solve the problem, municipal governments and higher levels of government administration have a responsibility to create a non-discriminatory living environment with equitable legal rights and social welfare for new urban residents, enabling them to settle down in urban areas. These are critical preconditions to sustainable development in underdeveloped rural areas.

Conclusion

In summary, cross-regional labour migration has significantly contributed to the reduction of regional income disparity and an overall improvement in economic efficiency. Nonetheless, the western region's higher birth rates, remaining barriers to migration, and massive capital inflow into eastern coastal regions attracted by higher productivity levels preferential policies there, have caused regional income disparities to increase, although at a diminishing rate. Low education levels and the lack of available vocational training for the migrant workers appear to be the most serious barriers to further labour migration.

Table 6.6   **Population density in major world urban centres**

	Tokyo	New York	London	Paris	Beijing
Population (million people)	8.0	7.4	6.8	2.2	7.1
Area (1000 km²)	0.61	0.83	1.60	0.11	4.57
Population density (per km²)	13,115	8,916	4,250	20,000	1,554
Greater city area					
Population (million people)	32.6	19.8	12.3	10.7	10.4
Area (1000 km²)	13.6	32.9	11.3	12.0	16.8
Population density (per km²)	2,406	603	1,092	891	619

Sources: Yang and Han, 2004. *An Anatomy of Urban Transport Development in Japan*, Tongji University. Available online at http://www.tongji.edu.cn/.

Compulsory primary and secondary education in rural areas needs further attention. In addition, vocational education at a secondary school level needs to be improved and expanded. In conjunction with education strategies, family-planning policies in the western regions need improvement. More balanced national treatment policies for foreign and domestic investment across regions should be adopted. Finally, improvement in living environments, equitable access to legal protection and social welfare for migrant workers residing in urban areas need to be provided. It is expected that the proposed policy adjustments will bring the trend of increasing regional income disparity under control in the near future.

There remains significant potential for the expansion of labour migration across China. Some underdeveloped areas have only just begun to export labour, while development and urbanisation are creating new destinations for labour flows along the eastern coastal regions. The Yangzi River Delta has become a new destination, following the experience of Guangdong province. Further increases in labour migration will contribute to the economic development of both developed and underdeveloped areas across China and gradually reduce regional income disparity.

Notes

[1] The weighted average of GDP growth rates of the 31 provinces, autonomous regions and municipalities under direct administration of the Central Government, as published by the NBS, is higher than the published GDP growth rate for China as a whole. This is possibly a result of differences in statistical methodologies employed and adjustments by the NBS at the national level to deal with widespread over-reporting of GDP and growth rates by local statistical offices. It is likely the real regional gap in growth rates is greater than indicated because over-reporting is likely to be more common in central and western provinces than in eastern provinces.

[2] The extrapolated size of floating labour may be biased downward because data was collected from migrant workers' family members remaining in rural areas. Workers who migrated with their family members may have been excluded. It is expected the structure of floating labour is reliable.

[3] There is evidence that urban employment statistics in some provinces are underreported. Data from 2000 at the provincial level is significantly less than the national total. National urban employment levels are calculated based on the national population census so are more reliable. The informal employment sector is most underreported in urban employment data at the provincial level. As a result, the ratio of immigrant workers to urban employment as mentioned above may be overstated.

[4] Municipalities under the direct central administration, that is, Beijing, Shanghai and Tianjin, are calculated based on their full territory, that is, including their suburb areas.

References

Beladi, H. and Naqvi, N., 1987. 'The theory of inter-industry wage differentials: an inter-temporal analysis', *Canadian Journal of Economics,* 20(2): 245–56.

Cai, F. and Wang, D., 2004. 'Regional comparative advantage in China: diversity, variety and the impact on regional disparity', in Wang and Fan (eds), *Regional Disparity in China: tendency and the influential factors in 20 years*, Economic Science Press, Beijing (Chinese Language).

Employment and Social Security Department of the Ministry of Labour and Social Security (MLSS), 2002. *The Situation of Employment and Flow of China's Rural Labour*, China Labour Market Web. Available online at www.lm.gov.cn (Chinese Language).

Harris, J. R. and Todaro, M. P., 1970. 'Migration, unemployment and development: a two-sector analysis', *American Economic Review*, 60(1):126–42.

Lewis, W.A., 1954. 'Economic development with unlimited supplies of labour', *Manchester School of Economic and Social Studies,* 22:139–91.

National Bureau of Statistics (NBS), various years. *China Statistical Yearbook*, China Statistics Press, Beijing.

——,1999. *Comprehensive Statistical Data and Materials on 50 Years of New China*, China Statistics Press, Beijing.

——, 2005. *China Statistical Abstract*, China Statistical Press, Beijing.

Wang, X. and Xia, X., 1999. 'Optimizing city scale and fueling economic growth', *Economic Research*, 9:22–29.

—— and Fan, G., 2004. 'Regional disparity in China: an overall analysis on tendency and the influential factors in 20 years', in Wang and Fan (eds), *Regional Disparity in China: tendency and the influential factors in 20 years*, Economic Science Press, Beijing (Chinese Language).

World Bank, 1996. *The Chinese Economy: controlling inflation, deepening reform*, World Bank, Washington D.C.

Yang, D. and Han, H., 2004. 'An anatomy of urban transport development in Japan', Tongji University Website. Available online at http://www.tongji.edu.cn/ (Chinese Language).

7

Rapid urbanisation and implications for growth

Ligang Song and Sheng Yu

Since the mid 1980s, China has experienced unprecedented urbanisation, generating rapid growth in the urban labour force. The reallocation of resources prompted by this labour migration has become an important source of growth and rising incomes. At the same time, however, 'history's largest flow of rural–urban migration' also brings about enormous economic, social, environmental, as well as political challenges that China will have to confront to avoid major disruptions to growth.

This chapter discusses why urbanisation poses a particular challenge for China, highlighting the size, scope and speed of urbanisation, as well as the institutional constraints on rural-to-urban migration. Urbanisation, particularly the impact of low-cost migrant workers entering urban labour markets and the increased demand for urban infrastructure, has been a key generator of economic growth in China in recent years.

The chapter then identifies a number of driving forces behind urbanisation by applying the disequilibrium-analysis method. Using this analysis, it then compares the relative strength of both the 'pull' and 'push' factors determining urbanisation, finding that the 'push' forces are stronger than the 'pull' forces over the period of reform. This insight raises the question of whether the anticipated rate of urbanisation in China is likely to be 'excessive'.

We conclude that China needs to maintain reasonably high growth to alleviate the unemployment problems associated with urbanisation and ongoing enterprise restructuring. This can be achieved by further encouraging and promoting private sector development. The services sector needs to be expanded further to absorb increased employment associated with urbanisation. Urban reforms such as equal opportunities and social protection of migrant workers need to be accelerated.

Finally, a balanced strategy, one that focuses on investment in physical and human capital to promote development of the agricultural sector and rural communities, is needed to mitigate the strong 'push' forces driving people from rural areas.

The classical migration model and its application to China: a review

In the 1950s, development economists saw the demand for labour created by a 'growing modern industrial complex' as the main pull factor in migration (Williamson 1988). Statistical data on unemployment and underemployment collected from developing countries, however, contradicted this paradigm. Todaro (1969) and Harris and Todaro (1970) observed chronic unemployment problems in urban areas and instead suggested the expected wage gap between rural and urban areas was the 'pull' factor. Migration, they argued, is stimulated by rational economic considerations of relative benefits and costs—the decision to migrate depends on 'expected' rather than 'actual' urban–rural real wage differentials, and the probability of obtaining an urban job is inversely related to the urban unemployment rate.

Rural–urban migration in developing countries, especially those with large rural populations, such as China, is driven by both 'push' and 'pull' factors—urban–rural income gaps, urban development, employment opportunities in both rural and urban areas, and rural labour surpluses, among other things. Studying the relative strengths of the two forces can reveal how migration has been driven by their interaction.

For example, in the process of industrialisation, the possibility of over-urbanisation, or migration rates in excess of urban job-opportunity growth rates, will not only be possible but indeed rational. This is exactly what happened in many developing countries in the 1960s and 1970s, when rising levels of open urban unemployment prompted developing-country policymakers to shift from trying to transfer surplus labour from agriculture to industry to trying to reduce 'excessive' rates of urbanisation in these countries (Todaro 1985).

Basu (1995), focusing on the 'push' factors in urbanisation, analysed the relationship between rural labour surpluses and unemployment. As he argued, the marginal productivity of rural labour in many developing countries, for a variety of reasons, was zero over certain ranges, implying that the withdrawal of part of the labour force would have no effect on rural output. Thus, given the constant 'pull' from urban areas due to the income gap between rural and urban areas, the existence of surplus labour will accelerate urbanisation.

A number of studies have focused on urbanisation issues in China since the 1980s. A critical argument that prevails in the literature is that approaches to shaping this transformation should be based on analysis of people's motivations for migrating and the conditions they encounter when they do so. Liang, Chen and Gu (2002) focused on the 'push factors' for migration, exploring the possibility that migration was possibly curtailed by the level of rural industrialisation. Chen and Coulson (2002), in contrast, focused on the 'pull factors' of destinations for migrant workers. They found that migrants were attracted not so much by high wages but by high gross incomes and entrepreneurial activity.

Some studies focused more specifically on rural–urban income gaps, urban employment and growth, and rural output and productivity. For example, Zhu (2002) modelled the impact of income gaps on migration in China and found that they were the most important positive factor from both the 'push' and 'pull' perspectives. Cai (1996) studied the ratio of local rural income to the average national rural income, finding that higher ratios are associated with lower migration. Using household level data, Hare (1999) found rural per capita production assets had no significant effect on the expenditure of migrant workers. These findings are generally consistent with the predictions of the Harris–Todaro two-sector model.

Zhang (2002) analysed urban development and employment by examining the cross-provincial pattern of urban growth after 1978. He found that economic growth fostered rural–urban migration and urban growth, rather than vice versa. Foreign direct investment was an especially strong causal factor, explaining much of the difference between coastal and inland provinces in urban growth rates. Song and Zhang (2002) showed that, despite China's recent extraordinary urban development, the distribution of city size was within expectations from research on urban development in other nations—somewhat more even than the average nation, precisely as expected for a large country, but not too different from the commonly observed Pareto distribution.

Liang, Chen and Gu (2002) looked at how changes in rural output and productivity affected migration by examining the relationship between the level of rural industrialisation and migration from rural to urban areas. As they argued, although the rural industrialisation could slow rural–urban migration by providing potential migrants with opportunities to remain at home, it could also promote migration since 'investments in machines, new crops, improved seeds…all reduce the number of workers needed to produce a unit of agricultural output' (Massey 1988:391). This result is also consistent with Fei and Ranis' (1969) analysis of small-town development strategies in China, as well as some empirical studies, such as Yang (1996) and Liang (2001).

Building on previous studies, this chapter aims to make use of the disequilibrium-analysis method to explore the determination of urbanisation in China from both 'push' and 'pull' perspectives. Three issues—the urban–rural income gap, urban development, and employment and changes in rural output and productivity—will be reconsidered as 'push' and 'pull' factors from the demand and supply sides respectively.

Size, speed, contributions and challenges of urbanisation

In the course of economic development, virtually all countries follow a broadly similar trajectory: as development gets under way, the share of agriculture in national employment falls and there is a rapid increase in the share of manufacturing (Rowthorn and Coutts 2004). China has basically followed this path, but rapid urbanisation in China in the past two decades is also an outcome of profound economic transformation that has introduced market forces into the economic system and forced changes in economic, social and political institutions. One consequence of this in China is the massive movement of migrant workers from rural to urban areas since the beginning of economic reform in the late 1970s.

China's urbanisation experience has passed through two distinct periods since 1960, demonstrating very different trends from what would have arisen in a free-market economy (Liang, Chen and Gu 2002). The first was the period of central planning, lasting from 1960 to 1978, when urbanisation was often suppressed and, for military reasons, channelled away from the eastern coastal cities. During that time, the total number of cities increased only by 26 and the urban population stabilised at 90–110 million, implying a national urbanisation level of about 11–12 per cent.

The second period was the reform era from 1979 to the present, when the first period's bias was dramatically reversed, the eastern coastal cities tapped an expansion in China's international trade, and urbanisation accelerated significantly. The total number of cities increased from 193 in 1978 to 667 in 2003, or 245 per cent. China's non-agricultural population in urban areas increased from 172 million in 1978 to 524 million in 2003, a 204 per cent increase—much greater than the national population growth rate of 30 per cent over the same period. As a result, China's urbanisation rate (the share of urban population in total population) increased from 18 per cent in 1978 to 40.5 per cent in 2003 (Figure 7.1).[1]

It should be noted, however, that the real size of China's urban population is not clear from the official statistics because of some fundamental data problems. For example, cities do not generally count migrant workers in their population figures as people are 'counted' as living in their places of registration, not their actual residence. Nontheless, we know that China already has, in absolute terms, the world's largest urban population.

Figure 7.1   **Urbanisation rate, 1960–2003** (per cent)

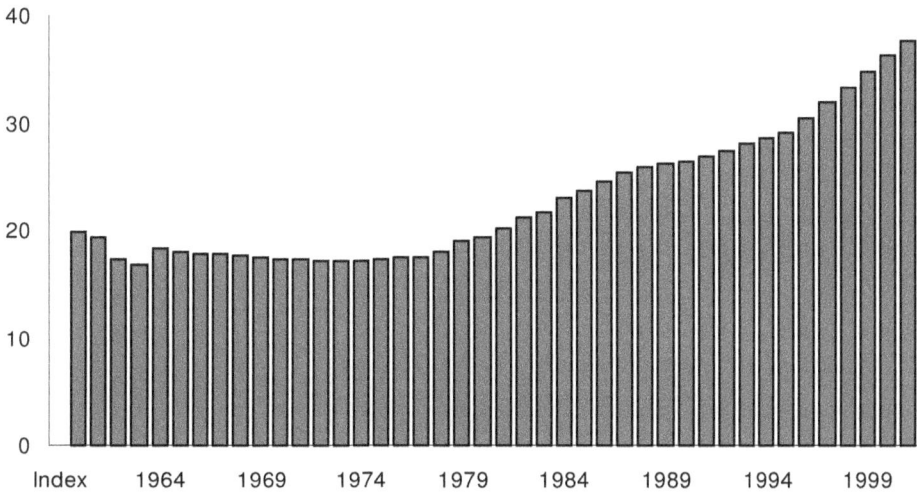

Source: Calculated using the figures from Appendix table A7.1

The rate of urbanisation differs greatly across various parts of the country. Appendix table A7.3 shows that major cities such as Beijing (77 per cent), Shanghai (88 per cent) and Tianjin (72 per cent), had much higher than average rates of urban growth (36 per cent) in 2000. In contrast, a large number of medium and small size cities still have relatively low rates of growth. The most rapid growth of urbanisation occurred between 1990 and 2000, with particular force in China's most dynamic areas, including Shanghai, Jiangsu, Fujian and Guangdong.

It can be expected that China's urban population will increase by another 100 million, probably surpassing the world average urbanisation level of 47 per cent around 2010. China's quantity of arable land per capita is less than half the world average and there is still a large supply of rural surplus labour (estimated at 200–250 million people). As a consequence, continuing urbanisation is important for increasing agricultural productivity and rural incomes and moving towards a more prosperous society for China.

Rapid urbanisation in China is the major factor in urban labour force growth and in optimising resource reallocation between the rural and urban areas, thereby enhancing economic growth. For example, the influx of rural migrants into urban areas has raised productivity because they have typically accepted relatively low wages, and this in turn has helped Chinese industries maintain competitiveness. Rural–urban migration also provides significant income supplements to the inland provinces through remittance flows.

Migrant workers' contribution to growth can be seen from rural migrant workers' rising employment share in China's dynamic non-state sector (Table 7.1). The role of SOEs and collectives in absorbing migrant workers fell rapidly between 1995 and 2002. By contrast, the share of rural migrants in non-state sector employment has been consistently increasing, from 14 per cent in 1995 to 53 per cent in 2002. In fact the non-state sector's share is probably even higher as private participation in SOEs' activities is now commonplace but not well captured by the statisticians (Garnaut et al. 2005).

The rapid pace of urbanisation has also resulted in a very high demand for basic urban infrastructure. As Davis and Henderson (2003:98) observed, '[u]rbanisation and economic development go hand-in-hand as a country moves from a rural-agricultural base to an urban-industrial base'. As a result, infrastructure development has become a fundamental driving force in China's recent growth (Table 7.2).[2]

However, the large scale of rural–urban migration also poses enormous challenges for the government. Many small cities and towns are now emerging, sprawling over previously arable land and reducing the amount of this scarce resource available (at 0.095 hectares per capita, China's level of arable land is already less than half the world average). The absolute decline in the quantity of arable land,

Table 7.1   **Employment of rural migrant workers in urban areas by ownership, 1995–2002** (10,000 person and per cent)

| | Employment | | | | Proportion (Total=100) | | |
	Total	SOEs	Collectives	Others[1]	SOEs	Collectives	Others
1995	1431	762	465	203	53	33	14
1996	1265	682	392	191	54	31	15
1997	1153	595	349	209	52	30	18
1998	913	400	240	274	44	26	30
1999	929	390	226	313	42	24	34
2000	897	341	201	355	38	22	40
2001	904	327	178	399	36	20	44
2002	1002	299	169	535	30	17	53

Note: [1] Others include all non-state (collective) enterprises including domestic private and foreign firms.
Source: Assembled and calculated using the data from the *Statistical Yearbook of China*.

coupled with lower growth rates among township and village enterprises (TVEs) since the 1990s, has put further pressure on rural employment and thereby strengthened the 'push' forces for urbanisation. The growing number of jobless and landless peasants presents a major concern for social stability, demanding firm measures to protect peasants' rights effectively in economic transition.

Those who do migrate into urban areas are often poorly paid and cannot enjoy the privileges that urban residents enjoy, such as state-subsidised unemployment and retirement benefits, schooling and medical care. This is largely because urban governments often view migrant workers as 'belonging' to their place of origin.

This attitude and the lack of institutional support pose various social and political problems for migrant workers in urban areas, such as general discrimination, constraints on jobs, legal vulnerabilities (lack of social protection), lack of access to services, and vulnerability to crimes.

Table 7.2   Infrastructure development in urban areas, 1990–2003

	1990	1995	2000	2003
City area				
Developed area(sq.m)	12856	19264	22439	28308
Floor space of buildings (100 mn sq.m)	40	57	77	141
Floor space of residence (100 mn sq.m)	20	31	44	89
Water supply, gas supply and heating				
Annual supply of tap water (100 mn tonnes)	382	482	469	475
Coal gas supply (100 mn cubic m)	175	127	152	202
Natural gas supply (100 mn cubic m)	64	67	82	142
Liquefied petroleum gas ('000 tonnes)	219	489	1054	1126
Length of gas pipeline (10,000 km)	2	4	9	13
Municipal infrastructure				
Length of road (10,000 km)	10	13	16	21
Area of road (100 mn sq. m)	9	14	19	32
Length of sewer pipeline (10,000 km)	6	11	14	20
Public transport				
Number of public vehicles for business transportation (10,000 units)	6	14	23	26
Taxis (10,000 units)	11	50	83	90
Afforestation				
Public green area (10,000 hectares)	48	68	87	121
Area of park and zoo (10,000 hectares)	4	7	8	11

Source: National Bureau of Statistics, 2004. *China Statistical Yearbook*. China Statistics Press, Beijing.

Given the significance of the issues involved, any policy response promoting development and industrialisation must identify what specifically is driving Chinese urbanisation.

Disequilibrium analysis and data

The method of disequilibrium analysis was originally developed by Dixit (1969), and is currently widely used for discussing transitional economies. The core of the method is to specify the determinants of equilibrium from both supply and demand perspectives separately and then combine them to identify their relative roles in affecting the equilibrium. Following Young and Deng (1998), we apply this method to analyse the factors determining urbanisation in China. The counterpart forces are specified as the 'push' force in rural areas and the 'pull' force exerted by urban areas.

The large wage or income differential between rural and urban areas is thought to be a fundamental cause of migration. In the Chinese case, one can decompose this fundamental cause into three factors: the urban–rural income gap, urban development and employment, and changes in rural output and productivity. The channels through which these factors affect urbanisation can be assumed as being the demand ('pull') and supply ('push') forces respectively.

First, from the supply perspective, urbanisation in China is affected by the release of rural surplus labour. There are three factors which influence the emigration of rural labour—agricultural sector output, rural employment, and the rural–urban income gap. Thus, the relationship can be written as follows

$$\ln US_t = \alpha_0 + \alpha_1 \ln RO_t + \alpha_2 \ln RE_t + \alpha_3 \ln GAP_t \\ + \alpha_4 DM78 + \alpha_5 DM89 + \varepsilon_t \tag{7.1}$$

where US represents the urbanisation determined from the supply side at time t, RO_t stands for agricultural output at time t, RE_t represents rural employment at time t, and GAP_t stands for the rural–urban income gap. Equation 7.1 shows that the labour supply resulting from urbanisation in China can be generally defined as the function of rural output, rural employment and the urban–rural income gap. From the demand perspective, urbanisation in China is affected by the absorption of labour in urban areas. Three factors determine the immigration of urban labour— urban employment, the natural growth rate of urban population and the rural– urban income gap. Thus, the relationship can be written as

$$\ln UD_t = \beta_0 + \beta_1 \ln UE_t + \beta_2 \ln NR_t + \beta_3 \ln GAP_t \\ + \beta_4 DM78 + \beta_5 DM89 + \varepsilon_t \tag{7.2}$$

where UD_t represents the urbanisation determined from the demand side at time t, UE_t represents urban employment at time t, NR_t represents the natural growth rate of the population in urban areas at time t, and GAP_t represents the rural–urban income gap. Equation 7.2 shows that the labour demand of urbanisation in China can be generally defined as the function of urban employment, the urban population natural growth rate, and the urban–rural income gap.

Meanwhile, in both the supply and demand equations, dummy variables for the specific years of 1978 and 1989 are used to test the impact of government policies and political changes on urbanisation.

Combining Equations 7.1 and 7.2, the equilibrium urbanisation level is jointly determined by both the demand and supply of rural labour.3 Since there is always some difference between the demand and supply forces of rural–urban migration at each time, the minimum of both forces represents the condition on which actual (equilibrium) urbanisation occurs.

$$UB_t = \min\ (US_t,\ UD_t) \tag{7.3}$$

where UB_t represents the urbanisation equilibrium shown in practice, US_t stands for urbanisation as determined by the supply forces at time t as shown in Equation 7.1, and UD_t represents urbanisation as it is determined by the demand forces at time t as shown in Equation 7.2.

Equations 7.1–7.3 constitute the disequilibrium method for analysing the determination of urbanisation. On the one hand, one can assume that the urbanisation rate is mainly determined by supply forces, estimated using Equation 7.1. On the other hand, one can assume that the urbanisation rate is mainly determined by demand forces, estimated using Equation 7.2. Comparing these two independently estimated results, the relative strength of both the 'push' and 'pull' forces in determining urbanisation in China at different periods of time can be discerned. The results can also be used to predict future changes in the urbanisation process.

Data used for the disequilibrium analysis are from three sources — *The Statistical Yearbook of China*, *The Urban Statistical Yearbook of China* and *The Labour Statistical Yearbook of China*. The sample is specified as the annual data series, taken in log form to reduce the time trend effects. The urbanisation index is defined in two forms: one follows Young and Deng (1998), measuring the ratio between urban population and total population, while the other is the ratio between the rural–urban migration over the total urban population. The agricultural output index at time t is defined as the ratio between the value of rural output and total GDP. Rural employment at time t is defined as the number of people employed in rural areas. Urban employment at time t is defined as the total number of people employed in urban areas. The natural growth rate of population in urban areas at time t is defined as the newly-born rate minus the death rate in urban areas. The rural–urban income gap is defined as the ratio of the real wage per capita in urban areas over the real income per capita in rural areas.

The determinants of urbanisation: estimation results

Table 7.3 shows the results of the analysis. The dependent variable in the disequilibrium regressions is defined as the urban–total population ratio and the migration–urban population respectively. The independent variables are defined as rural output, rural employment, and the urban–rural income gap for the supply side; and urban employment, the natural population growth rate in urban areas, and the urban–rural income gap for the demand side.

On the supply side, urbanisation is positively correlated with rural–urban income gaps, with the coefficients equaling 0.69 and 2.68 at the 10 per cent significance level respectively for the two model estimations. This finding supports the hypothesis that rural–urban income gaps are the most important motivation for people to migrate from rural to urban areas. Figure 7.2 shows the widening income gap between rural and urban households in terms of per capita disposable incomes over the period 1978–2003.

The coefficients of agricultural output are 0.03 and 0.16, and both are statistically significant at the 10 per cent level. This implies that the growth of agricultural output contributes positively to urbanisation. This is consistent with a number of studies on urbanisation. Perkins (1969) found that the need to obtain an agricultural surplus to supply urban residents' basic needs placed constraints on the size and location of urban centres. Chan (1994) showed that net rural–urban migration rates were positively related to urban grain supplies over the 1956–82 period and there were significant positive relationships between urbanisation and rural grain output per person.

The coefficients of the rural employment indices are –0.05 and –0.15 — statistically significant at 10 per cent level for the regression with the urban–total population ratio, but insignificant for the regression with the migration–urban population ratio. This suggests that the current level of rural employment is insignificant in affecting urbanisation. A possible explanation is that there might be potential over-employment in the rural areas, reflecting rural surplus labour in the agricultural sector.

The overall regression of urbanisation in China with respect to the supply factors is statistically significant (F-test is 12.37 and 7.09 respectively), providing some evidence that supply factors do play an important role in determining urbanisation.

Table 7.3   **Determining the pace of urbanisation from supply and demand perspectives, 1960–2003**

| | Supply equation | | | Demand equation | |
	Urban– population ratio	Migration– urban population ratio		Urban– population ratio	Migration– urban population ratio
Constant	−0.10	−0.74	Constant	0.42	1.05
	[−0.70]	[−0.94]		[1.53]	[0.73]
RO	0.03	0.16	UE	0.05	0.27
	[1.67]	[1.62]		[3.22]	[3.56]
RE	−0.05	−0.15	NR	−0.30	−1.05
	[−1.59]	[−0.95]		[−2.45]	[−1.66]
GAP	0.69	2.68	GAP	0.47	0.21
	[1.78]	[1.91]		[1.82]	[2.10]
DM78	0.82	4.08	DM78	0.82	3.09
	[3.52]	[4.85]		[4.37]	[3.16]
DM89	−0.74	−2.46	DM89	−0.65	−2.32
	[−3.29]	[−2.12]		[−3.43]	[−2.34]
Adjusted			Adjusted		
R-square	0.62	0.42	R-square	0.67	0.54
D-W tests	0.60	0.51	D-W tests	0.54	0.48
F-statistics	12.37	7.09	F-statistics	18.34	10.8

Source: Authors' own calculations.

Figure 7.2   **Rising per capita income gap between urban and rural areas in China: 1978–2003** (yuan)

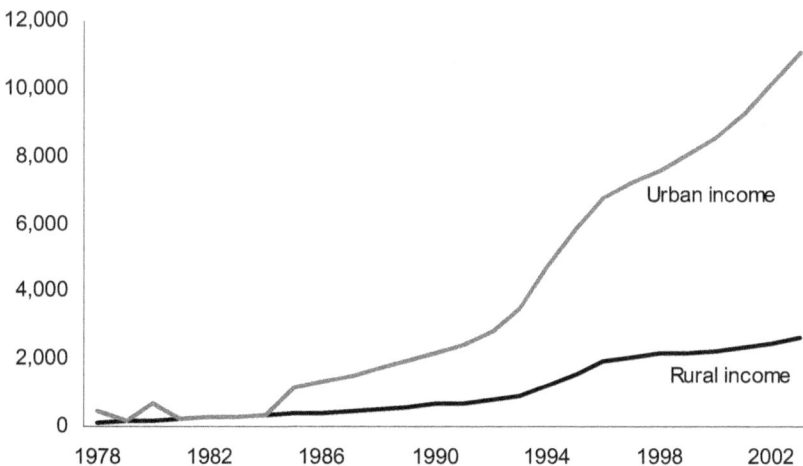

Source: Authors' own calculations using the data from the National Bureau of Statistics, 2004. *China Statistical Yearbook*. China Statistics Press, Beijing.

From the demand perspective, urbanisation is positively correlated with the rural–urban income gap and negatively correlated with the natural growth rate of population, and urban employment has a statistically significant effect on urbanisation. The coefficients of the rural–urban income gap and the natural growth rate of population are 0.47, 0.21 and –0.30, –1.05 respectively for both model estimations. Both are statistically significant. The coefficients for urban employment are 0.05 and 0.27, which are statistically significant at 5 per cent level.

These findings imply first that the rural–urban income gap is a critical factor in urbanisation in the reform era, supporting Anderson and Ge's (2004) conclusion that urban demand for rural labour is mainly motivated by economic incentives. Second, because rural immigrants compete with the urban population for jobs, the urban population growth rate is negatively correlated with urban–rural migration, suggesting there might be a constraint on urbanisation when both rural–urban migration and urban population increase at the same time. Third, and most significantly, employment opportunities in urban areas are the most important factor attracting new migrant workers to urban areas.

The dummy variables are statistically significant at the 5 per cent level in both the supply and demand equations, confirming that political factors could deter migrant workers from entering urban areas, while market-oriented reform could enhance the process of urbanisation.

The process of urbanisation in China has been determined by both supply (push) and demand (pull) forces (Figure 7.3). A clear pattern can be seen, however, in which each force has played a dominant role in determining the process of urbanisation. Rural–urban migration before 1978 was mainly dominated by demand factors. The urban labour demand force was much stronger than the calculated supply forces for most of the years in this period, suggesting that urbanisation before 1978 was driven largely by the 'pull' forces.

But this trend reversed after the initiation of reforms in 1978. The calculated 'push' forces of rural labour supply were consistently stronger than the 'pull' forces of labour demand, implying that the process of urbanisation over the period of reform was driven predominantly by the 'push' forces from the rural areas. An explanation on this phenomenon is that economic reform and its related policy changes have not only accelerated urban growth, but have also relaxed the various constraints on rural–urban migration. These constraints, the legacy of central planning, suppressed the 'push' forces in the period prior to economic reform, so their removal released pent-up pressures for migration and generated an unprecedented rush to the cities.

Figure 7.3   **The disequilibrium analysis on urbanisation in China, 1960–2003**

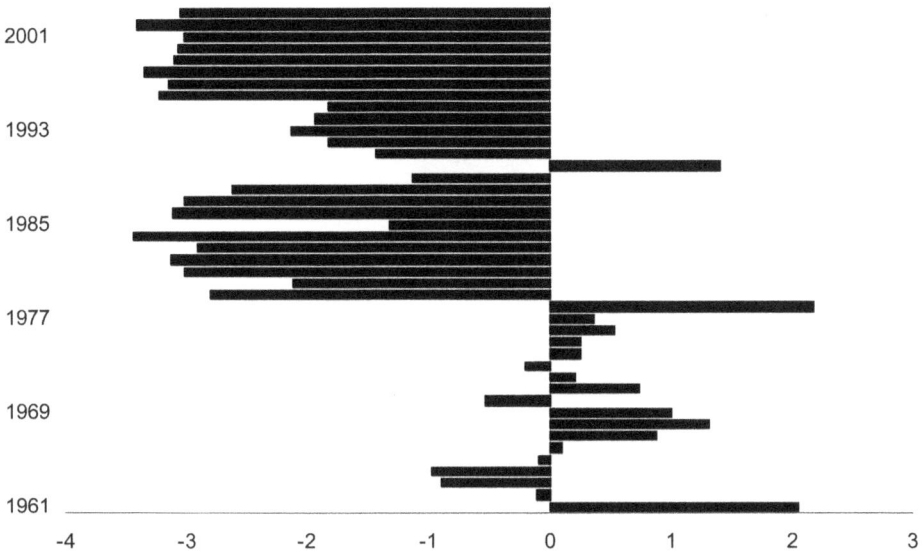

Source: Authors' calculations.

Second, precisely because of this unprecedented scale of migration, there is a danger of over-urbanisation. The dominance of supply-determined rather than demand-determined urbanisation since 1978 suggests that a major factor is the sheer scale of surplus labour in rural areas, built up by long-term policy discrimination against agriculture and associated restrictions on labour mobility. This surplus labour needs to be released and absorbed by the urban sectors in the process of economic transformation.

Dilemmas in managing the process of urbanisation

China is facing a dilemma in managing urbanisation. On the one hand, although great progress has been made, China's rate of urbanisation is still relatively low, not only compared with the world average, but also with the current level of industrialisation in China. The agricultural sector provides roughly half of all employment in China but contributes only about 14 per cent of the nation's GDP (Figures 7.4 and 7.5). According to Chinese statistics, the total rural labour force was about 490 million people at the end of 2002, of which 320 million worked in the agricultural sector. The actual demand for labour in agriculture, however, is estimated to be only about 170 million, which means that about 150 million people are therefore redundant. Some even estimate that, given the amount of arable land now available, the agricultural sector would need only about 60 million people to sustain current levels of grain production, which suggests that the real size of the rural labour surplus may be much higher (Chen 2004). Continuing to shift rural surplus labour out of the agricultural sector is the key to raising agricultural productivity and rural incomes, boosting domestic demand, especially in rural areas, and accelerating the pace of industrialisation in China.

China thus needs to accelerate the pace of urbanisation. An effective way of doing so is to reduce further the remaining institutional barriers raised by the *hukou* system (household registration system), which still restricts the mobility of labour, especially migrant workers. After more than twenty years' reform, the *hukou* system is no longer a prohibitive policy, but continues to act as an important institutional barrier to the free flow of workers and to cause segregation in the labour market. A consequence of the *hukou* system is that the 'pull' force from the urban areas tends to be weakened, thereby slowing urbanisation. Meanwhile, there are social, economic, political and environmental concerns associated with rural–urban migration that also tend to affect the process of urbanisation in China.

At the same time, the strong 'push' forces raise the risk of over-urbanisation, especially in the short to medium terms. This possibility raises a number of issues for the Chinese government. First, there are concerns over employment. As predicted by the Harris–Todaro model, an increase in the number of manufacturing jobs will lead to rural–urban migration so large that urban unemployment actually rises. China's urban areas already face increasing pressure to resolve employment problems for those who have just graduated and entered the labour market and those who have been laid off in enterprise restructuring. The different scenarios for urban labour force forecasts reported in Table 7.4 highlight the challenges of meeting China's employment targets in the next 10–15 years.

According to other developed countries' experiences, once a certain per-capita GDP is reached, the share of manufacturing product in total GDP increases, but following industrial structural adjustment and growing productivity, manufacturing employment falls. The estimated turning point, according to Rowthorn and Coutts (2004), is around US$9,500 (1995 PPP) per capita, which most OECD countries had reached by 1970, despite having a per-capita income of only US$1,000. However, China has already seen its industrial labour force share peak and stabilise since the mid 1990s (Figure 7.5). This indicates that China will have to rely more heavily on the development of service sectors to increase employment opportunities.

Figure 7.4   **Industrial structure of the economy, 1978–2003** (per cent)

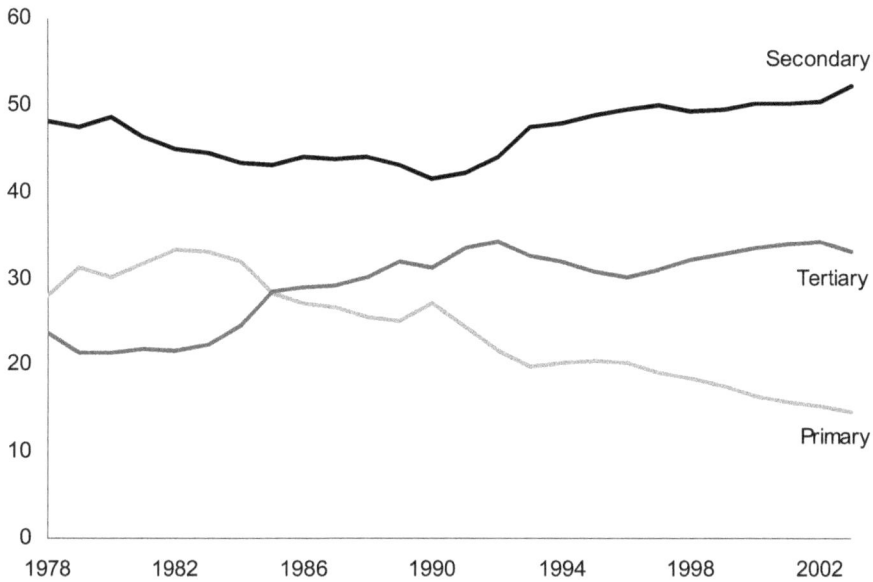

Source: National Bureau of Statistics, 2004. *China Statistical Yearbook.* China Statistics Press, Beijing.

Figure 7.6 shows the growth of urbanisation in China from 1960 to 2003. The growth rate of urbanisation in China has been decreasing over time, especially since 1996, suggesting that urbanisation has tended to slow in more recent years. A possible explanation is that the growth of the urban services sector has been insufficient to compensate for the slow growth of manufacturing-sector employment, and hence there are simply not enough jobs available. Further development of the services sector and encouragement of private sector development will strengthen the 'pull' force from the urban areas, facilitating a faster pace of urbanisation.

Second, smooth and stable urbanisation will also depend on whether the agricultural sector can remain sustainable. Uneven development between a relatively modern and high-wage industrial sector and a poor traditional agricultural sector within a single economy is usually described as 'economic dualism' (Todaro 1985). Economic dualism tends to diminish as a country's level of urbanisation increases. This phenomenon, however, has not taken place in China. Figure 7.2 shows that income gaps between urban and rural areas in China have been widening,

Table 7.4   **Three scenarios for urban labour force forecasts, 1995–2020**
(number of net urban migration: million people in five years)

Urbanisation	With an increase rate of 1 per cent per year	With an increase rate of 2.5 per cent per year between 2001–10 and 2 per cent between 2011–20	With an increase rate of 4 per cent per year between 2001–10 and 3 per cent between 2011–20
	Conservative	Moderate	Radical
1996–2000	45.9	45.9	45.9
2001–05	47.3	49.5	51.7
2006–10	49.7	56.3	62.9
2011–15	52.2	63.3	74.3
2016–20	54.9	70.5	86.1

Source: Taken from Table 7.1 and Xu, Y., 2000. *Forecasting Labour Supply in Urban China: integrating demographic dynamics and socioeconomic transition*, Interim Report, International Institute for Applied Systems Analysis, Laxenburg.

particularly in recent years. The urban–rural income ratio increased from 2.93 in 1978 to 3.23 in 2003, which implies that the urban–rural income gap has not fallen through urbanisation.

The growth rate of agricultural output has also been falling in recent years (Figure 7.7), which will reduce rural employment opportunities and thereby strengthen the 'push' forces in urbanisation. To weaken the 'push' forces in order to achieve a more balanced process of urbanisation, the government needs to deepen rural reform by providing more incentives for engaging in agricultural production, encouraging technological change, and increasing agricultural inputs.

Another measure aimed at adjusting 'push' forces is to revive rural industries. Taiwan's experience shows that an increase in rural industrialisation tends to promote urbanisation (Parish 1994). This can be achieved by further transforming the ownership of the TVEs, developing appropriate means of rural finance, investing in both physical and human capital in rural areas, and building rural infrastructure.

Conclusion

Urbanisation in China has been regarded as the most solid indication that China's economic growth will continue for many years to come. Expanding the labour force in the modern urban sector by shifting labour out of agriculture enhances productivity and thereby contributes to growth. The disequilibrium analysis used here shows that urbanisation in China since 1978 has been driven mainly by 'push' factors. An important implication is that there might be a possibility of over-

Figure 7.5   **Employment structure of the economy, 1978-2003** (per cent)

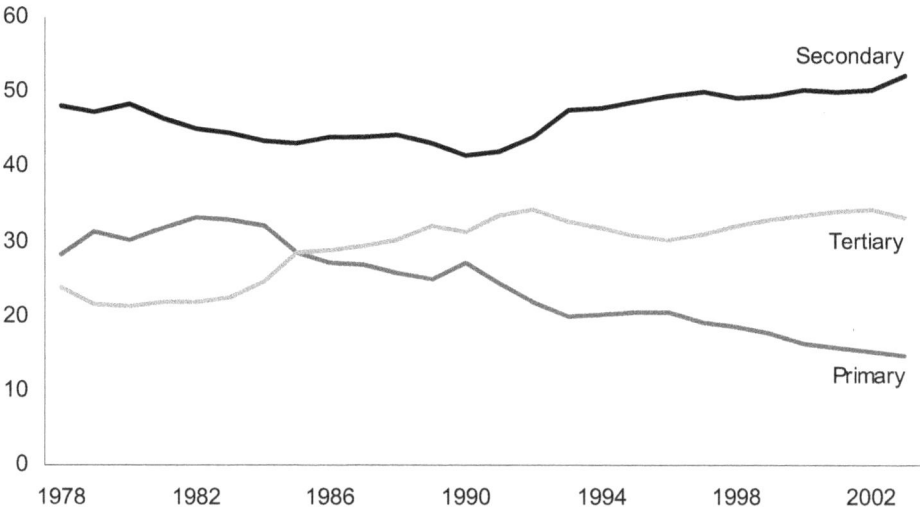

Source: National Bureau of Statistics, 2004. *China Statistical Yearbook.* China Statistics Press, Beijing.

Figure 7.6   **Growth rate of urbanisation in China 1960–2003**

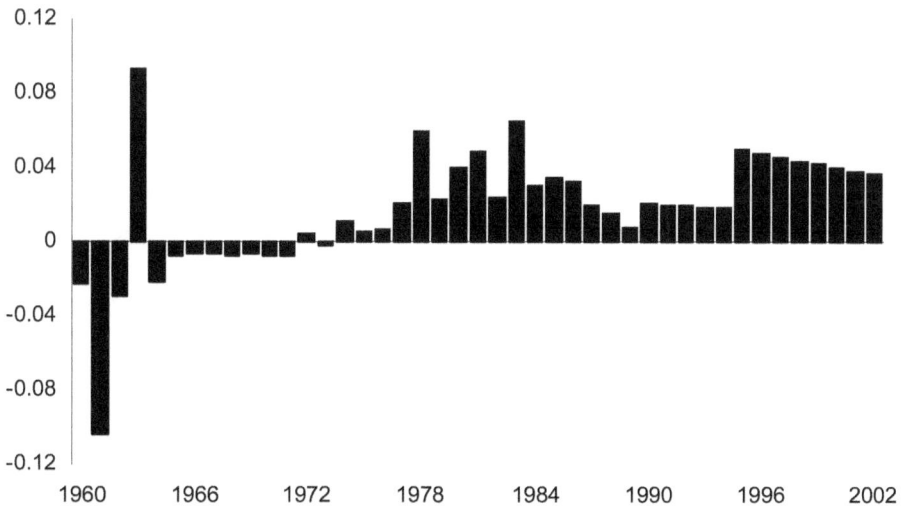

Source: Authors' calculations using the data from National Bureau of Statistics, 2004. *China Statistical Yearbook.* China Statistics Press, Beijing.

Figure 7.7   **Growth rates of agricultural outputs, 1961–2003** (per cent)

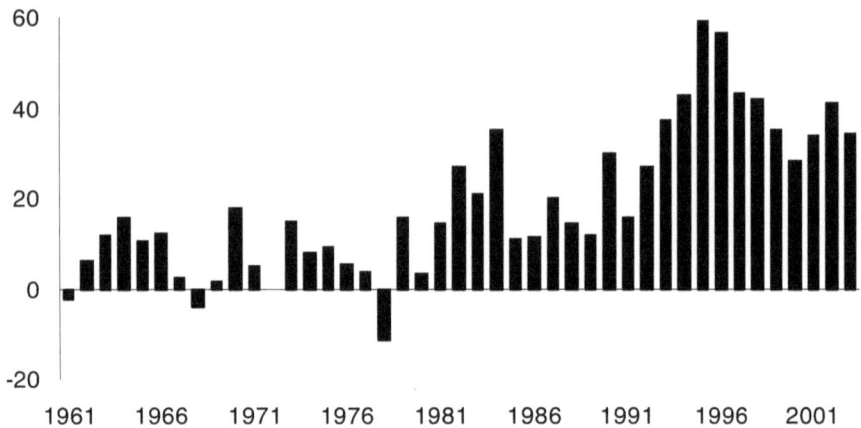

Source: National Bureau of Statistics, 2004. *China Statistical Yearbook.* China Statistics Press, Beijing.

urbanisation, especially in the short to medium term, given the increasing income differential between rural and urban areas, the rapid loss of arable land, and the growing rural labour surplus. At the same time, rural–urban migration is central to the problem of growing urban unemployment. There are, therefore, huge demands for employment, urban infrastructure development, institution building and policy adjustment to cope with the massive movement of migrant workers.

China needs to maintain a reasonably high growth rate in order to solve its unemployment problem. This can be achieved by encouraging and promoting further private sector development. The services sector in particular needs to be expanded to provide more employment opportunities. Urban reforms such as equal opportunity and social protection of migrant workers will have to accelerate. Finally, a balanced strategy that develops agriculture through investment in both physical and human capital and increased public expenditure to build rural communities is needed to mitigate strong pressure resulting from the 'push' forces in migration.

Notes

[1] The rate of urbanisation rose to 42 per cent in 2004 and the urban contribution to GDP increased to 70 per cent (*The People's Daily*, Overseas Edition, 12 May 2005).

[2] Although Zhang and Song's (2003) finding shows that the causal link runs from economic growth to migration.

[3] In each time period, either demand (pull) or supply (push) forces could play a more important role in determining the process of urbanisation.

References

Anderson, G. and Ge, Y., 2004. 'Do economic reforms accelerate urban growth? The case of China', *Urban Studies*, 41(11):2197–210.

Basu, K., 1995. *Analytical Development Economics: the less developed economy revisited*, The MIT Press, Cambridge.

Chan, K.W., 1994. 'Determinants of urbanisation in China: empirical investigations', in L. Day and X. Ma (eds), *Migration and Urbanisation in China*, M.E. Sharpe, Armonk, New York:241–66.

Chen, H., 2004. On the transfer of China's surplus labour from rural areas, China Economic Information Network. Available online at http://www.cei.gov.cn/.

Cai, F., 1996. 'Comparative advantage and the internationalisation of China's agriculture', in R. Garnaut, S. Guo and G. Ma (eds), *The Third Revolution in Chinese Countryside*, Cambridge University Press, Cambridge:173–84.

Chen, A. and Coulson, N.E., 2002. 'Determinants of urban migration: evidence from Chinese cities', *Urban Studies*, 39(12):2189–97.

Davis, J.C. and Henderson, J.V., 2003. 'Evidence on the political economy of the urbanisation process', *Journal of Urban Economics*, 53(1):98–125.

Dixit, A., 1969. 'Public finance in a Keynesian temporary equilibrium', *Journal of Economic Theory*, 12(2):242–58.

Fei, J. and Ranis, G., 1969. 'Economic development in historical perspective', *American Economic Review*, 59(2):286–400.

Garnaut, R., Song, L., Tenev, S. and Yao, Y., 2005. *China's Ownership Transformation: process, outcomes, prospects*, The International Finance Corporation and the World Bank, Washington, DC.

Hare, D., 1999. '"Push" versus "Pull" factors in migration outflows and returns: determinants of migration status and spell duration among China's rural population', in S. Cook and M. Maurer-Fazio (eds), *The Workers' State Meets the Market: labour in China's transition*, Frank Cass Publishers, London:45–72.

Harris, J.R. and Todaro, M.P., 1970. 'Migration, unemployment and development: a two-sector analysis', *American Economic Review*, 60(1):126–42.

Li, H. and Zahniser, S., 2002. 'The determinants of temporary rural-to-urban migration in China', *Urban Studies*, 39(12):2219–35

Li, B., 2004. *Urban Social Exclusion in Transitional China CASE Paper 82*, Centre for Analysis of Social Exclusion, London School of Economics, London.

Liang, Z., 2001. 'The age of migration in China', *Population and Development Review*, 27(3):499–524.

——, Chen, Y. and Yanmin Gu, Y., 2002, 'Rural industrialisation and internal migration in China', *Urban Studies*, 39(12):2175–87.

Lin, J.Y., Cai, F. and Li, Z., 1996. 'The lessons of China's transition to a market economy', *Cato Journal*, 16(2):201–31.

Massey, D.S., 1988. 'Economic development and international migration in comparative perspective', *Population and Development Review*, 14(3):383–413.

National Bureau of Statistics, 2004. *China Statistical Yearbook*, China Statistics Press, Beijing.

Parish, W, 1994. 'Rural industrialisation in Fujian and Taiwan', in T. Lyons and V. Nee (eds), *The Transformation of South China*, East Asian Series No. 70, Cornell University, New York:119–40.

Perkins, D., 1969. *Agricultural Development in China: 1368–1968*, Aldine Publishing Company, Chicago.

Rowthorn, R. and Coutts, K., 2004. 'De-industrialisation and the balance of payments in advanced economies', *Cambridge Journal of Economics*, 28(5):767–90.

Song, S. and Zhang, K.H., 2002. 'Urbanisation and city size distribution in China', *Urban Studies*, 39(12):2317–27.

Todaro, M.P., 1969. 'A theoretical note on labour as a "inferior" factor in less developed economies', *Journal of Development Studies*, 5(4):252–61.

——, 1985. *Economic Development in the Third World*, Longman, New York and London (Third Edition).

Xu, Y., 2000. *Forecasting Labour Supply in Urban China: integrating demographic dynamics and socioeconomic transition*, Interim Report, International Institute for Applied Systems Analysis, Laxenburg.

Yang, D., 1996, *Calamity and Reform in China: state, rural society, and institutional change since the Great Leap famine*, Stanford University Press, Stanford.

Young, D. and Deng, H., 1998. 'Urbanisation, agriculture and industrialisation in China, 1952–91', *Urban Studies*, 35(9):1439–55.

Zhang, K.H., 2002. 'What explains China's rising urbanisation in the reform era?', *Urban Studies*, 39(12):2301–15.

—— and Song, S., 2003, 'Rural-urban migration and urbanisation in China: evidence from time-series and cross-section analysis', *China Economic Review*, 14(4):386–400.

Zhao, Z., 2003. *Rural–urban migration in China—what do we know and what do we need to know?*, China Centre for Economic Research, Peking University, Peking.

Zhu, N., 2002. 'The impacts of income gaps on migration decision in China', *China Economic Review*, 13(2–3)213–30.

Appendix Table A7.1   **Urban and rural population and their proportions in total population (urbanisation) in China, 1960–2003** (millions and per cent)

	Population		Proportion (per cent)	
	Urban	Rural	Urban	Rural
1960	130.7	531.3	19.8	80.2
1961	127.1	531.5	19.3	80.7
1962	116.6	556.4	17.3	82.7
1963	116.5	575.3	16.8	83.2
1964	129.5	575.5	18.4	81.6
1965	130.5	594.9	18.0	82.0
1966	133.1	612.3	17.9	82.1
1967	135.5	628.2	17.7	82.3
1968	138.4	647.0	17.6	82.4
1969	141.2	665.5	17.5	82.5
1970	144.2	685.7	17.4	82.6
1971	147.1	705.2	17.3	82.7
1972	149.4	722.4	17.1	82.9
1973	153.5	738.7	17.2	82.8
1974	156.0	752.6	17.2	82.8
1975	160.3	763.9	17.3	82.7
1976	163.4	773.8	17.4	82.6
1977	166.7	783.1	17.6	82.4
1978	172.5	790.1	17.9	82.1
1979	185.0	790.5	19.0	81.0
1980	191.4	795.7	19.4	80.6
1981	201.7	799.0	20.2	79.8
1982	214.8	801.7	21.1	78.9
1983	222.7	807.3	21.6	78.4
1984	240.2	803.4	23.0	77.0
1985	250.9	807.6	23.7	76.3
1986	263.6	811.4	24.5	75.5
1987	276.7	816.3	25.3	74.7
1988	286.6	823.7	25.8	74.2
1989	295.4	831.6	26.2	73.8
1990	302.0	841.4	26.4	73.6
1991	312.0	846.2	26.9	73.1
1992	321.8	850.0	27.5	72.5
1993	331.7	853.4	28.0	72.0
1994	341.7	856.8	28.5	71.5
1995	351.7	859.5	29.0	71.0
1996	373.0	850.9	30.5	69.5
1997	394.5	841.8	31.9	68.1
1998	416.1	831.5	33.4	66.6
1999	437.5	820.4	34.8	65.2
2000	459.1	808.4	36.2	63.8
2001	480.6	795.6	37.7	62.3
2002	502.1	782.4	39.1	60.9
2003	523.7	768.5	40.5	59.5

Source: National Bureau of Statistics, 2004. *China Statistical Yearbook*, China Statistics Press, Beijing.

Appendix Table A7.2   **Urban and rural employment and their proportions in total employment, 1952–2003**
(millions and per cent)

| | Employment | | Proportion (per cent) | |
	Urban	Rural	Urban	Rural
1952	24.9	182.4	12.0	88.0
1957	32.1	205.7	13.5	86.5
1962	45.4	213.7	17.5	82.5
1965	51.4	235.3	17.9	82.1
1970	63.1	281.2	18.3	81.7
1971	68.7	287.5	19.3	80.7
1972	72.0	286.5	20.1	79.9
1973	73.9	292.6	20.2	79.8
1974	76.9	296.8	20.6	79.4
1975	82.2	299.5	21.5	78.5
1976	86.9	301.4	22.4	77.6
1977	91.3	302.5	23.2	76.8
1978	95.1	306.4	23.7	76.3
1979	100.0	310.3	24.4	75.6
1980	105.3	318.4	24.8	75.2
1981	110.5	326.7	25.3	74.7
1982	114.3	338.7	25.2	74.8
1983	117.5	346.9	25.3	74.7
1984	122.3	359.7	25.4	74.6
1985	128.1	370.7	25.7	74.3
1986	132.9	379.9	25.9	74.1
1987	137.8	390.0	26.1	73.9
1988	142.7	400.7	26.3	73.7
1989	143.9	409.4	26.0	74.0
1990	166.2	472.9	26.0	74.0
1991	169.8	478.2	26.2	73.8
1992	172.4	483.1	26.3	73.7
1993	175.9	487.8	26.5	73.5
1994	184.1	487.9	27.4	72.6
1995	190.9	488.5	28.1	71.9
1996	198.2	490.4	28.8	71.2
1997	202.1	493.9	29.0	71.0
1998	206.8	492.8	29.6	70.4
1999	224.1	489.8	31.4	68.6
2000	231.5	489.3	32.1	67.9
2001	239.4	490.9	32.8	67.2
2002	247.8	489.6	33.6	66.4
2003	256.4	487.9	34.4	65.6

Source: National Bureau of Statistics, 2004. *China Statistical Yearbook*, China Statistics Press, Beijing.

Appendix Table A7.3   **Comparison of urbanisation by region, 1990–2000**
(millions and per cent)

	Urban population		Urban population in total		Growth rate (per cent)
	1990	2000	1990	2000	1990–2000
National	296.5	455.9	26.2	36.1	9.9
Beijing	7.9	10.7	73.1	77.5	4.5
Tianjin	6.0	7.2	68.7	72.0	3.3
Hebei	11.7	17.6	19.1	26.1	7.0
Shanxi	8.3	11.5	28.7	34.9	6.2
Inner Mongolia	7.8	10.1	36.1	42.7	6.6
Liaoning	20.1	22.3	50.9	54.2	3.4
Jilin	10.5	13.6	42.7	49.7	7.0
Heilongjiang	16.6	19.0	47.2	51.5	4.4
Shanghai	8.8	14.8	66.2	88.3	22.1
Jiangsu	14.2	30.9	21.2	41.5	20.3
Zhejiang	13.6	22.8	32.8	48.7	15.9
Anhui	10.1	16.7	17.9	27.8	9.9
Fujian	6.4	14.4	21.4	41.6	20.2
Jiangxi	7.7	11.5	20.4	27.7	7.3
Shandong	23.1	34.5	27.3	38.0	10.7
Henan	13.3	21.5	15.5	23.2	7.7
Hubei	15.6	24.2	28.9	40.2	11.3
Hunan	11.1	19.2	18.2	29.8	11.5
Guangdong	23.1	47.5	36.8	55.0	18.2
Guangxi	6.4	12.6	15.1	28.2	13.1
Hainan	1.6	3.2	24.1	40.1	16.1
Chongqing	5.0	10.2	17.4	33.1	15.7
Sichuan	16.7	22.2	21.3	26.7	5.4
Guizhou	6.1	8.4	18.9	23.9	4.9
Yunnan	5.4	10.0	14.7	23.4	8.6
Tibet	0.3	0.5	12.6	18.9	6.3
Shaanxi	7.1	11.6	21.5	32.3	10.8
Gansu	4.9	6.2	22.0	24.0	2.0
Qinghai	1.2	1.8	27.4	34.8	7.4
Ningxia	1.2	1.8	25.7	32.4	6.7
Xinjiang	4.8	6.5	31.9	33.8	1.9

Source: National Bureau of Statistics, 2004. *China Statistical Yearbook*, China Statistics Press, Beijing.

8

Corporate governance and firm performance

Mei Wen

Industrial competition and ownership diversification have contributed significantly to China's industrial growth since economic reforms began (Wen 2002a).[1] Although no large-scale transformation of ownership took place in the state industrial sector before 1995 and growth occurred mainly outside the state-planned sector (Naughton 1994), the development of non-state owned industrial firms and market-based competition have raised the prominence of China's industry in the world economy. The majority of state-owned enterprises (SOEs) made either apparent or genuine losses in the 1990s, and, according to the third national industrial census, held in 1995, many manufacturing industries had excess production capacity. Further fundamental reforms to SOEs are required to remove remaining inefficiencies. The industrial policy guideline 'keep the large and let the small go' for the reform of SOEs was a major policy response to the situation and commenced in 1995.

Since the 1980s, SOE reform has involved forms of contracting, leasing, merger and even bankruptcy, but large-scale transformation of ownership structures did not begin until 1996. The newly legislated township and village-owned enterprises (TVE) law provided private TVEs with the same legal protection as collective TVEs. Since 1996, *gaizhi* has become a popular term to describe the SOE reforms. *Gaizhi*, directly interpreted as 'transforming system', implies the reform of state-owned enterprises towards economic entities that compete in a market system. The market-supporting institutions and market mechanisms that developed after the systematic introduction of markets since 1992 has laid a stronger base for the transformation of SOEs' ownership structures. The establishment of two stockmarkets in Shanghai and Shenzhen enabled SOEs to transform their ownership structure by gradually reducing the state-owned shares through listing and trading. SOE inefficiencies have forced the government to introduce more fundamental reforms in the sector, even though the social security system is still insufficient to assist the large numbers of workers who have been and will be laid-off during the reform process.

In most cases, *gaizhi* of SOEs implies a degree of ownership transformation, in many cases experimental or gradual. While the majority of firms that undertook *gaizhi* sought to transform their ownership structure, a small group of firms in the IFC survey (Garnaut et al. 2005) tried instead to improve performance by mimicking private-sector corporate governance and financial practices. According to Garnaut et al. (2005), around 80 per cent of SOEs had transformed ownership in some way by the end of 2001, with partial or total transfer of ownership to private entities occurring in approximately 70 per cent of the *gaizhi* cases.

Ownership structure has implications for efficiency due to incomplete information, transaction costs and different operational objectives. Because of incomplete information, imperfect contracts and vaguely defined property rights, agency costs are usually much higher in SOEs than in privately-owned firms. In transitional economies, the soft budget constraints faced by SOEs (Li and Liang 1998, Qian and Roland 1996) provide larger scope for increasing agency costs. Some studies on transitional economies regard privatisation as a necessary condition for firms to tighten budgets (Kornai 1986, Kornai et al. 2003, Earle and Estrin 2003). Distribution of the rights to claim residual income and to control the firm has strong implications for efficiency. Improvement in enterprise internal efficiency must be based on the efforts of managers to reduce production costs. However the separation of the rights of control from the rights to claim residual income indicates that owners and managers have conflicting objectives. Due to information asymmetries, the behaviour of managers cannot be fully observed. To improve internal efficiency, owners can design incentive contracts to induce managers to reduce production costs, align management objectives with the interests of owners or strengthen the monitoring of management behaviour.[2] In SOEs, chief managers retain residual control rights. They are the risk takers. The nominal owners of SOEs and final bearers of the consequences of risky behaviour, however, are the 1.3 billion Chinese people. Due to the great number of nominal owners, there is little incentive for managers to protect owners' interests. Monitoring by government officials has little effect when personal gains from rent seeking are not caught and punished, and the negative phenomena are reinforced when banks are also state-owned and directed by rent-seeking managers and government officials

(Che 2002; Lin 2005; Zhu 1998)—ownership transformation becomes essential to improve the performance of SOEs.

Different methods of transforming the ownership structure lead to different *ex post* ownership and governance structures. As the 'keep the large and let the small go' policy guideline indicates, the majority of firms to be privatised were SOEs within industries that did not have strongly increasing returns to scale. The *ex post* ownership and governance structure and market conditions are the major determinants of post-privatisation performance.

Different methods of *gaizhi*

When the SETC and IFC conducted a survey of SOE *gaizhi* in 11 Chinese cities in 2002, they identified ten broad types of *gaizhi*

1) listing through public offering
2) internal restructuring without ownership transfer
3) bankruptcy before restructuring
4) change into companies with shares through internal privatisation
5) sale
6) leasing, contracting or takeover
7) leasing with internal share division
8) combination of sale and leasing
9) transforming into joint venture by inviting foreign investment
10) other types.

Among these ten categories, internal restructuring without ownership transfer, privatisation through internal distribution of shares, sale and leasing includes sub-types according to changes in management form, restructuring, new financing approaches for internal restructuring without ownership transfer, the registered enterprise forms after *gaizhi* for change into companies with shares through internal privatisation, different buyers for sale, and the different agents for leasing, contracting or takeover.

Owing to concerns over the sample size, four *gaizhi* types were chosen to study relative effectiveness. The first type is category one *gaizhi* reforms, where firms undertook stocklisting and incorporation.

The second type occurred when firms underwent internal restructuring without transferring ownership. This type of *gaizhi* reform mimics the governance approach of corporations by setting up boards of directors and company rules and regulations. Although companies remain owned by the state, the *gaizhi* reforms allow firms to function more as independent legal entities and reduce state intervention.

The third type of *gaizhi* reform was internal privatisation of firms, after which firms registered as limited liability companies. Under the fourth type of *gaizhi* reform, the enterprise privatised internally but registered as cooperative or collectives. Both types are the subcategories of change into companies with shares through internal privatisation.

Company Law requires that the maximum number of shareholders in a limited liability company to be 50. The major *ex post* difference between firms that undertook the third and fourth type of *gaizhi* reforms is that the maximum number of internal shareholders after the third type of reform is 50, while the number of shareholders after the fourth type of reform exceeds 50. In other words, ownership concentration in the former would be much higher than in the latter, which resemble collectives, and employees have a say in enterprise decision-making.

From an economic point of view, comparisons between type 1 and 2 reforms reveal differences in corporate governance between firms that privatise through public listing and firms that mimic trading counterparts while transforming without changing ownership. Comparison between type 1 and types 3 or 4 illustrates the difference between privatisation through public listing and internal privatisation. Differences in ownership concentration after type 3 and type 4 reforms can cause differences in performance.

Sample methodology

The sample used is from a survey of *gaizhi* firms in 11 Chinese cities—Harbin, Fushun, Tangshan, Lanzhou, Weifang, Xining, Zhenjiang, Huangshi, Chengdu, Hengyang, and Guiyang—conducted by the China Economy and Business Program of The Australian National University for IFC . The survey was administered by the State Economic and Trade Commission (SETC) of the State Council and its counterparts in the sample cities. The 11 city economic and trade commissions (ETCs) sent out 1,100 questionnaires to firms and registered a high return rate, with 683 questionnaires collected, predominantly from manufacturing firms (81 per cent).[3] Among the responses, 375 firms provided details about the one or more forms of *gaizhi* reform they had pursued between 1986 and 2003. The survey questionnaire, however, only asked about the firm's accounting and financial situation between 1995 and 2001; *gaizhi* reforms undertaken before 1995 or after 2001 were excluded. This left 239 firms available for comparison. This study compares the change in performance from observations between 1995 and 2001, so firms that undertook reforms in only 1995 or only in 2001 must be excluded, leaving 222 firms that experienced different forms of *gaizhi* reforms from 1996 to 2000. Among these, the four types of *gaizhi* reforms incorporate a fraction of firms from the total sample. A sample of 109 firms that experienced form 1, form 2, form 3 or form 4 *gaizhi* reforms from 1996 to 2000 was examined.[4]

Pre-*gaizhi* performance

The 109 firms' pre-*gaizhi* performance in terms of average labour productivity, profit–asset ratio and the ratio of sum of profits and taxes to assets was compared. Labour productivity is calculated by dividing the firm's value-added by the number of employees on duty. The profit–asset ratio is the ratio of total profits after tax to total assets. The ratio of the sum of total profits and total taxes to total assets is denoted as the (profit+tax)–asset ratio. Many firms did not report at least one of these accounting variables so individual sample size is included in the three average pre-*gaizhi* performance tables (Tables 8.1–8.3).[5]

Type 1 firms had the highest average pre-*gaizhi* labour productivity and profit–asset ratio, as well as the second highest average pre-*gaizhi* (profit+tax)–asset ratio. On average, only firms that undertook type 1 *gaizhi* reforms were making a profit prior to reform, the other firms were making losses (Table 8.2).

These two observations indicate that better-performing SOEs were chosen to be included in the type 1 *gaizhi* reform. Firms that undertook type 4 reforms had the highest average pre-*gaizhi* (profit+tax)–asset ratio, although on average they were making losses. Their contribution in taxes may have guaranteed government

Table 8.1   **Average pre-*gaizhi* labour productivity**

Form of ownership transformation	Form 1	Form 2	Form 3	Form 4
Labour productivity (10,000 yuan/per employee)	3.814035	1.251437	1.675711	1.578685
Number of observations	8	22	11	11

Table 8.2   **Average pre-*gaizhi* profit-asset ratio**

Form of ownership transformation	Form 1	Form 2	Form 3	Form 4
Profit–asset ratio	0.008952	−0.022782	−0.057536	−0.027654
Number of observations	8	23	19	11

Table 8.3   **Average pre-*gaizhi* (profit+tax)-asset ratio**

Form of ownership transformation	Form 1	Form 2	Form 3	Form 4
(Profit+tax)–asset ratio	0.037976	0.028533	−0.033776	0.043079
Number of observations	8	20	19	11

Source: Based on data from Garnaut et al., 2005. *China's Ownership Transformation: process, outcomes and prospects*, the World Bank and International Finance Corporation, Washington, DC.

support for financing and reduced the risk of being closed down. This may be a major reason why more than 50 people in the firm owned shares in the firm and firms registered as cooperatives rather than limited liability companies after undertaking privatisation. Although firms that undertook type 2 reforms were also making losses, the contribution of taxes was significant with an average profit–asset ratio of −0.0228, but average (profit+tax)–asset ratio of 0.0285. This may be one reason why these firms did not experience ownership transformation. They also had a large number of employees. These firms have undertaken internal restructuring that emphasised enterprise governance.

The average performance of firms that undertook type 3 reforms was the worst in terms of the pre-*gaizhi* reform profit–asset and (profits+taxes)–asset ratios. This may be due to genuinely poor economic performance or accounting manipulation for low share prices during internal privatisation. The average labour productivity of these firms, however, was the second highest, so there may be scope to improve their profit–asset and (profits+taxes)–asset ratios. A smaller number of employees probably played some role in the choice of reform strategy in these organisations.

Post-*gaizhi* performance

First, on average, *gaizhi* forms 1 and 3 improved firms' profit–asset and (profit+tax)–asset ratios, with type 3 reforms delivering the more significant improvements. While *gaizhi* forms 1 and 3 improved firms' performance on average, the difference could be partly due to the *ex post* differences in the match between control rights and rights to claim residual income, and partly due to differences in the scope for improvement.

Second, average labour productivity increased following all forms of *gaizhi*, especially strongly among firms that undertook type 1 reforms. *Gaizhi* reforms undertaken after 1995 resulted in firms laying off large numbers of workers. In 1997, the Ministry of Labour projected 4.3 million employees being laid off annually from SOEs over the following three years. Most firms did not have the optimal number of workers prior to reform, but type 1 firms gained far more autonomy over employment decisions in the transformation process, which likely explains their exceptional performance in labour productivity.

Third, on average, the profit–asset ratio and the (profit+tax)–asset ratio of firms that undertook type 2 or 4 *gaizhi* reforms decreased (Tables 8.4–8.6).

Determinants of changes in enterprise performance

To further confirm the effects of different forms of *gaizhi* reforms on firm performance, *gaizhi* form and year dummies are used in a regression analysis to explain the changes labour productivity. Observations about the percentage of

Table 8.4   **Average change in labour productivity**

Form of ownership transformation	Form 1	Form 2	Form 3	Form 4
Change in labour productivity (10,000 yuan/per employee)	2.1194	0.3759	0.4315	0.9487
Number of observations	9	20	10	8

Table 8.5   **Average change in profit-asset ratio**

Form of ownership transformation	Form 1	Form 2	Form 3	Form 4
Change in profit-asset ratio	0.00358	−0.00877	0.05393	−0.06978
Number of observations	8	21	13	9

Table 8.6   **Average change in (profit+tax)-asset ratio**

Form of ownership transformation	Form 1	Form 2	Form 3	Form 4
Change in (profit+tax)-asset ratio	0.01827	−0.01452	0.07075	−0.06843
Number of observations	8	21	13	9

Source: Based on data from Garnaut et al., 2005. *China's Ownership Transformation: process, outcomes and prospects*, the World Bank and International Finance Corporation, Washington, DC.

company shares owned by the CEO were added to these variables to examine the determinants of the profit–asset and (profit+tax)–asset ratios (Table 8.7).

Form 1 *gaizhi* is significantly more effective at raising labour productivity than other types of *gaizhi* reform. Firms that undertook *gaizhi* in 1996 had smaller changes in labour productivity than those who undertook *gaizhi* in 1999. Form 1 *gaizhi* was less effective at raising labour productivity in 1997 while form 2 *gaizhi* reforms were less effective in 1999.

The percentage of shares owned by the CEO has a positive effect on the change in the firm's profit–asset and (profit+tax)–asset ratios, significant at the 0.01 and 0.10 level respectively. Form 2 *gaizhi* reforms significantly decrease the firm's profit–asset ratio, except during 1999. Similarly, form 4 *gaizhi* reforms have a significant negative effect on the firm's profit–asset ratio. In addition, form 3 *gaizhi* increases the firm's (profit+tax)–asset ratio at the 0.10 significance level, with the effect less significant in 2000. Form 4 *gaizhi* reforms decrease the firm's (profit+tax)–asset ratio.

Internal privatisation towards a limited liability company or form 3 *gaizhi* reforms significantly increased firms' profitability, although the average pre-*gaizhi* reform profitability of these firms was the lowest. The improvement can be attributed to more clearly-defined property rights, better governance structures and stronger incentives for CEOs that own shares in post-reform firms.

Table 8.7   **Determinants of change in enterprise performance**

	Labour productivity	Profit-asset ratio	(Profit +tax)– asset ratio
Dform1	6.734***		
	(5.256)		
Dform2		−0.0885***	
		(−2.6603)	
Dform3			0.0486*
			(1.8518)
Dform4		−0.0962***	−0.0635*
		(−3.7682)	(−1.7974)
D1996	−11.154***		
	(−5.649)		
D1998		0.0794***	0.033
		(3.5932)	(1.2171)
D1999	3.845***		
	(3.465)		
D2000			
Percentage of shares held by CEO		0.0024***	0.0019*
		(4.0033)	(2.0343)
Dform2*d1999	−3.519**	0.0871**	
	(−2.569)	(2.1564)	
Dform1*d1997	−6.150*		
	(−3.467)		
Dform3*d2000			−0.0414*
			(−0.9322)
Number of observations	43	30	30
R-squared	0.60	0.49	0.35
Adjusted R-squared	0.56	0.41	0.25

Notes: (1) The number in brackets is the t-statistic. (2)* , ** and *** indicate significance higher than 0.10 0.05 and 0.01 levels, respectively.

Source: Based on data from Garnaut et al., 2005. *China's Ownership Transformation: process, outcomes and prospects*, the World Bank and International Finance Corporation, Washington, DC.

While superficially similar to fully privatised firms, firms that undertook partial privatisation or became cooperatives experienced a decline in profitability. The positive effects of CEO shareholdings slightly counteracted this overall decline. The overall negative effects arose from high agency costs in the collective ownership structures, from higher coordination costs incurred through employee decision-making and the loss of former advantages from government support. These firms' average pre-reform (profit+tax)–asset ratio was the highest among the four types of firms.

Partial privatisation of SOEs through listing and trading in financial markets, form 1 *gaizhi*, improved profitability by facilitating the adoption of high-powered contracts and CEO share purchases. A significant increase in labour productivity among these firms was observed. It is ineffective for SOEs to mimic modern corporations, however, because the limited scope for improving the alignment between control and the right to claim residual income generates few incentives to improve performances. Governance changes provide the CEOs with greater control rights than prior to reforms, but increasing management's control without simultaneously increasing its ownership provides larger scope for managers to squander the SOE's assets. In fact, these firms experienced a decline in profitability after undertaking type 2 *gaizhi* reforms.

The effectiveness of enterprise governance is closely related to the ownership structure, especially when industrial competition is fierce. Further effieciency gain from strengthening market competition will be small in the short-run gain. Emphasising governance without accompanying changes to the ownership structure will not be effective (Table 8.7). In addition, the appropriate form of privatisation and choice of privatisation mechanism are more important for increasing efficiency (Wen 2002b, 2004). Some forms of privatisation may actually decrease firms' profitability. Without appropriate *ex post* governance, privatisation will fail to improve efficiency (Table 8.7).

Conclusion

Unlike papers that compared either the labour productivity, total factor productivity or technical efficiency between firms with different ownership types (Jefferson and Singh 1999, Wen et al. 2002, Zhang et al. 2001), this paper has compared the change in performance by firms that have undertaken different types of *gaizhi* reforms. The type of reform undertaken directly affects the labour productivity and profitability of the firm.

However, this study is limited by a small sample size and lack of some desirable variables. Further investigation of industry-specific factors that examine the effects of different approaches of privatisation on internal efficiency and market performance are needed. A recent study by Bai et al. (2004) constructed a governance index to test the effect on the performance of stockmarket listed firms, which offers a useful tool for further studies on the effects of privatisation on firm performance.

Notes

[1] According to State Statistical Bureau (various years), pure-industrial SOEs and enterprises with state-holding controlling shares dropped from around 118,000 units in 1995 to 34,280 units comprising either pure state ownership or state-held shares in 2003. The latter includes enterprises where the state does not hold controlling shares, which indicates that the influence of the state in the industrial sector has decreased more than the figure suggests. The share of pure-industrial SOEs and enterprises with state-holding controlling shares of the value of total industrial output in 1995 was 0.34, while the 34,280 units with either pure-state ownership or state-holding shares in 2003 had a share of 0.37 of the value of total industrial output.

[2] China's SOE reform before 1995 was by and large along the lines of using various contracts to provide management with stronger work incentives.

[3] See Garnaut et al. (2005) for more details.

[4] One firm that undertook two of the four types of *gaizhi* reforms from 1996 to 2000 is excluded.

[5] Construction of the pre-*gaizhi* and post-*gaizhi* variables is as follows: if there is only one year before or after the *gaizhi* reforms, then the value of the calculated variable in that particular year is used. When two or even three years of data is available before or after *gaizhi* reforms, then the two year or three year average value of the calculated variable is used.

References

Bai, C., Liu, Q., Lu, J., Song, F. M. and Zhang, J., 2004. 'Corporate governance and market valuation in China', *Journal of Comparative Economics*, 32:599–616.

Che, J., 2002 .'Rent seeking and government ownership of firms: an application to China's township-village enterprises', *Journal of Comparative Economics*, 30(4):787–811.

Earle, J.S. and Estrin, S., 2003. 'Privatisation, competition, and budget constraints: discipline enterprises in Russia' *Economics of Planning*, 36:1–22.

Garnaut, R., Song, L., Tenev, S. and Yao, Y., 2005. *China's Ownership*

Transformation: process, outcomes and prospects, the World Bank and International Finance Corporation, Washington, DC.

Jefferson, G.H. and Singh, I., 1999. *Enterprise Reform in China: Ownership, Transition and Performance*, Oxford University Press, Oxford.

Kornai, J., 1986. 'The soft budget constraint', *Kyklos*, 39(1):3–30.

Kornai, J., Maskin., E. and Roland, G., 2003 .'Understanding the soft budget constraint', *Journal of Economic Literature*, 41(4):1095–136.

Li, D. and Liang, M., 1998. 'Causes of soft budget constraint: evidence on three explanations', *Journal of Comparative Economics*, 26(1):104–116.

Lin, S., 2005. 'Excessive government fee collection in China', *Contemporary Economic Policy*, 23(1): 91–106.

Naughton, B., 1994. *Growing Out of Plan: Chinese economic reform, 1978–93*, Cambridge University Press, New York.

Qian, Y. and Roland, G., 1996. 'The soft budget constraint in China', *Japan and the World Economy*, 8(2):207–23.

State Statistics Bureau, *China Statistical Yearbook*, China Statistical Publishing House, Beijing.

Wen, M.,2002a 'Competition, ownership diversification and industrial growth of China', in *China 2002*, (eds) by R. Garnaut and L. Song, Canberra: Asian Pacific Press: 63 – 80.

— —, 2002b. 'Privatisation: theory and evidence' in Guoqiang Tian (ed.), *Frontier Development of Modern Economics and Finance*, Shangwu Press, Beijing:564–609.

— —, Li, D. and Lloyd, P., 2002 .'Ownership and technical efficiency—a cross-section study on the third industrial census of China', *Economic Development and Cultural Changes*, 50(3):709–34.

— —, 2004. 'Bankruptcy, sale, and mergers as a route to the reform of Chinese SOEs', *China Economic Review*, 15(3):249–67.

Zhang, A., Zhang, Y. and Zhao, R., 2001. 'Impact of ownership and competition on the productivity of Chinese enterprises', *Journal of Comparative Economics*, 29:327–46.

Zhu, T., 1998. 'A theory of contract and ownership choice in public enterprises under reformed socialism: the case of China's TVEs', *China Economic Review*, 9(1):57–71.

9

Restructuring state-owned enterprises—labour market outcomes and employees' welfare

Xin Meng

State-owned enterprises (SOEs) have undergone reform over the past few decades, with the objective to increase the economic efficiency of enterprises. It was not until the mid 1990s that privatisation began, and even then it was a piecemeal rather than a 'big bang' approach. By the end of 1990s, most SOEs had experienced some form of restructuring. At the extreme end of the spectrum firms were fully privatised. Most firms, however, were leased out, becoming shareholding companies or joint venture partners with other enterprises. These dramatic changes to the structure of SOEs had significant effects on the employment, wages and welfare of workers.

Background to restructuring

State sector reform took a significant step in the mid 1990s when a large number of SOEs experienced losses and could not afford to continue operations. In 1995, the central government implemented a 'keep the large and let go of the small' policy that left the structure of between 500 to 1000 large state enterprises unchanged, but allowed most SOEs to be leased or sold.

Since then, the share of the state sector in the economy has quickly shrunk. The number of state enterprises in the industry sector was 118,000 in 1995 and by 2001, had fallen to 46,800—an annual reduction rate of 15 per cent. Total state sector employment decreased from 113 million in 1995 to 76 million in 2001—a reduction of almost 50 per cent (National Bureau of Statistics, various years). Within the state sector, most enterprises experienced some internal restructuring, resulting in some arrangement of partial privatisation. According to a national survey, 87 per cent of industrial SOEs had undergone restructuring by the end of 2001. Among them, 70 per cent were partially or fully privatised (China Economy and Business Program and China Center for Economic Reform 2003).

Such significant restructuring has no doubt affected enterprise behaviour in many important ways. Several important issues arise for the labour market. Previous research on the behaviour of SOE firms suggests that state ownership, when coupled with soft budgetary constraints, induced SOEs to behave like labour-managed firms, maximising workers' income and welfare. As a result, the inability to fire redundant workers was a common problem for SOE firms (Walder 1989, Byrd 1992, Sicular 1994, Meng 2000). The question naturally arises—did SOEs change their behaviour with regard to hiring, firing and wage determination after restructuring? In addition, has restructuring caused significant retrenchment and a reduction in the welfare conditions of workers?

The negative effects of SOE restructuring on employment are commonly acknowledged. As early as 1993, the central government set up a security fund to cover the costs of compensation for retrenched workers, and to reduce adjustment costs (China Economy and Business Program and China Center for Economic Reform 2003). In 1998, when large-scale retrenchment began, the State Council issued an eight-point document to ensure that retrenched workers were properly protected (State Council 1998). New rules were established that covered retrenched workers with the 'retrenched worker living allowance' for no more than three years, before becoming eligible for unemployment benefits for no more than two years. The burden of supporting retrenched workers and their social welfare payments was mainly shouldered by the enterprises themselves, with some assistance from the central and local governments. Many enterprises already faced financial crisis due to poor economic performance. As a result, many firms became indebted to their current and retrenched workers for wages, living allowances and social welfare payments.

Retrenchment and the inability to pay wages and welfare payments are directly related to the process of restructuring and the factors that induced restructuring. As mentioned, the restructuring of state enterprises was initiated because many small and medium-sized enterprises were making losses. In 1995–96, approximately 50 per cent of SOEs were making a loss (East Asian Analytical Unit 1997).

Facing financial difficulties and increased market competition, many enterprises laid off workers and delayed the payment of entitlements long before formal restructuring began. If this was the case, restructuring was not the cause for retrenchments and delayed entitlement payments. On the contrary, both restructuring and retrenchments were caused by poor performance by the SOE sector.

The effect of restructuring on employment has also raised some important issues for female workers. It is commonly believed that firms prefer to lay off female rather than male workers when facing retrenchment decisions. Using household level data, many studies have found that women are more likely to be retrenched or dismissed than men (Meng 2003, Giles, Park and Cai 2003). However, it is not clear that the restructuring of SOEs in China is responsible for the disproportionate dismissal of women workers.

Methodology and data

The behavioural changes induced by the restructuring of SOEs, with regard to employment and wage determinants, are of particular interest. Previous studies have found that SOEs aimed to maximise income per worker rather than profit, implying that part of the profit earned was to be shared among workers. In addition, because managers were responsible for the welfare of employees, firing was seldom used to achieve optimal labour demand. Instead, SOEs were overstaffed (Walder 1989, Byrd 1992, Sicular 1994, Meng 2000). These factors contributed to the collapse of the SOE sector.

Increasing market competition and tighter budgetary constraints have made it difficult for SOEs to survive. The objective of SOE restructuring therefore was to change the behaviour of firms. The key to evaluating the effect of SOE restructuring lies in examining counterfactuals—that is, the effects on labour market outcomes and employee welfare had restructuring not taken place. This is expressed as

$$\Delta_i = (Yi_1 - Yi_0 \mid Di = 1) \tag{9.1}$$

Where Y_{i1} is firm i's outcome after restructuring and Y_{i0} is firm i's outcome had restructuring not taken place. Δ_i indicates the effects of SOE restructuring on outcome Y, and $D_i = 1$ indicates that firm i has undertaken SOE restructuring.

Fortunately, the SOE Restructuring Survey 2002 (SRS) has data for seven years. Each firm was asked about employment, wage, financial indicators and production details for the period of 1995 to 2001. Firms, having undertaken restructuring, can compare the pre and post-restructuring circumstances and observe the effects of restructuring.

Labour demand and wage equations are specified to examine the behavioural changes with regard to employment and wage determination.

$$\ln(L_{it}) = \alpha_{11} + \alpha_{12}gz_{it} + \beta_{11}\ln(OP_{it}) + \beta_{12}\ln(W_{it}) + \beta_{13}\ln(OP_{it})^*gz_{it} + \beta_{14}\ln(W_{it})^*gz_{it} + \varepsilon_{it} \quad (9.2)$$

$$\ln(W_{it}) = \alpha_{21} + \alpha_{22}gz_{it} + \beta_{21}LP_{it} + \beta_{22}(\pi/L)_{it} + \beta_{23}LP_{it}^*gz_{it} + \beta_{24}(\pi/L)_{it}^*gz_{it} + \in_{it} \quad (9.3)$$

Where L_{it} and W_{it} are firm-level employment and average wages at time t, gz_{it} is the dummy variable indicating whether firm i at time t has restructured $(gzit = 1)$ or not $(gz_{it} = 0)$, OP_{it} is output of firm i at time t, LP_{it} is firm-level labour productivity, and $(\pi/L)_{it}$ is the average profit per worker for firm i at time t. ε_{it} and $\in_{it}$ are the residual terms for the labour demand and wage equations respectively. In these equations, α_{12} and α_{22} capture the effect of restructuring at the level of labour demand and wages, while β_{13}, β_{14}, and β_{23}, β_{24} indicate the additional effects of the restructuring on the relationship between the explanatory variables and dependent variables. In addition to the variables specified, year dummy variables, regional dummy variables and industry dummy variables are also controlled.

Due to the panel nature of the data, equations 2 and 3 are estimated using a fixed effect model. The fixed effect model controls for all unchanging firm-specific effects not included in the explanatory variables, for example, the degree of product markets competition, quality of management and level of human capital. In addition, controlling for the firm-specific effects results in an unbiased estimator of the restructuring effects, if firm-specific effects are correlated to restructuring.

The effects of restructuring on the welfare of workers are also of interest. Welfare measures examined include the proportion of workers laid-off or dismissed, and the proportion of female workers laid-off or dismissed as a proportion of total retrenchment and arrears of wages, salary and social welfare payments workers.

To ensure that the estimated effects of restructuring are within the firm effects, the sample size is restricted to firms that undertook restructuring during the timeframe of the dataset. Firms needed to have both pre and post-restructuring data to allow the effects of restructuring to be evaluated. Firms that had not undertaken or experienced restructuring prior to the timeframe were excluded. The SRS survey was conducted in 2002–03 and included 683 enterprises from 11 cities. However less than one-half of the surveyed firms or 311 enterprises indicated that they had undertaken restructuring and among them, only 229 enterprises revealed the exact timeframe of restructuring, allowing the pre and post-restructuring periods to be identified. Of the 229 firms, 24 undertook a process of restructuring prior to 1995 and 21 after 2001. These timeframes were outside the dataset period and the 45 firms were excluded from the calculations. Only 184 firms were included. The final, restricted sample includes 70 to 90 firms, depending on the variables considered. It is a small sample and may not be representative, which is regrettable.

The sensitivity of the sample exclusions was tested on all firms that had indicated their restructuring timeframe, an unrestricted sample, to estimate equations 2 and 3.

The distribution of the region, industry and firm ownership at the survey year were compared between the restricted sample and the unrestricted samples (Figure 9.1a) Relative to the total sample, distribution was more concentrated in Tangshan, Huangshi and Chengdu and less concentrated in Haerbin and Hengyang.

The proportion of firms corporatised in the total sample is less than the proportion of firms corporatised in the restricted sample, while the number of limited-liability firms in the restricted sample is greater than the number in the total sample (Figure 9.1b). This is because most uncorporatised firms have not undertaken restructuring.

There are very few differences in the distribution of industry between the three samples (Figure 9.1c). The degree of representation of the restricted sample is high when compared to the total sample, but differs more significantly for location and ownership structure.

Firms in the restricted sample are on average larger than those in the total sample, have fewer retired, laid-off and dismissed workers and have a higher level

Figure 9.1a **Distribution of region, ownership and industry for three samples, regions**

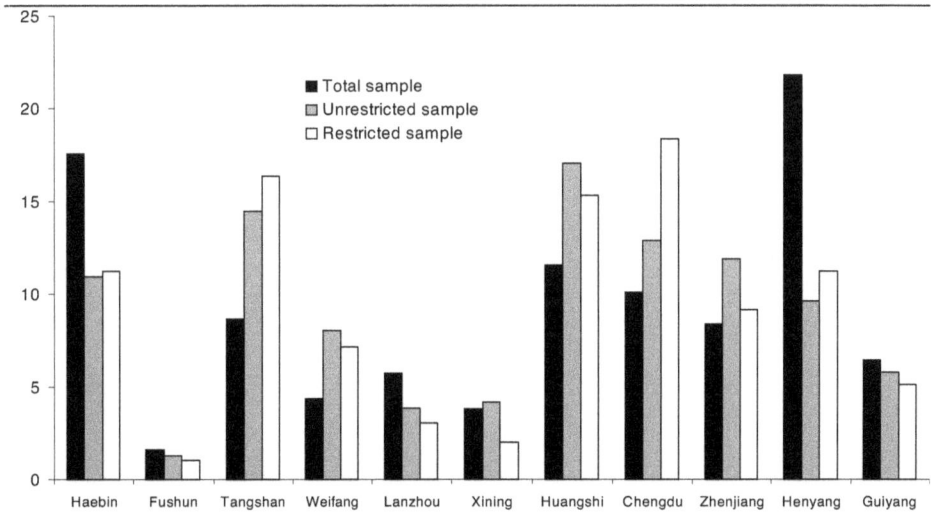

Source: Author's calculations.

Figure 9.1b **Distribution of region, ownership and industry for three samples, ownership**

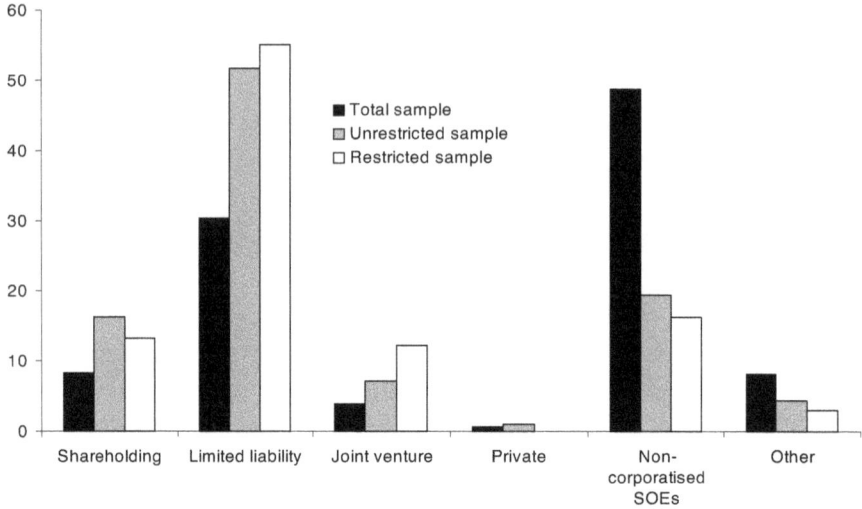

Source: Author's calculations.

Figure 9.1c **Distribution of region, ownership and industry for three samples, industry**

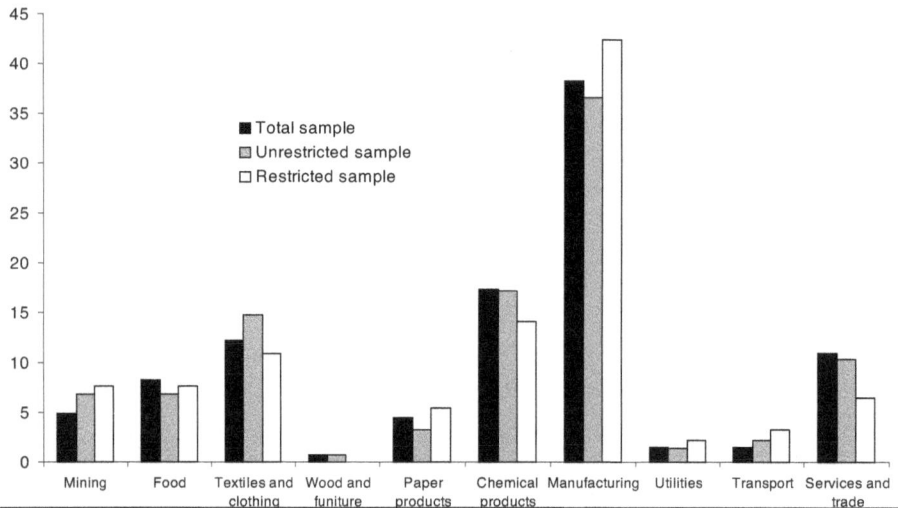

Source: Author's calculations.

of value-added (Table 9.1a). Internal restructuring and shareholding companies account for the majority of firms that undertook restructuring, in both the restricted and unrestricted sample (Table 9.1b). The share of internal restructuring was slightly higher for the restricted sample than the unrestricted sample.

Empirical results

OLS and fixed-effect estimates were calculated (Table 9.2). Although the magnitude of the coefficients differed between the restricted and unrestricted samples, and between the OLS and fixed-effect estimations, the signs of the coefficients and significant levels were consistent across the two samples and between the two different estimations

The fixed-effect estimation from the restricted sample is of particular interest. The model fits well. The adjusted R^2 is 0.73 for the OLS estimation and between R^2 is 0.46. All variables have the expected sign. Output, as measured by the value-added, has a positive effect, and price (or wages) has a negative effect on labour demand. In addition, there is a negative time trend for labour demand. Since 1998, demand for labour has diminished. Between 1998 and 1999, the demand for labour decreased by 9 per cent. By 2000, demand had fallen a further 6 per cent and in 2001 another 5 per cent. Firms that had not undertaken restructuring experienced the same diminishing demand. In fact, data from a sample of 177 firms that did not undertake restructuring reveals that the reduction in labour demand was larger than for firms that had undertaken restructuring.

Table 9.1a **Summary statistics of the three samples**

	Total sample		Unrestricted sample		Restricted sample	
	Mean	CV	Mean	CV	Mean	CV
Total number of on-duty workers	657.28	1.75	876.52	1.74	1022.76	1.85
Retired workers	271.38	1.94	318.52	2.07	384.13	2.25
Retired as per cent of on-duty workers	41.29		36.34		37.56	
Layoff workers	205.39	1.51	156.39	1.81	168.78	1.69
Layoff as per cent of on-duty workers	31.25		17.84		16.50	
Dismissed workers	22.18	2.75	9.58	5.23	12.11	4.62
Dismissed as per cent of on-duty workers	3.37		1.09		1.18	
Value added	1185.78	2.26	1637.40	1.98	1667.62	2.24

Source: Author's calculations.

Table 9.1b   Distribution of the forms of the restructuring

	Restricted sample	Unrestricted sample
Float	6.17	6.88
Internal restructuring	32.10	22.48
Bankruptcy and reorganisation	6.17	10.09
Shareholding	32.10	33.03
Open sales	12.35	11.47
Leasing	7.41	11.01
Joint venture	3.70	5.05

Source: Author's calculations.

The most important estimator is the effect of restructuring, which reduces the demand for labour. In addition, the effect of output on labour demand is stronger after restructuring has taken place than before. Restructuring increases labour productivity significantly, particularly for smaller firms (Figure 9.2).

Prior to restructuring, firms that produced 30,000 yuan value-added per annum hired on average 235 workers. After restructuring, the number of workers hired was 137 workers—a 42 per cent reduction. The reduction of hiring for firms that produce 200,000 yuan value-added per annum was about 32 per cent—from 317 to 217 workers. At 23 million value-added per annum, the effects of restructuring on the demand for labour disappeared.

The most notable change in enterprise behaviour is revealed in the wage equation estimations (Table 9.3). Prior to restructuring, wages at the enterprise level were determined by both productivity and profitability. This is indicated by positive and significant coefficients per worker value-added and profits. The equation is specified as a semi-log form so the coefficients indicate the percentage change. The restricted sample indicates that prior to restructuring, every 10,000 yuan increase in value-added and profit per worker led to the average firm-level wage increasing by 4 and 5 per cent, respectively. Restructuring reduced average firm-level wages by 9 per cent and the impact of the value-added per worker on wages after restructuring was 7 per cent (0.04+0.03). Although the joint significance test (see F-test) indicicates a significant effect, it is not statistically different from the period prior to restructuring (insignificant t-test).

Thus, from the restricted sample we find that before the restructuring every 10,000 yuan increased in value-added and profit per worker increases average firm level wages by 4 and 5 per cent, respectively. The restructuring reduced

Figure 9.2   **Effect of the restructuring on demand for labour**

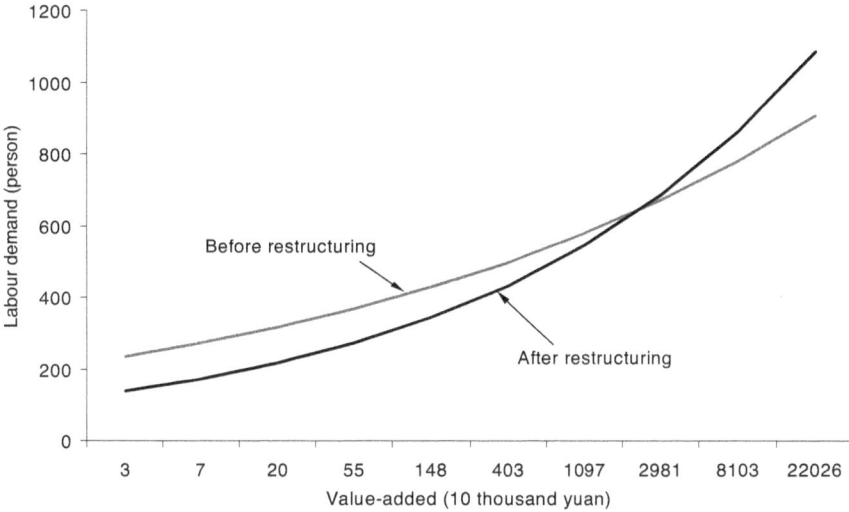

Source: Author's estimations.

average firm level wages by 9 per cent (row (3)). The impact of the value-added per worker on wages for the post-restructuring period is 7 per cent (0.04+0.03). Although the joint significant test (see F-test) indicates that this is a significant effect, it is not statistically different from the pre-restructuring period (insignificant t-test).

The main difference is the impact on the profit per worker. The coefficient for the interaction term between the profit per worker and the restructuring dummy variable is negative and statistically significant. The joint significance test indicates that after restructuring the relationship between the profit per worker and the average firm-level wages is negative. This may be an accounting relationship—that is low costs and high profits. These results suggest that in the post-restructuring period, the objective of enterprises shifted from maximising the income per worker to profit maximisation, where wages were determined solely by labour productivity. The findings that profit-sharing behaviour diminished following restructuring is consistent with previous studies. Meng (2000) found using a panel dataset for 1990–93 that firm average profits were positively and significantly related to wages in the state sector but had no effect on wages in the private sector. Meng (2002) later found, using data from urban workers and rural migrant workers within state enterprises

Table 9.2   **Estimated labour demand equation**

	Restricted sample				Unrestricted sample			
	OLS		Fixed effects		OLS		Fixed effects	
	Coef.	Std. Err.	Coef.	Std. Err.	Coef.	Std. Err.	Coef.	Std. Err.
Constant	3.04***	0.36	5.31***	0.17	2.66***	0.31	5.15***	0.13
Log value added	0.51***	0.03	0.15***	0.02	0.56***	0.02	0.15***	0.02
Log wage	−0.34***	0.09	−0.44***	0.06	−0.40***	0.07	-0.44***	0.05
Dummy for gz[a]	−0.62***	0.27	−0.62***	0.15	−0.46***	0.22	-0.75***	0.14
Log value added*gz	0.07	0.04	0.08***	0.02	0.05	0.03	0.10***	0.02
Log wage*gz	−0.08	0.10	0.00	0.05	−0.04	0.08	−0.16***	0.05
1996	0.02	0.10	0.01	0.04	0.02	0.08	−0.02	0.04
1997	−0.03	0.10	−0.03	0.04	−0.01	0.08	−0.05	0.04
1998	−0.07	0.10	−0.09**	0.05	−0.05	0.08	−0.10***	0.04
1999	−0.16	0.10	−0.09**	0.05	−0.10	0.08	−0.13***	0.04
2000	−0.16	0.11	−0.14***	0.06	−0.13	0.08	−0.15***	0.04
2001	−0.18*	0.11	−0.19***	0.06	−0.17**	0.08	−0.20***	0.04
Regional effect	Yes				Yes			
Industry effect	Yes				Yes			
Number of observations	586		527		878		937	
Number of firms	90				184			
Adjusted or within R^{2b}	0.73		0.46		0.74		0.48	
Between R^2	0.43				0.34			
Overall R^2	0.37				0.32			

Note: a. 'gz' is the abbreviation for 'restructuring'. b. This row indicates adjusted R^2 for the OLS estimation and between R^2 for the fixed-effects estimation.
Source: Author's calculations.

Table 9.3　Estimated wage determination equation

| | Restricted sample | | | | Unrestricted sample | | | |
| | OLS | | Fixed-effects | | OLS | | Fixed-effects | |
	Coef.	Std. Err.	Coef.	Std. Err.	Coef.	Std. Err.	Coef.	Std. Err.
Constant	-1.40***	0.21	-0.75***	0.05	-1.39***	0.18	-0.77***	0.04
Value added/Tworker (1)	0.05	0.03	0.04**	0.02	0.06***	0.02	0.05***	0.02
Profit/Tworker (2)	0.07	0.04	0.05**	0.03	0.08***	0.03	0.07***	0.02
Dummy for gz[a] (3)	0.06	0.08	-0.09**	0.05	-0.01	0.06	-0.06	0.04
Value added/Tworker*gz (4)	0.02	0.03	0.03	0.02	0.02	0.02	0.02	0.02
Profit/Tworker*gz (5)	-0.07*	0.04	-0.10***	0.03	-0.09***	0.04	-0.07***	0.02
1996	0.05	0.08	0.09**	0.05	0.07	0.07	0.09***	0.04
1997	0.15*	0.08	0.17***	0.05	0.18***	0.07	0.18***	0.04
1998	0.13*	0.08	0.20***	0.05	0.18***	0.07	0.21***	0.04
1999	0.30***	0.09	0.37***	0.06	0.30***	0.07	0.35***	0.04
2000	0.29***	0.09	0.40***	0.06	0.31***	0.07	0.36***	0.05
2001	0.33***	0.10	0.45***	0.07	0.40***	0.07	0.44***	0.05
Regional effect	Yes				Yes			
Industry effect	Yes				Yes			
F-test for (1)+(4)=0	12.86 (p=0.00)		23.49 (p=0.00)		65.88 (p=0.00)		67.16 (p=0.00)	
F-test for (2)+(5)=0	0.02 (p=0.88)		36.50 (p=0.00)		0.12 (p=0.73)		0.03 (p=0.87)	
Number of observations	441		469		650		691	
Number of firms			74				143	
Adjusted or within R^2 [b]	0.45		0.37		0.48		0.36	
Between R^2			0.07				0.23	
Overall R^2			0.17				0.23	

Note: [a] 'gz' is the abbreviation for 'restructuring', and it is equal to one for after restructuring period. [b] This row indicates adjusted R^2 for the OLS estimation and between R^2 for the fixed-effects estimation.
Source: Author's estimations.

that profit sharing behaviour only applied to urban workers but not rural migrant workers, who were treated as outsiders. These studies confirm the effectiveness of restructuring in changing the objective function of former state enterprises.

Welfare measures, before and after restructuring, including retrenched and dismissed workers as a proportion of total employed workers, retrenched and dismissed female workers as a proportion of total retrenched and dismissed workers and wages and welfare payments per worker in areas were compared (Table 9.4). The results indicate that apart from wages in arrears, restructuring appears to have reduced the welfare of workers for every measure. Restructuring takes place at different times for firms so the comparison may be contaminated by factors such as year effects and the length of time before and after restructuring.

Column two attempts to eliminate differences in the length of time before and after restructuring by comparing the year restructuring took place with that prior to restructuring (Table 9.4). The differences in welfare measures are no longer statistically significant. Firms that have never undertaken restructuring have on average a higher proportion of retrenched workers and owe more wages to workers for the period (Figure 9.3a).

Regression analysis for the restricted sample controls for the effect of profit per workers, debt per worker, firm size and year effects on welfare measures (Table 9.5). Larger and more profitable firms retrenched a smaller proportion of workers while firms with high levels of debt retrenched more workers. Compared with 1995, firms retrenched more workers over the period of the study. This trend is not the result of the time period (Figure 9.3b) because the time trend was observed for firms that had undertaken restructuring and for those that had not undertaken restructuring. In addition, profitable firms dismiss more workers but there is no time trend.

Restructuring has a negative effect on the proportion of retrenched workers but no effect on the dismissal rate for firms. Do these results contradict findings from the labour demand equation that indicates that restructuring reduces labour demand? Not necessarily. An increase in production or decrease in wages will generate a higher demand for labour, which may offset the effect of retrenchment. Controlling for the year effect, restructuring increased value-adding by an average of 5.8 million yuan for the restricted sample. Controlling for firm size, the figure is approximately 6 million yuan (Appendix B). Restructured firms also pay on average lower wages. When these two facts are combined, it is not suprising that after restructuring, labour productivity increased but the proportion of retrenched or dismissed workers did not increase (Table 9.3).

Currently-employed female workers, as a proportion of the total employed workforce, were included to control for the gender ratio within the firm (Table 9.5).

Figure 9.3a   **Welfare comparisons between restructured and non-restructured firms, proportion of retrenched workers**

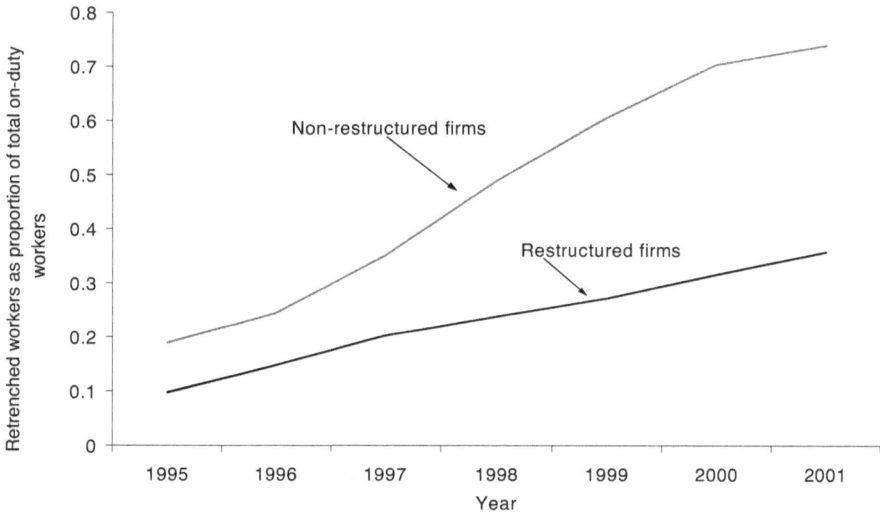

Source: Author's calculations.

Figure 9.3b   **Welfare comparisons between restructured and non-restructured firms, arrears of wages**

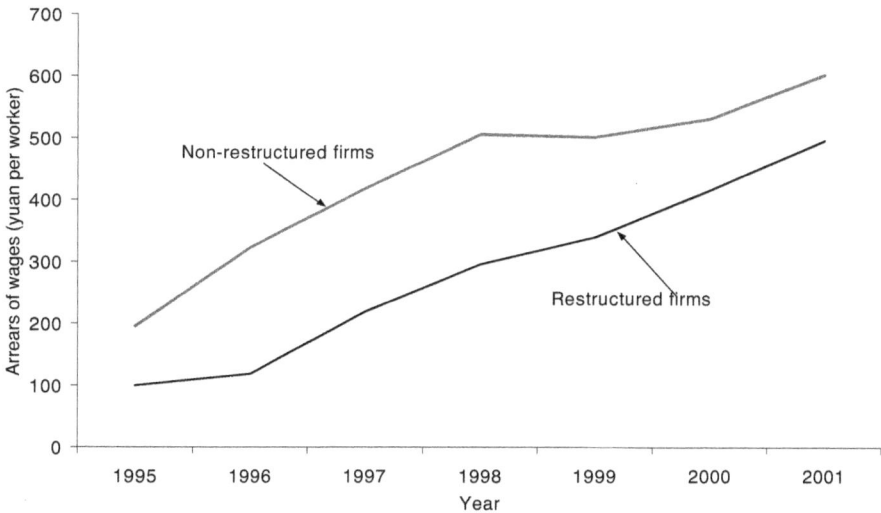

Source: Author's calculations.

Table 9.4   **Differences in various welfare measures before and after the restructuring**

| | After restructuring | | Before restructuring | | | |
	mean	sd	mean	sd	difference	t-ratio
Proportion of layoff workers	0.155	0.187	0.092	0.126	0.063	4.08
Per cent of female layoffs	0.351	0.285	0.268	0.274	0.083	3.13
Proportion of dismissed workers	0.037	0.152	0.007	0.025	0.030	2.76
Per cent of female dismissals	0.086	0.188	0.039	0.110	0.047	3.15
Arrear of wages per worker	0.019	0.063	0.018	0.060	0.001	0.18
Arrear of welfare per worker	0.039	0.098	0.023	0.056	0.015	2.01
	The year of restructuring		1 year before restructuring			
	mean	sd	mean	sd	difference	t-ratio
Proportion of layoff workers	0.143	0.179	0.141	0.165	0.002	0.07
Per cent of female layoffs	0.336	0.293	0.332	0.265	0.003	0.07
Proportion of dismissed workers	0.026	0.097	0.009	0.022	0.017	1.38
Per cent of female dismissals	0.059	0.141	0.056	0.141	0.003	0.10
Arrear of wages per worker	0.020	0.075	0.026	0.072	−0.007	−0.51
Arrear of welfare per worker	0.031	0.073	0.033	0.070	−0.002	−0.14

Source: Author's calculations.

Table 9.5   Fixed-effects estimation of the effect of SOE restructuring on employees' welfare

	Proportion of laid-off workers		Proportion of dismissed workers		Proportion of females laid-off		Proportion of females dismissed		Arrears of wages per worker		Arrears of welfare payments per worker	
	Coef.	Std. err	Coef.	Std. err	Coef.	Std. err	Coef.	Std. err	Coef.	Std. err	Coef.	Std. err
Constant	0.138***	0.018	0.030	0.024	0.362***	0.085	0.033	0.061	-0.008	0.012	-0.008	0.024
Dummy for restructuring[a]	-0.021**	0.011	0.009	0.015	0.002	0.026	-0.005	0.019	-0.007	0.005	-0.005	0.009
Profit per worker	-0.021***	0.004	0.014***	0.005	0.010	0.010	0.010	0.007	0.000	0.002	-0.010***	0.004
Debt per worker*10^-2	0.226***	0.028	0.211***	0.038	0.075	0.068	-0.010	0.049	0.022	0.014	0.033	0.026
Firm size*10^-3	-0.091***	0.014	-0.037**	0.019	-0.023	0.033	0.002	0.024	0.004	0.007	-0.006	0.013
Per cent of female workers					-0.443**	0.214	-0.021	0.155				
Per cent of laid-off workers									0.167***	0.023	0.022	0.045
Per cent of retired workers									0.000	0.043	0.116	0.084
1996	0.004	0.012	0.003	0.016	0.044	0.029	0.022	0.021	0.004	0.005	0.008	0.010
1997	0.042**	0.012	0.002	0.016	0.089***	0.029	0.018	0.021	0.006	0.005	0.012	0.010
1998	0.063***	0.013	0.007	0.017	0.112***	0.030	0.030	0.022	0.004	0.006	0.014	0.011
1999	0.076***	0.014	0.001	0.018	0.110***	0.033	0.063***	0.024	0.005	0.006	0.016	0.012
2000	0.091***	0.015	0.002	0.020	0.168***	0.036	0.067***	0.026	0.004	0.007	0.022	0.014
2001	0.083***	0.017	0.001	0.022	0.139***	0.040	0.062**	0.029	0.007	0.008	0.044***	0.015
Number of observations	430		430		430		423		429		429	
Number of groups	71		71		71		70		71		71	
R-sq: within	0.54		0.13		0.16		0.05		0.27		0.15	
Between	0.08		0.01		0.11		0.020		0.34		0.00	
Overall	0.16		0.04		0.013		0.003		0.35		0.03	

Note: [a] after restructuring period=1.
Source: Author's estimations.

If a firm has more female workers than male, then the gender ratio for retrenched workers may vary in accordance with the overall gender ratio, but it does not indicate gender bias. Interestingly, firms with more male workers retrench more female workers—indicating male dominated firms may discriminate in the retrenchment of female workers more than female dominated firms. In addition, there also appears to be a strong time trend with retrenched and dismissed female workers. However, restructuring did not have an effect on the retrenchment and dismissal of female workers, which is indicated by a statistically insignificant coefficient for the restructuring dummy variable.

The results suggest that there is no relationship between the time trend and restructuring.

The estimated results for the arrears of wages and welfare payment equations include additional control variables—average wages of the firm, the proportion of retrenched workers, and the proportion of retired workers relative to the on-duty workers (Table 9.5). Firms with a higher proportion of retrenched workers owe more wages and salaries to employees, and perhaps to retrenched workers as well. While the coefficients for the proportion of retrenched and retired workers are positive for the arrears in welfare payment equation, it is not statistically significant. Profitability significantly contributes to the amount of welfare payments owed to employees. More profitable firms owe less in welfare payments to employees. There is no effect from restructuring on wages and welfare payments in arrears. In fact, both coefficients are negative but not significant.

Conclusion

The restructuring of SOEs has changed the behaviour of firms for employment and wage determination. After undertaking restructuring, firms use fewer workers to produce the same amount of output. In other words, the problem of overstaffing has been tackled. Prior to restructuring, SOEs shared profits with employees. After restructuring, no profit-sharing behaviour has been observed. These significant findings indicate that firms are behaving more like capitalist firms than SOEs, even though full privatisation has not yet been achieved.

Restructuring does not worsen the welfare of employees as commonly believed. In fact, there is a negative effect of restructuring on the rate of retrenchment of workers, indicating that firms retrenched more workers prior to restructuring than after. It should be noted, however, that due to data limitations, the study used a very small sample size, which limits the representative areas of the study.

Notes

[1] Walder indicated that a state enterprise is 'a socio-political community' and the managers are the leaders of that community. They are responsible for community welfare and they are judged both by their superiors and subordinates on their effectiveness in all areas concerning community welfare including employment, 'not just on meeting production and financial plans' (Walder 1989).

[2] For detailed information on sampling and survey design, see China Economic and Business Program and China Center for Economic Reform (2003).

[3] See Appendix A for estimated labour demand equation using a sample of firms which did not experience the restructuring.

[4] The prediction follows the following formula

$e^{ln}(L_{it}) = \alpha_{11} + \alpha_{12}*gz_{it} + \beta_{11}*ln(OP_{it}) + \beta_{13}*ln(OP_{it})*gz_{it}$.

[5] The variable profit per worker appears to be endogenous, and there is no attempt to establish a causal relationship between the profitability and dependent variables.

References

Byrd, W.A.,1992. 'Chinese industrial reform, 1978–89', in W.A. Byrd (ed.). Chinese Industrial Firms Under Reform, Oxford University Press, Oxford:1–32

China Economy and Business Program and China Center for Economic Reform, 2003. *The Technical Report—Study on Restructured SOEs*, Australian National University and Beijing University for International Finance Corporation, Canberra and Beijing.

East Asia Analytical Unit,1997. *China Embraces the Market*, Department of Foreign Affairs and Trade, Canberra.

Giles, J., Park, A. and Cai, F., 2003. 'How has economic restructuring affected China's urban workers?', unpublished manuscript.

Meng, X., 2000. *Labour Market Reform in China*, Cambridge University Press, Cambridge.

——, 2001. 'Are rural migrants outsiders in urban Chinese enterprises? An alternative interpretation for the earnings gap between urban workers and rural migrants', The Australian National University, Canberra (unpublished).

——, 2003. 'Unemployment, consumption smoothing, and precautionary saving in urban China', *Journal of Comparative Economics*, 31(3):465–85.

National Bureau of Statistics, (various years). Chinese Statistical Yearbook, Chinese Statistics Press, Beijing.

Sicular, T., 1994. 'Going on the dole: why China's state enterprises choose to lose', Department of Economics, University of Ontario, Ontario (unpublished).

State Council, 1998. 'Eight point notice on ensure basic living standard for redundant workers and their re-employment issue, *People's Daily*, 23 June 1998.

Walder, A., 1989. 'Factory and manager in an era of reform' *China Quarterly*, 118:242–64.

Appendix table A9.1 **Labour demand equation for a sample of firms without restructuring**

	Coefficient	Std. Err	T-Ratios
Constant	4.74	0.09	50.20
Log value added	0.15	0.01	10.23
Log wages	−0.51	0.03	−17.42
1996	0.00	0.03	0.10
1997	−0.05	0.03	−1.37
1998	−0.13	0.03	−3.88
1999	−0.22	0.04	−6.14
2000	−0.27	0.04	−7.56
2001	−0.34	0.04	−9.32
Number of observations		963	
Number of groups		177	
Within R^2		0.53	
Between R^2		0.38	
Overall R^2		0.34	

Source: Author's calculations.

Appendix table B9.1   **Effect of the restructuring on value added**

	Without control for firm size			With control for firm size		
	Coefficient	Std. Err	T-Ratio	Coefficient	Std. Err	T-Ratio
Constant	1810.11	194.65	9.30	1317.12	388.09	3.39
Dummy for restructuring	570.08	246.83	2.31	609.83	247.93	2.46
Firm size				0.46	0.31	1.47
1996	6.68	268.87	0.02	2.48	268.47	0.01
1997	−12.98	268.11	−0.05	4.28	267.95	0.02
1998	−241.93	276.21	−0.88	−199.61	277.29	−0.72l
1999	−400.49	297.74	−1.35	−350.27	299.24	−1.17
2000	−409.61	326.64	−1.25	−344.29	329.16	−1.05
2001	−932.00	360.52	−2.59	−833.45	366.16	−2.28
Number of observations	452			452		
Number of groups	75			75		
Within R²	0.03			0.03		
Between R²	0.00			0.67		
Overall R²	0.01			0.53		

Source: Author's calculations.

10

Foreign banks—can Chinese banks compete?

Zhenya Liu, Hanene Hamdoun and David Dickinson

China finally joined the World Trade Organization in December 2001, after 14 years of negotiation. Accession makes Chinese enterprises subject to the authority of international rules and competition, including banks. At the same time, China will be open to the risks and uncertainties of international financial markets. The domestic financial structure and banking sector will change dramatically and become stronger and more stable in the long term.

China has committed to a four-step process of reform for the banking sector on accession to the WTO. Foreign-funded banks will be permitted to provide international financial services to foreign companies in China. One year after the accession, foreign-funded banks will be permitted to provide international financial services to Chinese companies and social agencies. After two years, foreign-funded banks can administer renminbi (RMB) financial services to institutions. Finally, five years after accession, foreign-funded banks will be permitted to supply individual financial services to the Chinese population.

After China entered the WTO, Nanjing Ericsson acted in an interesting fashion. In March 2002, the Nanjing Ericsson Company repaid all its loans, worth about US$2 billion, to their Chinese lenders, the Bank of Communications, the Industrial and Commercial Bank of China and the Bank of China and reborrowed the amount from Citibank. Clearly, the level of competition between foreign and Chinese banks had become more significant.

The Chinese government has undertaken reform in the banking sector in an effort to improve the financial sector as a whole. The People's Bank of China made five commitments to foreign financial institutions to ensure entry into the Chinese market (Dai 2001). First, China will revoke existing regulations stating that foreign-funded financial institutions in China were to be approved by the State Council. Foreign-funded institutions will then be able to establish commercial institutions in any city. Second, China will remove controls over targets for foreign exchange services provided by foreign-funded financial institutions. Third, current business scale limitations, concerning the regulations foreign firms face when being admitted into the RMB, will be removed. However, foreign financial institutions must follow three requirements to operate a RMB business—businesses must have been operating for over three years, have made a profit for two consecutive years and have met requirements set by the People's Bank of China. Fourth, China will abandon control over the establishment of joint venture banks or joint venture financial firms. Foreign financial firms will be able to select any Chinese company as their partner. Finally, China will increase the business scope for RMB operations by foreign financial companies and make RMB business services more available in regional areas.

The deadline for the five-year commitment approaches—foreign-funded banks have been guaranteed equal treatment with Chinese banks by 2006. In light of this, an assessment of the banking sector is particularly timely.

Current circumstances for Chinese banks

After twenty years of banking reforms, the main banking infrastructure in China is operational. Competition between Chinese and foreign-funded banks has become fierce. As the deadline for the banking sector to admit foreign competitors approaches, the growing pressure on Chinese banks is becoming more evident.

The market structure is divided into four parts—assets structure, deposits structure, loans structure and profits structure. Three important changes to the structure of banking assets have occurred during the past decade (Table 10.1). The market-share percentage of the 'big-four' banks has been reduced from 86 per cent in 1995 to 73 per cent in 2003. The 'big-four' banks still dominate the assets structure of the banking sector in China. Non-state commercial banks, such as the Bank of Communications, have grown fast over the last ten years, from RMB 484.6 billion in 1995 to RMB 4,002 billion in 2003—an increase of eight times. Finally, foreign-funded banks in China have also grown steadily in the past decade, from RMB 158.8 billion in 1995 to RMB 400.1 billion in 2003.

Similar changes in the deposits structure have also taken place (Table 10.2). Three important changes have taken place in the banking deposits structure over

Table 10.1 Assets structure of major banks (100 million RMB)

	1995	1996	1997	1998	1999	2000	2001	2002	2003
The Industrial and Commercial Bank of China	19,357.2	22,565.9	24,901.3	32,387.0	35,398.7	39,737.7	43,180.7	47,342.4	52,399.6
The Agricultural Bank of China	9,772.5	11,742.3	13,423.9	20,224.0	22,758.4	21,848.9	25,279.9	29,765.7	34,940.2
Bank of China	5,710.2	6,477.6	7,292.6	7,437.9	9,102.7	26,851.1	25,966.4	28,500.5	31,402.1
Construction Bank of China	9,523.0	11,482.5	13,756.0	19,236.0	22,010.7	25,317.0	27,649.6	30,832.0	35,542.8
Total	44,362.9	52,268.3	59,373.8	79,284.9	89,270.5	113,754.7	122,076.6	136,440.5	154,284.7
Bank of Communications	2,104.6	2,500.78	3,084.5	4,839.2	5,380.5	6,281.8	6,690.7	7,668.7	9,504.4
CITIC Industrial Bank	350.4	559.0	741.0	1,336.1	1,573.3	2,352.9	3,004.0	3,351.6	4,198.0
China Everbright Bank	211.7	432.5	413.6	747.23	1,678.9	2,042.0	2,654.1	3,192.2	3,944.2
Hua Xia Bank	92.5	196.2	257.8	498.7	611.3	951.1	1,366.4	1,781.5	2,468.3
Guangdong Development Bank	513.5	708.3	505.2	1,069.2	1,219.0	1,487.4	1,912.0	2,191.8	3,017.3
Shenzhen Development Bank	270.3	379.3	204.2	390.1	458.7	660.1	1,201.3	1,661.7	1,928.5
Shenzhen Merchants Bank	564.9	874.0	670.0	1,509.1	1,802.8	2,195.1	2,663.2	3,716.6	5,038.9
Pudong Development Bank	386.8	641.6	641.1	849.3	1,032.1	1,297.4	1,736.9	2,793.0	3,710.6
Fujian Industrial Bank	351.6	258.1	215.3	355.8	491.8	856.1	1,248.4	1,910.6	2,600.0
Mingsheng Bank		68.1	150.0	252.4	363.9	697.2	1,389.0	2,466.6	3,610.6
Total	4,846.1	6,618.0	6,882.7	11,847.0	14,612.4	18,821.0	23,865.8	30,734.3	40,021.0
Total of City Commercial banks	646.5	2,141.9	2,744.8	3,723.1	4,516.8	6,998.0	8,730.4	11,661.4	14,653.7
Foreign banks	1,588.6	2,483.4	3,147.4	2,836.9	2,638.6	2,857.7	3,749.9	3,210.6	4,001.6
Total assets	51,444.1	63,511.6	72,148.7	97,691.9	111,038.3	142,431.3	158,422.8	170,578.4	212,961.0

Sources: Jiao, J., 2002. *Study on International Competitiveness of China's Banking Industry, Chinese Modern Economic Publishing House,* Beijing:69–77. Association of China's Finance and Banking, 2002–04. *Almanac of China's Finance and Banking (2002–2004),* Chinese Finanical Publishing House, Beijing.

the past decade. The market-share percentage of the 'big-four' banks has been reduced from 89 per cent in 1995 to 82 per cent in 2003. The 'big-four' banks still dominate the deposits structure of the banking sector, dropping only 7 per cent— small when compared to the assets structure. Non-state commercial banks grew rapidly over the past ten years, from RMB 348 billion in 1995 to RMB 2,805 billion in 2003—increasing over eight times. Foreign-funded banks in China also grew steadily during the past decade, from RMB 26 billion in 1995 to RMB 72.7 billion in 2003.

Similar changes have occurred in the loans structure (Table 10.3). At least three important changes have occurred in the banking loans structure over the past decade. The market-share percentage of the 'big-four' banks has been reduced from 90 per cent in 1995 to 81 per cent in 2003. However, the 'big-four' banks still dominate the loans structure of the banking sector. Second, non-state commercial banks grew rapidly over the last ten years, from RMB 231.1 billion in 1995 to RMB 1,964.3 billion in 2003—an increase of over eight times. Finally, foreign-funded banks in China grew steadily over the past decade, from RMB 105.8 billion in 1995 to RMB 193.7 billion in 2003. It increased only 1.8 times during the period.

At least three changes have occurred in the structure of banking profits over the past decade (Table 10.4). The percentage of the 'big-four' banks is not considered stable. The 'big-four' banks did not dominate the profits structure in 2003, taking in only 41 per cent of the total. The profits of non-state commercial banks have increased over the last ten years, from RMB 7 billion in 1995 to RMB 16 billion in 2003—over 50 per cent of the total market. Finally, the profits of foreign-funded banks in China has remained stable during the past decade, from RMB 2.1 billion in 1997 to RMB 1.8 billion in 2003—less that 10 per cent of the total market.

The four state commercial banks occupy an important place in the banking sector. Two indices, the concentration ratio CRn and the Herfindahl index H are used to determine whether a monopoly exists.

The concentration ratio of the industry is used as an indicator of the relative size of firms in relation to the industry as a whole (Table 10.5). The four firm concentration ratio is commonly used, where n=4, the 'big-four'

$$CRn = \sum_{i=1}^{n} X_i / \sum_{i=1}^{N} X_i$$

Using J-S Bain Analysis, the market structure is divided into six categories. The 'big-four' banks have retained a monopoly with a CR4 above 75 per cent until

Table 10.2 Deposits structure of major banks (100 million RMB)

	1995	1996	1997	1998	1999	2000	2001	2002	2003
The Industrial and Commercial Bank of China	14,443.0	17,974.6	21,611.7	25,032.1	28,335.1	32,485.2	35,804.7	40,569.0	456,81.6
The Agricultural Bank of China	6,939.3	8,950.1	11,189.4	13,348.6	15,492.1	18,089.0	20,914.1	24,796.9	29,972.8
Bank of China	3,904.2	4,864.3	5,864.3	7,308.8	8,652.2	16,854.8	17,988.6	20,830.5	24,271.1
Construction Bank of China	7588.9	10333.3	12555.2	14689.4	16845.5	20102.8	22,655.6	25,996.5	29,712.8
Total	32,875.3	42,122.3	51,220.5	60,378.8	69,325.0	875,31.8	97,363.1	112,192.2	129,638.5
Bank of Communications	1,824.2	2,277.4	2,698.3	3014.6	3,385.1	3,169.7	3,673.1	4,547.7	5,875.9
CITIC Industrial Bank	337.1	540.4	692.8	790.5	938.2	1,275.5	2,266.9	2,648.7	3,442.4
China Everbright Bank	133.8	248.8	300.7	411.6	565.6	1,338.6	1,790.5	2,342.7	2,995.5
Hua Xia Bank	55.6	140.7	239.2	339.3	442.1	686.0	973.2	1,328.1	1,869.8
Guangdong Development Bank	298.0	362.0	475.5	614.8	698.1	988.7	1,361.8	1,496.2	2,050.4
Shenzhen Development Bank	107.4	164.1	182.1	249.5	308.8	447.3	738.9	929.9	1,120.6
Shenzhen Merchants Bank	357.4	521.0	500.0	673.3	904.7	1562.0	2018.7	2,816.1	37,06.4
Pudong Development Bank	228.3	371.8	522.5	632.7	722.7	984.1	1348.4	2,078.0	2641.8
Fujian Industrial Bank	138.7	168.8	170.3	224.2	286.1	475.5	777.5	1,277.2	1,810.3
Mingsheng Bank	--	35.9	123.5	160.8	260.8	478.2	1020.9	1,734.5	2537.33
Total	3,480.4	4,830.8	5,904.9	7,111.3	8,512.2	11,405.4	15,969.9	21,199.1	28,050.4
Total of City Commercial banks	506.2	1,470.6	2,536.7	3,629.5	4,387.4	--	6,816.7	8,988.24	11,747.6
Foreign banks	260.6	323.7	371.8	373.1	431.6	482.5	552.5	727.6	--
Total deposits	37,122.5	48,47.4	60,034.0	71,492.7	82,656.2	98,937.3	120,702.2	143,107.1	169,436.5

Sources: Jiao, J., 2002. Study on International Competitiveness of China's Banking Industry, Chinese Modern Economic Publishing House, Beijing:69–77. Association of China's Finance and Banking, 2002–04. Almanac of China's Finance and Banking (2002–2004), Chinese Finanical Publishing House, Beijing.

Table 10.3 **Loans structure of major banks** (100 million RMB)

	1995	1996	1997	1998	1999	2000	2001	2002	2003
The Industrial and Commercial Bank of China	14,054.1	16,331.3	19,092.8	21,705.5	23,334.9	24,135.9	26,594.7	29,578.4	33,469.2
The Agricultural Bank of China	6,553.8	7,712.9	9,809.2	13,666.1	15,527.5	14,843.6	16,461.8	19,129.6	22,683.9
Bank of China	4,179.3	4,751.5	5,630.0	6,503.8	7,318.2	115,01.5	12,461.9	14,023.1	16,873.3
Construction Bank of China	6,135.3	7,457.2	10,291.7	11,735.6	11,275.6	13,863.9	15,059.1	17,663.9	21,221.3
Total	30,922.5	36,252.9	44,823.7	53,611.0	574,56.2	64,344.8	70,577.4	80,394.9	94,247.8
Bank of Communications	1,210.9	1,486.6	1,824.21	2,148.7	2,435.4	2,633.7	29,98.4	3,580.9	4,669.1
CITIC Industrial Bank	154.4	244.0	374.5	459.6	607.9	1,207.4	1,607.0	1,393.6	1,871.3
China Everbright Bank	66.4	159.9	235.3	297.0	366.8	698.5	996.1	1,366.6	1,971.5
Hua Xia Bank	39.8	83.7	125.4	201.4	267.6	454.5	622.3	7,98.4	1,223.0
Guangdong Development Bank	220.2	266.1	310.7	413.3	500.9	710.7	1,022.9	857.8	1388.1
Shenzhen Development Bank	76.9	102.8	128.7	177.9	210.9	231.4	415.2	537.3	862.6
Shenzhen Merchants Bank	285.2	414.0	366.9	493.7	618.6	766.1	989.1	1,493.0	2,301.7
Pudong Development Bank	154.8	231.2	341.8	415.6	479.9	591.7	852.4	1,358.5	2,204.4
Fujian Industrial Bank	102.52	116.7	121.7	150.4	210.0	302.7	491.7	901.8	1,390.0
Mingsheng Bank		19.7	50.4	98.9	150.3	301.1	526.7	998.5	1,761.5
Total	2,311.0	3,124.7	3,879.4	4,856.3	5,848.23	7,898.0	10,524.7	13,286.54	19,643.3
Total of City Commercial banks	202.2	779.8	1,491.3	2,193.0	2,704.0	3,481.0	4,257.7	5,924.8	7,743.7
Foreign banks	1,058.3	1,612.7	2,280.0	2,162.2	1,782.0	1,548.4	1,538.5	1,525.5	1,936.8
Total loans	34,493.9	41,770.1	52,474.5	62,822.5	67,790.4	77,272.2	86,898.3	101,131.7	123,571.5

Sources: Jiao, J., 2002. *Study on International Competitiveness of China's Banking Industry*, Chinese Modern Economic Publishing House, Beijing:69–77. Association of China's Finance and Banking, 2002–04. *Almanac of China's Finance and Banking (2002–2004)*, Chinese Finanical Publishing House, Beijing.

Table 10.4 Profits structure of major banks (100 million RMB)

	1995	1996	1997	1998	1999	2000	2001	2002	2003
The Industrial and Commercial Bank of China	46.7	58.1	30.5	34.5	41.3	173.6	148.1	62.2	21.1
The Agricultural Bank of China	19.4	21.0	5.3	−9.1	−3.6	2.9	11.5	21.2	19.4
Bank of China	47.0	52.1	39.4	35.2	29.0	28.0	31.1	110.6	70.4
Construction Bank of China	61.7	48.3	18.8	16.4	49.6	84.8	51.9	43.4	4.5
Total	174.8	179.6	93.9	86.2	119.9	289.4	242.6	237.3	115.4
Bank of Communications	37.7	36.2	37.7	26.7	26.9	26.7	25.6	15.9	1.7
CITIC Industrial Bank	6.8	10.6	13.7	20.0	11.4	14.5	15.7	22.4	24.5
China Everbright Bank	3.1	7.0	11.0	13.0	6.8	3.7	4.2	6.1	8.2
Hua Xia Bank		4.4	5.3	4.9	5.1	7.5	9.2	11.5	13.8
Guangdong Development Bank	4.2	1.7	2.8	2.7	2.2	3.6	4.3	4.6	5.3
Shenzhen Development Bank	4.4	7.8	8.6	8.1	6.0	5.0	5.6	5.1	3.5
Shenzhen Merchants Bank	11.5	18.7	19.4	20.0	15.2	12.0	21.1	25.7	34.5
Pudong Development Bank		12.5	13.3	10.4	11.8	9.9	14.4	18.7	23.4
Fujian Industrial Bank	2.1	2.7	3.5	5.5	4.4	4.6	7.3	9.2	16.3
Mingsheng Bank		0.1	3.9	2.5	3.6	3.7	9.0	12.2	19.4
Total	69.7	101.8	119.2	113.9	93.3	91.2	116.3	131.4	150.6
Total of City Commercial banks			21.2	17.8	−12.9	0.6	24.1	38.0	54.2
Foreign banks							16.3	15.1	18.5
Total profits	244.5	281.4	234.3	217.9	213.2	381.2	399.4	421.8	338.6

Sources: Jiao, J., 2002. *Study on International Competitiveness of China's Banking Industry*, Chinese Modern Economic Publishing House, Beijing:69–77. Association of China's Finance and Banking, 2002–04. *Almanac of China's Finance and Banking (2002–2004)*, Chinese Finanical Publishing House, Beijing.

Table 10.5   **'Big-four' concentration ratio**

	1995	1996	1997	1998	1999	2000	2001	2002	2003
Assets	86.2	82.3	82.3	81.2	80.4	79.9	77.1	79.9	72.5
Deposits	88.6	86.4	85.3	84.5	83.9	88.5	80.7	78.4	76.5
Loans	89.6	86.8	85.4	85.3	84.8	83.3	81.2	79.5	76.3
Profits	71.3	63.8	40.1	39.6	56.2	75.9	60.8	56.3	34.1

Sources: Jiao, J., 2002. *Study on International Competitiveness of China's Banking Industry,* Chinese Modern Economic Publishing House, Beijing:69–77. Association of China's Finance and Banking, 2002–04. *Almanac of China's Finance and Banking (2002–2004)*, Chinese Finanical Publishing House, Beijing.

2002, classified as oligopoly one (Table 10.6). However, the monopoly has gradually decreased since 1995, from an average of 85 per cent to 75 per cent. Moreover, the monopoly degree of deposits and loans, around 76 per cent, is starting to shift to an oligopoly of two, while the monopoly degree of assets is already oligopoly two. The 'four concentration ratio' for profits is around 34 per cent, suggesting Chinese banks are ready to face international competition.

The Herfindahl index is also a measure of the size of firms in relation to the industry and an indicator of the level of competition among banks. It is defined as the sum of the squares of the market shares of each individual firm.

$$H = \sum_{i=1}^{n} (X_i/T)^2$$

The United States uses the Herfindahl index to determine whether mergers are equitable—increases of over 100 points generally provoke scrutiny, although it varies between cases (Table 10.7). The Department of Justice considers Herfindahl indices between 1000 and 1800 to be moderately concentrated and indices above 1800 to be concentrated. As the market concentration increases, competition and efficiency decrease and the chance of collusion and monopoly increase.

In 2003, the H index for assets, loans and profits was below 1800 points, which suggests the 'big-four' banks are losing their monopoly (Table 10.7). However, the H index for deposits is still above 1800 points, suggesting concentration. In 1995, the H index for profits was already showing moderate levels of concentration.

The degree of monopoly by the 'big-four' banks has gradually decreased over the past ten years for assets, loans and profits, while deposits still demonstrate a monopoly. The monopoly of deposits may be explained by the wide spread of bank branches across the country. High operation costs incurred by bank branches may explain the decreasing monopoly of profits.

Table 10.6   **Market structure**

Market structure	CR4
Oligopoly 1	75 ≤CR4
Oligopoly 2	65 ≤CR4≤ 75
Oligopoly 3	50 ≤CR4≤ 65
Oligopoly 4	35 ≤CR4≤ 50
Oligopoly 5	30 ≤CR4≤ 35
Competition	CR4 ≤ 30

Source: Jiao, J., 2002. *Study on International Competitiveness of China's Banking Industry,* Chinese Modern Economic Publishing House, Beijing:69–77.

Current circumstances for foreign-funded banks

There was no significant change in the number of foreign-funded banks in China between 1999 and 2003 (Tables 10.8 and 10.9). Foreign-funded bank branches totalled 156 at the end of 1999 and 157 at the end of 2003. Japanese banks closed 28 branches in 1999 and only 20 branches at the end of 2003. South Korean banks opened 5 new branches in the period from the end of 1999 to the end of 2003. In the current climate, the location of foreign-funded banks became more balanced. The number of foreign-bank branches across China is not expected to dramatically increase in the forseeable future.

Current performance of Chinese banks

Chinese banks have many desirable features—good sales networks, a wide distribution of branches across the country, the 'big-four' banks are ranked among the largest 100 banks in the world, and have significant customer numbers, extensive local knowledge and government support. Flourishing banks, such as Mingsheng and CITIC Industrial Bank, are considered serious competitors to foreign-funded banks.

Less desirable characteristics include poor management, underdeveloped human resources and service skills, unclear ownership structures, the non-profit orientation and a tendency to be overly reliant on government support.

Foreign-funded banks have several advantages—profit-orientated attitude, the low level of non-performing loans (0.67 per cent (Liang 2003)), they have better understanding of financial innovations and enjoy important connections with international markets, highly-qualified staff, and incentive-based salaries. As such, foreign-funded banks are able to attract Chinese staff in an attempt to offset the lack of local knowledge. Most of the large foreign institutions are global banks.

Table 10.7   **Herfindahl index**

	1995	1996	1997	1998	1999	2000	2001	2002	2003
Assets	2275	2083	2059	2028	1952	1743	1639	1773	1466
Deposits	2421	2288	2248	2220	2214	2137	2116	2263	2587
Loans	2508	2351	2192	2094	2142	1930	1850	1771	1625
Profits	1703	1385	1047	1058	1444	2716	1786	1253	1075

Source: Jiao, J., 2002. *Study on International Competitiveness of China's Banking Industry,* Chinese Modern Economic Publishing House, Beijing:69–77.

Foreign-funded banks have a high potential to succeed against and compete with Chinese banks, yet there are several potential weaknesses — limited local knowledge, a small customer base, a limited number of branches across China, and the fact that they remain subject to the domestic clearing system.

Since China's accession to the WTO, foreign-funded banks have been able to do the same business as Chinese banks, with the ability to set up branches like Chinese banks without restriction and provide financial services to Chinese companies and individuals.

Anderson (2005) proposed six criteria to judge improvements in the banking sector
- size of the non-performing loans
- quality of internal controls
- ownership and privatisation
- deregulation and structural change
- level of government interference
- quality of macroeconomic management.

The size of non-performing loans is important because bad loans damage the banking system by directly reducing the bank's profitability and cash flows. Non-performing loans also divert new real resources to rolling-over bad asset exposure. Banks can become weakened and more sensitive to shocks in the economy.

After the economic bubble burst in 1996–97, the non-performing loan ratio for financial systems was approximately 55 per cent to 65 per cent. The current non-performing loan ratio is approximately 25 per cent to 30 per cent — still high but decreasing. The decrease in the ratio is due to government reform and improved performance of flows. Moreover, the quality of official non-performing loan data is becoming more accurate with the adoption of a standard five-tier classification system in 2001.

Problems in the balance sheet were previously hidden with false reporting of non-performing loans.

Table 10.8 Regional distribution of foreign-funded bank branches in China, end of 1999

	Shanghai	Beijing	Shenzhen	Guangzhou	Tianjin	Xiamen	Dalian	Other regions	Total
Hong Kong	4	2	9	4	1	3	3	10	36
Japan	9	3	3	1	3	0	6	3	28
France	5	1	3	3	3	1	0	1	17
United States	4	4	1	2	1	1	0	0	13
Singapore	4	1	1	1	1	2	0	1	11
South Korea	2	1	0	0	4	0	1	0	8
Germany	5	1	1	1	0	0	0	0	8
United Kingdom	1	1	1	0	1	1	0	3	8
Belgium	1	0	1	1	0	0	0	0	3
Thailand	1	0	1	0	0	1	0	2	5
Netherlands	3	1	2	0	0	1	0	0	7
Other countries	7	1	0	2	0	1	0	1	12
Total	46	16	23	15	14	11	10	21	156

Source: Association of China's Finance and Banking, 2000. *Almanac of China's Finance and Banking (2002–2004)*, Chinese Finanical Publishing House, Beijing.

Table 10.9   **Regional distribution of foreign-funded bank branches in China, end of 2003**

	Shanghai	Beijing	Shenzhen	Guangzhou	Tianjin	Xiamen	Dalian	Other regions	Total
Hong Kong	4	3	8	4	1	3	3	12	38
Japan	4	3	3	1	3		4	2	20
France	5	2	2	3	3	1	0	1	17
United States	4	4	1	2	2	1	0	0	14
Singapore	3	2	1	1	1	2	0	1	11
South Korea	5	2	0	0	4	0	1	1	13
Germany	5	1	0	1	0	0	0	0	7
United Kingdom	2	1	1	0	1	1	0	2	8
Belgium	2	0	1	1	0	0	0	1	5
Thailand	1	0	1	0	0	1	0	2	5
Netherlands	3	1	1	0	0	0	0	0	5
Other countries	7	3	0	2	0	0	0	2	14
Total	45	22	19	15	15	9	8	24	157

Source: Association of China's Finance and Banking, 2004. *Almanac of China's Finance and Banking (2002–2004)*, Chinese Finanical Publishing House, Beijing.

Internal governance and supervision controls have improved with cooperation between the government and banks. Restructuring, raising controls and procedures for regulatory agencies, the adoption of international accounting procedures, risk management practices and better trained employees also contributed to this.

Questions over the ownership structure of banks still remain. This is a delicate issue because managers of the 'big-four' banks have appointed civil servants with close attachments to the central and local governments. As a result, it is unclear where the real control of banks lies.

There have been two major structural changes. Liberalisation has taken place since the early 1990s; however, with recent support by the government for the consolidation of the financial sector, the economy is stronger and more stable than in the post-bubble period.

The share of the state in total lending and government interference has fallen over the past decade. This is due to both the rising share of non-state lending firms and the improving quality of state borrowers.

Anderson (2005) believes that the overall macroeconomic environment is optimistic. Authorities were able to react efficiently during the period 2002–04, which was characterised by rapid lending and overheated growth. Interest rates remain rigidly fixed at low levels but don't indicate that authorities are unable to make changes. The People's Bank of China is focused on setting the quantity of money rather than price. This focus has advantages because they have succeeded

Figure 10.1 **An index of progress in China's banking system**

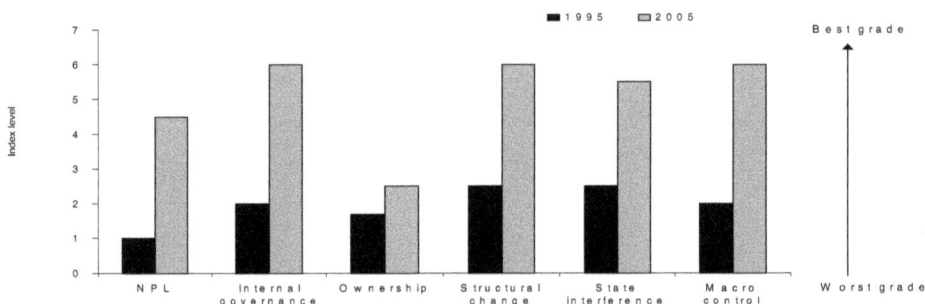

Source: Anderson, J., 2005. 'Which way out for the banking system?', *Asian Economic Perspectives*, UBS Investment Research, June:16.

Table 10.10 **Comparison between Chinese and international banks, 1998**

	Tier one capital	Staff	Per capita profit	Per capita tier one capital	Per capita assets
China					
Bank of China	14,712	202,147	2.1	72.8	1,479.2
The Industrial and Commercial Bank of China	22,213	576,230	0.5	39.2	689.7
The Agricultural Bank of China	4,802	538,800	0.9	8.9	352.8
Construction Bank of China	5,988	386,000	3.1	15.5	526.2
France					
Credit Agricole Group	25,930	86,100	43.7	301.2	5,308.2
Banque Nationale de Paris	12,824	52,404	33.2	244.7	7,233.1
Societe Generale	12,521	58,600	34.3	213.7	7,637.3
Credit Mutuel	10,737	45,300	26.2	237.0	6,323.6
Germany					
Deutsche Bank	18,680	75,306	62.6	248.0	9,727.4
Dresdner Bank	13,042	48,948	31.9	266.5	8,728.9
Hypo Vereinsbank	11,853	25,146	108.9	471.4	13,409.6
Commerzbank	11,760	27,912	51.9	421.3	13,662.9
United States					
Citigroup	41,889	184,914	50.1	226.5	3,616.0
Bank America Corporation	36,877	170,975	47.1	215.7	3,612.7
Chase Manhattan Corporation	24,121	72,683	82.3	331.9	5,033.8
Bank One Corporation	19,654	88,628	50.4	221.8	2,950.3
United Kingdom					
HSBC Holdings	29,352	132,285	49.8	221.9	3,663.7
Barclays Bank	13,495	78,600	40.6	171.7	4,495.8
National Bank	13,389	64,400	55.3	270.9	4,804.7
Royal Bank of Scotland	12,111	77,200	65.0	156.9	3,109.7

Source: Huang, P. and Wang, G., 2003. *Institutional Reforms and Approach Options of the State-Owned Banks*, Economic Science Publishing House, Beijing:260.

Table 10.11 **Comparison between Chinese and international banks, 2003**

	Tier one capital	Staff	Per capita profit	Per capita tier one capital	Per capita assets
China					
Bank of China	21,916	192,468	8.7	1,13.9	2,255.90
The Industrial and Commercial Bank of China	21,530	405,558	2.1	53.1	1,423.0
The Agricultural Bank of China	16,435	--	--	--	--
Construction Bank of China	12,955	306,809	1.7	42.2	1,214.1
France					
Credit Agricole Group	35,660	955,37	39.7	373.3	6,375.1
Banque Nationale de Paris	24,119	87,685	64	275.1	8,495.0
Societe Generale	16,000	88,278	29.6	181.3	5,954.5
Credit Mutuel	13,156	54,300	37.6	242.3	6,710.7
Germany					
Deutsche Bank	23,848	77,442	48.1	307.9	10,269.0
Dresdner Bank	20,056	65,926	−13.4	304.2	10,993.9
Hypo Vereinsbank	12,259	36,566	−10.7	335.3	12,106.2
Commerzbank	9,950	9,605	23.8	1,036.0	37,262.3
United States					
Citigroup	59,012	250,000	91.1	236.0	4,388.8
Bank America Corporation	43,012	133,944	97.0	321.1	4,930.8
Chase Manhattan Corporation	37,570	94,335	26.7	398.3	8,043.7
Bank One Corporation	23,918	73,685	64.6	324.6	3,764.4
United Kingdom					
HSBC Holdings	38,949	184,406	52.3	211.2	4,177.2
Barclays Bank	27,651	111,800	68.7	247.3	5,808.6
National Bank	23,836	60,000	78.1	397.3	8,536.1
Royal Bank of Scotland	22,895	74,700	69.2	306.5	8,540.1

Source: Wei, C. and Zhu, F., 2005. *Commercial Banking Competitiveness*, China Financial Publishing House, Beijing:7–9.

reigning in liquidity by lowering base money growth in recent periods. Moreover, administrative controls have been successful in the past few years. Since 2004, the state has lifted step-by-step controls on bank lending rates.

Conclusion

Between 1998 and 2003, for the Chinese 'big-four' banks (Tables 10.10 and 10.11)
- tier one capital increased
- staff numbers gradually decreased
- per capita profit improved from 1998 to 2003 for the Bank of Communications,

and the Industrial and Commercial Bank of China but not for the Construction Bank of China
- per capita tier one capital and per capita assets increased.

However, there were several problems
- per capita profit wass low compared to international standards
- per capita assets were extremely low compared to the international standard
- the 'big-four' banks were overstaffed.

The Chinese banking sector has undeniably become more competitive in the last decade, in loans, deposits, assets and profits. However, while Chinese banks are becoming stronger and more stable they have some distance to go to match international standards. There are three objectives for Chinese banks—bank balance sheets must be cleaned up, the Chinese government should reshape the ownership structure of banks and, finally, the government should further liberalise the financial sector. As the deadline approaches in 2006, we expect that dramatic changes in the market players or structure of the Chinese banking sector are not likely to occur.

References

Anderson, J., 2005. 'Which way out for the banking system?', *Asian Economic Perspectives*, UBS Investment Research, June:16.

Association of China's Finance and Banking, 2004. *Almanac of China's Finance and Banking (2002–2004)*, Chinese Finanical Publishing House, Beijing.

Dai, X., 2001. 'Five commitments on foreign financial institutions entry into China' *People's Daily*, 31 December.

Huang, P. and Wang, G., 2003. *Institutional Reforms and Approach Options of the State-Owned Banks*, Economic Science Publishing House, Beijing.

Jiao, J., 2002. *Study on International Competitiveness of China's Banking Industry,* Chinese Modern Economic Publishing House, Beijing.

Liang, W., 2003. *Chinese Financial Industry Reforms and Openness after Entry into WTO*, Chinese Social Science Publishing House, Beijing.

Wei, C. and Zhu, F., 2005. *Commercial Banking Competitiveness*, China Financial Publishing House, Beijing.

11

How are equity markets performing in China?

Ted Rule

Stockmarkets were first established in China in the late nineteenth century to trade the shares of companies involved in foreign trade. All treaty ports had premises where share transactions were carried out. In the early 1920s, it is estimated that China had 150 stockmarkets with the key markets in Shanghai. The 1928 *China Yearbook* reported that the operations of the Shanghai Gold Exchange were so vast that it was 'at times capable of influencing the destiny of other countries' currencies' (Woodhead 1929:229). Speculation was fierce and the practices ethically questionable. In 1925, the Peking Government telegraphed the Shanghai Municipal Council asking the Shanghai Consular Corps to exercise greater control over local exchanges (Woodhead 1929). A by-law that brought stock exchanges under existing by-laws was submitted unsuccessfully to special ratepayers' meetings in 1922, 1924 and 1925 (Pott 1928). Representatives of the local Chinese community vigorously opposed the measures whilst foreign ratepayers 'manifested no interest in the matter' (Pott 1928:254).

Shanghai remained the centre of wild speculation throughout the 1930s and 1940s. In 1934, interested readers were told that 'for those who wish to "play the market", Shanghai offers a wide variety of entertainment'—as well as the London, Paris or New York Stock Exchanges, you could play local issues 'of which there are many, both bonds and shares' (Lethbridge1934:107).

When the communists entered Beijing in 1949, most of the exchanges had already closed—victims of the hyperinflation and civil unrest that had occurred during previous years. For a brief period before 1952, several exchanges reopened under the 'mixed economy' policy, permitting capitalists known as the 'National Bourgeoisie' to trade, however the policy had a limited lifespan. By the end of 1956, 99.6 per cent of total production was under state or 'mixed' control (State Statistical Bureau 1959) and the 'National Bourgeoisie' ceased to exist (Liu and Wu 1986).

Paradoxically, securities played a role eliminating the 'National Bourgeoisie'. Nearly RMB 4 billion (A$760,500) of State Treasury bonds were issued between 1950 and 1958. The 'National Bourgeoisie' had been allowed to keep 5 per cent of profits from their enterprises on condition that the majority of profits were compulsorily reinvested in state bonds (Guillermaz 1972). Thus the Party maintained the fiction of a 'mixed economy' and retained the services of managers, while redirecting profits towards state objectives.

The market system was replaced during the Great Leap Forward, where a fully developed economy and state of communism were to be achieved through class struggle. The political ascendancy of Liu Shaoqi and Deng Xiaoping (1960–66) following the disasters of the Great Leap Forward introduced several semi-market measures aimed at restoring a measure of prosperity. But the political left remained strong and prevented the government from introducing market forces. Small-market measures completely disappeared with the outbreak of the Cultural Revolution in 1966.

At the end of the Cultural Revolution in the late 1970s, China was controlled by politicians that understood the inherent weaknesses in the Soviet-style economic system, and thus the need for economic reform. Much of the success of the early reforms, especially the spectacular successes in the agricultural sector, were due to the realisation that economic progress was impossible without some element of personal reward and the reintroduction of limited markets. The success of agricultural markets resonated with a body of economists with whom the modern history of the shareholding system in China begins.

The birth of the shareholding system[1]

In 1979, regulations were promulgated that permitted the establishment of Sino-foreign joint ventures, with the Ministry for Foreign Economic Relations and Trade (MOFERT) responsible for implementation. The regulations provided for a system based on equity shareholding. The first joint venture, Beijing Air Catering, was established in Beijing in 1979 and became the first 'shareholding' company in China since 1956.

Joint ventures rapidly became very popular amongst Chinese enterprises, including state-owned enterprises. Privileges offered to joint venture partners included favourable tax treatment, overseas travel for managers, the right to withhold foreign earnings and the ability to escape the planning net.

The State Commission for the Restructuring of the Economic System (SCRES) approached shareholding from the perspective of economic efficiency. For political reasons, SCRES emphasised the 'experimental' nature of the system and initial experiments were confined within special economic zones. In Shenzhen, the 'Leading Committee on the Shareholding Experiment' was established in the early 1980s to oversee the establishment of joint venture companies.

In November 1982, Shenzhen established three joint ventures—Bao'an Investment Company, Yin Hu and San He. These joint venture arrangements were not a share of ownership in the companies, as in industrial economies, but an arrangement between shares and bonds. Joint ventures guaranteed dividends and capital and permitted the refund of capital. In the early 1980s, the defining element in the value of a share was the dividend rate compared with the bank savings rate.

Outside the special economic zones, SCRES experimented with the joint venture model for merging enterprises and issuing shares. The first experiment was Beijing Tianqiao Department Store, which merged three state-owned retail department stores by assessing the net book worth and dividing it into 1 RMB shares for issue of new shares. The original three department stores made up 51 per cent of the expanded capital, which became state shares. The new shares were issued to banks—26 per cent, other institutions—19 per cent and the public. Essentially, 96 per cent of Beijing Tianqiao remained owned by the state, which owned the shareholding banks and institutions. SCRES established a new class of shares called 'legal person shares' that promoted the benefits of spreading ownership. Any entity with a business registration was treated as a legal person with limited liability. Thus, the legal person rather than the state received the benefits of ownership.

Share trading

In 1986, SCRES instituted share trading of shares, which previously had occurred only on a small scale. Shanghai was the first city in China to introduce the over-the-counter (OTC) trading of shares. The first publicly traded shares in China were in Yanzhong and Fei Le, which commenced trading over the counters of Shanghai securities companies on 9 September 1986.

The popularity of capital markets in Shanghai spread between 1986 and 1988. The Bank of Communications popularised shares and was responsible for most of the new issues, worth approximately RMB 1.7 billion (A$323 million). The bank became the first financial institution to adopt the shareholding system and similarly to other contemporary companies, the form of incorporation was non-standard and the rights and obligations of shareholders were unclear. Capital markets quickly developed between mid 1988 and late 1990. The first OTC trading house was the Jing'an branch of the Industrial and Commercial Bank of China. Other trading counters were located at Hai Tong Securities, the Bank of China Securities and Shanghai International Securities. The six shares listed were Yanzhong, Xiao Fei Le, Shanghai Vacuum Electron Device, Ai Shi, Shen Hua and Da Fei Le.

Trading developed simultaneously in Shenzhen during this period, and in November 1986, the Shenzhen City Government published 'Regulations Governing Experimental Corporatisation of State Owned Enterprises' to initiate a local shareholding system.

The first company to list publicly in Shenzhen was the Shenzhen Development Bank in March 1987. It became the model for future listings with clearly defined shareholders rather than the issuing of bonds by an enterprise. Shareholders could participate in management through general meetings and had rights to the distribution of profits. Liability for the company's debts was limited to the share capital. The Shenzhen Development Bank's issue of 10 million 20 RMB shares was approved in May 1987. Until the end of 1988, trading remained stagnated with no movement in prices and a total turnover of only RMB 4 million (A$760,500). The price/earnings ratio for the Shenzhen Development Bank was 0.2 to 0.3. The Shenzhen City Government approved a RMB 38 million (A$7.2 million) issue by technology property company, Vanke, in December 1988 and quickly followed with the RMB 10.7 million (A$2 million) listing of textile company Gin Tian, with an issue in February 1989.

In 1988, the Shenzhen Development Bank's profit announcement boomed at three times the previous year's figure. Investors who had expected little better than bank interest received large dividends and a bonus share issue. As word spread quickly, 'hot money' from all over China poured into the Shenzhen Stock Exchange. Turnover exploded from RMB 32.5 million (A$2 million) for the whole year of 1988 to monthly volumes of RMB 110 million (A$21 million) in May 1990 and RMB 260 million (A$49 million) by June. The Shenzhen Development Bank's share price jumped from its issue price of RMB 20 (A$3.80) to RMB 120 (A$22.80) and market capitalisation rose from RMB 200 million (A$38 million) in December 1989 to RMB 2 billion (A$380 million) in December 1990. In addition, an enormous volume of capital illegally changed hands outside securities companies amongst massive crowds. Frantic trading occurred despite the lack of registration of most transactions and impossibility of verifying ownership of shares. Instead, shareholders commonly exchanged photocopies of identification cards as a form of guarantee on the title of shares. Share prices rose widely, the star performer was the Shenzhen Development Bank which peaked at RMB 79 (A\$15) representing a price/earning ratio of 57, while Vanke's price/earning ration was 66 and Gin Tian's price/earning ratio was 42.

The emergence of the stock exchanges

It became obvious that OTC trading was inadequate and the establishment of properly constituted markets was necessary. On 14 April 1989, a meeting was held to recommend the establishment of a Shenzhen Securities Exchange. A preparatory group for the Shenzhen Stock Exchange was set up under the leadership of Wang Jian, formerly a lecturer in economics at Tianjin's Nankai University and Deputy General Manager of the Shenzhen Development Bank.

In Shanghai, the People's Bank appointed Wei Wenyuan from their internal Financial Management Department as head of the preparatory group. During 1990, the Shenzhen and Shanghai preparatory groups drafted new regulations for approval by the State Council. Rivalry was fierce between the two groups for the honour of opening the first exchange.

Preparatory work for the Shanghai Exchange progressed smoothly with the support of Jiang Zemin, the former Mayor of Shanghai and the administrative and political skills of Mayor Zhu Rongji. The Shanghai Securities Exchange was officially established on 16 November 1990 within premises in the Pujiang Hotel on the north side of Suzhou Creek. The official opening ceremony was held on 19 December 1990.

Shenzhen's preparatory work progressed less smoothly because the form of regulations was reportedly constantly returned for amendments by Wang Zhen. Approval to open was only achieved after the direct intervention of Jiang Zemin.[2] The Shenzhen Stock Exchange had its soft opening on 1 December 1990 in the small, modern premises on the 15th floor of the Shenzhen ITIC building. The official opening of the Shenzhen Exchange was held on 3 June 1991.

Foreign participation in markets

Foreign participation in Chinese equity markets began early. The first listed Chinese company to sell shares to foreigners was Shenzhen's Vanke in mid 1988. As part of Vanke's IPO process, Shenzhen City Government requested its Hong Kong adviser, Sun Hung Kai Securities, produce an international standard prospectus. Sun Hung Kai arranged that its Hong Kong listed associate, Tian An, subscribe for over 25 per cent[3] of Vanke's capital, allowing Vanke's management to apply for joint venture status immediately. As Vanke's price continued to rise, Tian An sold its holding share to less than 25 per cent. Authorities were confronted with a dilemma—the joint venture arrangement was suddenly no longer a joint venture and circumstances were beyond their control.[4]

Many investors favoured foreign participation in the Chinese markets but opinions differed on the form of this participation. Some supported the Taiwanese model that restricted participation to a limited number of listed foreign funds, while others favoured a more direct approach. Meanwhile, the joint venture issue required resolution. Economic nationalism in Thailand and the Philippines, where stockmarkets were open to direct foreign investment, had inspired upper limits for foreign participation. China had struggled with guaranteeing minimum levels and finally established the minimum 25 per cent foreign participation requirement for joint venture arrangements, allowing enterprises to benefit from taxation and other provisions under the Joint Venture Law.

The issue of foreign participation received its first direct public airing in May 1990 at a seminar on the development of the securities market held in Shanghai under the auspices of the Stock Exchange Executive Council and the People's Bank of China. During the conference there was strong support for the proposal from the Standard Chartered Bank (Rule 1990), which identified the lack of renminbi (RMB) convertibility and privileges afforded to foreign ownership as the two main obstacles to foreign participation in Chinese markets. The proposal suggested the creation of a separate class of shares denominated in foreign currency with the subscription and all other foreign payments converted at the swap rate. Strong support from participants such as Zhou Xiaochuan, then a commissioner of SCRES, currency specialist Cao Fengqi of Peking University and Liu Hongru ensured further consideration of the proposal.

The Shenzhen Stock Exchange announced in early June 1991 that it would launch several new issues with B Share, and by September, 13 companies had received approval to issue B Shares.[5] Shanghai had only one approved company, an unattractive manufacturer of black and white televisions called Shanghai Vacuum Electron Limited. The company had the advantage of high-level political support from Jiang Zemin and Zhu Rongji and it became obvious that despite the merits or otherwise of listing candidates, the Shanghai Vacuum Electric would be the first company to list B Shares in Shanghai. The listing occurred on 2 February 1992. Despite the desire of involved Chinese and foreign professionals that international standards and practice be followed, political pressure to complete the deal on an unrealistic timetable meant the complete project was of poor quality. The listing documents failed to include an audit of Shanghai Vacuum Electron's results—in response to concerns about the quality of accounting information, Arthur Andersen produced a non-binding calculation of Vacuum's possible profits under international accounting standards in a single weekend. Underwriters then made their decisions on the basis of these quickly calculated figures. Sadly, these procedures became a precedent for the future development of the B Share market. Ad hoc, slap-dash practices and gross political interference became the guiding principles of the B Share market.

The market became less rational on 2 December 1991, with the fully subscribed issue of 100,000 B Shares at RMB 420 (A$79.80) per share as a placement to institutions on an information memorandum. The inability to register the prospectus in Hong Kong was sidestepped. The price represented a price/earnings ratio of 80, at a discount of Vacuum's A Share price of RMB 700 (A$133) (Sun Hung Kai Securities 1991).

The B Share has not been a success for the Chinese securities markets, remaining small and illiquid. Markets never became more than a device to allow foreign participation in markets to circumvent the maze of conflicting tax, currency and joint venture requirements and were viewed as a temporary measure until the yuan became convertible. This seemed more likely, paradoxically, at the opening of markets in the early 1990s than it subsequently became 11 years ago, when the People's Bank pegged the currency to the US Dollar, and even less likely during the East Asian financial crisis, when the People's Bank retreated further.

By the end of 1999, 108 companies had issued B Shares—almost all were universally poor quality companies. A study of the results of the 54 B Shares listed in Shanghai in 1999 revealed that only 24 companies made profits above the rate of inflation (Green and Wall 2000). Following the East Asian financial crisis, widespread concern in international financial circles about investment in East Asia meant international capital stayed away from the Chinese B Share market in droves. B Shares traded at a discount of 80–90 per cent of corresponding A Shares. There was little reason for companies to enter international markets when the necessary capital was available from the A Share market at more attractive prices.

Local capital sustained the B Share market during the period and illegal trading in B shares was ignored. Chinese citizens with foreign currency represented a large proportion of trade and ownership of B Shares. Shares were acquired on the speculation that a change in regulations to officially permit Chinese nationals to own and trade these shares, culminating in a rise in the market. By the end of 1999, the Shenzhen B Share index was languishing at 53.6 compared with a 1992 figure of 142, but by the end of 2000 the figure had risen to 85 (Shenzhen Fact Book 2003).

In July 2001, the prayers of speculators were answered when B Share markets became open to domestic investors and the price and volume of B Shares traded suddenly spiked. By the end of 2001, the Shenzhen B index had risen to 137.6, at end 2002 to 265.7 and at end 2004, 271.7 (Shenzhen Fact Book 2004). Trading volume in Shanghai and Shenzhen rose from RMB 6 billion (A$1.1 billion) in 1998 to RMB 69 billion (A$13 billion) in 2001, before settling around RMB 20 billion (A$3.8 billion) (China Securities Regulatory Commission 2004).

Further speculation has occurred in 2005, as international investors scramble for local assets on the expectation that China will revalue the yuan (as it has done in July, *Editor's note*). B Shares remain a blunt instrument for raising capital in China because of the mismatch between Chinese and foreign perceptions about investment in China and foreign suspicions that Chinese regulations and supervision is inadequate. The quality of regulation has been put into sharp relief by the highly professional supervision of H Shares and Red Chips in Hong Kong and the generally higher quality of Chinese stocks listed in Hong Kong. Hong Kong is perceived to be a better option for foreign investors who want exposure to Chinese assets. At the same time, the enormous volume of yuan available for investment in the A Share market overshadows the B Share market, given that it is cheaper capital. Between 1993 and 2004, RMB 762 billion (A$145 billion) was raised on the Shanghai and Shenzhen markets via A Shares and HK$ 603 billion (A$114 billion) was raised by Chinese enterprises on the Hong Kong market (China Securities Regulatory Commission 2004). In the same period, only RMB 36 billion (A$6.8 billion) was raised through B Share issues (China Securities Regulatory Commission 2004). China's enormous foreign exchange reserves mean there is no practical shortage of foreign exchange that might encourage companies to prefer B Share issues because they can purchase foreign currency at the bank.

The weak position of the B Share was further confirmed in December 2002 with the promulgation of the Qualified Foreign Institutional Investor Law, under which qualified investors, initially Citigroup, HSBC, UBS, Nomura Securities, Deutsche Bank, Morgan Stanley, Goldman Sachs and JP Morgan, were permitted to invest in A Shares in the US$50 to 800 million range. The foreign currency share is an anachronism that waits to take its place in history when the yuan becomes convertible.

The role of Hong Kong

Hong Kong has been a major winner, possibly the major winner, from the development of equity and other financial markets in China. After the frenzied development of the last 15 years, it is difficult to understand just how uninvolved the Hong Kong financial world was in Chinese finance in the mid 1980s. This is partly due to the lack of financial activity that occurred in China. In the mid 1980s, depending on the statistics consulted, the economy of Hong Kong at nominal exchange rates was between one-third and one-half the size of the total economy of the mainland.

Despite its claims to international status, in the mid 1980s Hong Kong was a medium-sized, deeply parochial market heavily weighted towards property.[6] Stock exchange statistics in 1986 indicate finance was the leading sector of the market with 21.7 per cent of total market capital, but almost three-quarters was attributed to the Hong Kong and Shanghai Bank and its associate the Hang Seng Bank, accounting for 15 per cent of total market capitalisation. In 1986, 9 of the top 20 Hong Kong companies were land developers and the bulk of the market was small family companies that had listed the minimum 25 per cent of their capital but were relatively illiquid.

In 1986, 20 of the 258 companies listed in Hong Kong were classed as 'international' but these were almost all parallel listings of Malaysian and Singapore companies and rarely traded. Daily turnover was similar to that of Singapore. There were no Chinese stocks listed in Hong Kong and disgraced Hong Kong Stock Exchange Chairman Ronald Li Fook-siu was reported to have suggested to various enterprises in China that they should list assets in Hong Kong via holding companies (Rowley 1987). In March 1987, Tian An China Development Ltd[7] was the first real Chinese play listed in Hong Kong, and, true to local traditions, it was a property play. It listed the foreign interests in several Chinese real estate developments, which had been injected into a Hong Kong holding company. China and Eastern Investment, a fund for Chinese investment sponsored by Baring Bros, followed shortly after.

The first listing in Hong Kong that set new parameters for future development was CP Pokphand Ltd in 1988. Assets were almost completely Chinese[8] and included industrial and, for the first time in Hong Kong, agricultural assets. The first IPO after the stock exchange crash of 1987, it was attractively priced and oversubscribed 297 times. Subscriptions of HK$27.9 billion (A$5.3 billion) were received by the company selling shares valued at HK$100 million (A$19 million), subsequently setting off a mania for Chinese assets. The appetite was aggressively fed by CP Pokphand's sponsor, Standard Asia, which over the next four years brought a steady stream of small manufacturers, mainly based in the Pearl River Delta, to market. As a result, the market began to move away from local property towards China-based manufacturing and reflected the broader trends in the Hong Kong economy. As the market began to change, Standard Chartered Asia actively prompted the raising of equity capital through Hong Kong-listed enterprises to large state enterprises and government economic regulatory bodies. In mid 1989, a large textile enterprise in Shenyang began to prepare to list in Hong Kong—the events of 4 June derailed the process.[9]

Prior to 1991, there was no official contact between the Hong Kong Stock Exchange and mainland financial regulators. Suggestions that Chinese enterprises should list in Hong Kong were first raised seriously in a meeting between the author and SCRES Chairman Liu Hongru in early 1991. At the same time, a group of Hong Kong brokers led by Victor Chu Lap-lik pushed for official discussions with mainland regulators. The first official meeting between the SEHK and the Financial Management Bureau of the People's Bank of China at that time the regulator of markets in China took place in Shenzhen on 5 September 1991.[10]

Following the meetings, the Hong Kong Stock Exchange concentrated on establishing a set of rules that would allow Chinese state enterprises to list Chinese shares governed by Chinese law directly on the Hong Kong Stock Exchange. These H Shares were established on the analogy of the B share and Sinopec, Tsingtao Brewery, Guangzhou Shipyard and Beiren Printing, were handpicked and prepared for listing.

The criteria used by the SCRES and People's Bank to select these companies illustrated the main disconnects between official thinking in China and the market reality, a contradiction that has not completely disappeared. Chinese government officials described the four companies as being amongst their best companies, however on close questioning it became clear that 'best' referred to production criteria and not necessarily to profitability or the efficient and financially productive use of funds.[11] Much of the preparatory work between the Hong Kong stock exchange and Chinese officials revolved around asset productivity issues, such as resolving unfunded pension liabilities, housing, health and other welfare provisions that remained the direct responsibility of work units.

The first two issues were listed in Hong Kong on 26 July 1993 for Sinopec and Tsingtao Brewery and were followed on 6 August by Guangzhou Shipyard and Beiren Printing.

At the same time, several state-owned enterprises followed a scheme of injecting assets into Hong Kong or Bermuda shells, thus creating what are now known as the Red Chips. In 1992 and 1993, companies such as COSCO, Shougang and Oriental Metals[12] were listed on the Hong Kong market. The listing of Chinese companies has transformed the Hong Kong sharemarket. In the early 1990s, the daily market turnover in Hong Kong was worth approximately HK$3 billion (A$570 million), similar to Singapore. By 2005, the daily turnover rose to about HK$15 billion (A$2.8 billion), while Singapore turnover remains in the HK$3–4 billion range (A$570–760 million).

The proportion of the increased turnover attributable to trading in China stocks has risen consistently over the past 12 years. Between 1993 and 2004, total turnover on the Hong Kong Stock Exchange grew 3.3 times. Non-China turnover or the turnover of stocks not officially nominated by the Exchange as Red Chips or H shares grew by 2.05 times.[13] During the same period, turnover in Red Chips and H shares grew by a massive 12.8 times. In 1993, the turnover of China-related stocks was worth HK$121 billion (A$23 billion) or 11.9 per cent of total turnover however by 1998 the turnover had grown to HK$443 billion (A$84 billion) or 28 per cent of total turnover. In 2000, trading was worth HK$839 billion (A$160 billion) or 29 per cent of total turnover, and in 2004 it worth HK$1 549 billion (A$294 billion) or 46 per cent of turnover (Hong Kong Exchanges and Clearing 2004). In April 2005, 10 of Hong Kong's top 20 stocks by turnover were Chinese stocks, in particular China Mobile, Petro China, China Life, CNOOC, Bank of China Hong Kong, China Telecom, Yanzhou Coal, Huaneng Power and CSCL.

In terms of market capitalisation, there are now 72 listed H Shares with a total market capitalisation of HK$445 billion (A$84 billion) and 83 listed Red Chips with a total market capitalisation of HK$1 439 billion (A$273 billion) (Hong Kong Exchanges and Clearing 2005). Market capitalisation has also grown rapidly. Chinese stocks made up 5 per cent of total market capitalisation in 1993, in 1998 the proportion had grown to 14 per cent, by 2000 it was 27 per cent and in 2004 it was 28 per cent of total market capitalisation. Six of the top 20 companies by market capitalisation, China Mobile, CNOOC, Bank of China Hong Kong, Petro China, China Unicom and China Netcom, were China-related stocks. These companies accounted for 16.5 per cent of the total market capitalisation of the Hong Kong stock exchange (Hong Kong Exchanges and Clearing 2005).

Ten of the 33 Hang Seng Index component companies are now China-related stocks, China Merchants Holdings, Denway Motors, CITIC Pacific, China Resources, China Unicom, CNOOC, China Mobile, COSCO Pacific, Bank of China Hong Kong and Lenovo Group.

The listing of Chinese companies has significantly broadened the range of industries represented on the Hong Kong board, with the appearance of completely new categories. New categories include the energy and resources sector with companies like CNOOC, Yanzhou Coal and Sinopec, iron and steel companies such as Chongqing Iron and Steel and Ma'anshan Iron and Steel. Petrochemical companies are now listed with Sinopec Shanghai Petrochemical, and China Petroleum and Chemical. Motor vehicles are newly represented by Denway, Brilliance China and Great Wall Automobile and the insurance sector is represented by Ping An and China Life. The utilities sector has been particularly broadened with the addition of several Chinese power generator enterprises and of a number of toll-road and airport construction companies.

Hong Kong remains one of the favourite platforms for raising funds for Chinese companies (Table 11.1).

Shanghai Securities Exchange Fact Book 2004

There is no obvious pattern in these statistics and it is difficult to predict the future for Hong Kong as a source of funds for China. The numbers are skewed by the fact that Shanghai has had an average sixty IPOs per year for the past 14 years. Hong Kong has had a very creditable performance in comparison.

For H Shares in particular, as Shanghai and Shenzhen price/earning ratios continue to correct, raising capital in the Hong Kong market becomes more attractive. At the peak of the bubble in China, A Shares of the same companies listed in Shanghai traded at the inflated price/earning ratios in the 40s and 50s while H shares, with price/earning ratios in the mid teens, were closer to their

Table 11.1 **Funds raised by the market 1993–2004**

	Hong Kong (HK$ billion)	Shanghai (yuan billion)
1993	15.0	9.3
1994	13.0	15.0
1995	6.6	5.8
1996	19.0	20.2
1997	81.0	47.5
1998	17.0	37.7
1999	55.0	48.6
2000	294.0	91.4
2001	19.0	95.7
2002	52.0	61.4
2003	5.0	56.1
2004	26.0	45.7

Note: HK$1 = ¥1.06
Sources: Hong Kong Exchanges and Clearing, 2005. Available online at www.hkex.com.hk/.

Hong Kong peers. As Shanghai prices/earning ratios correct towards the 20s, the gap between A Shares and H Shares narrows and the Hong Kong market becomes correspondingly more attractive.

Companies listed in Hong Kong remain more attractive to international capital than China-listed equivalents because international capital trusts the quality of supervision and regulation in Hong Kong, particularly following the widely reported disciplinary actions against Hong Kong-listed Chinese companies. The market believes Hong Kong is immune from the corruption, petty and otherwise, the political interference and the uneven supervision which dogs the efforts of Chinese administrative bodies. International capital is correspondingly prepared to support fundraising by Hong Kong-listed companies over those of non-Hong Kong-listed companies.

Even a cursory examination shows that Red Chips have been more successful than H Shares on the Hong Kong market. This is not surprising given they have generally escaped the state net in various ways and have greater flexibility than large SOEs. At the most basic level, they do not have to endure the long and complicated approval measures to which H Shares are subject.

These trends are entirely in keeping with the general liberalisation of Chinese industry since the initiation of reforms in 1978 and are likely to continue. It should be noted, that a State Administration of Exchange Control regulation of 24 January 2005, requiring government approval for establishing businesses overseas and swapping shares with foreign companies may make the process difficult or even impossible. The author's discussions with the State Administration of Foreign Exchange in May 2005 suggest that it is an unintended consequence of currency regulations and may be subject to further revision.

The development of local markets

The Shanghai and Shenzhen equity markets must be counted as an enormous success when the overall criteria for markets are applied. After 13 years of operation, they now rank amongst the largest in the world. At the end of 2004, the two markets collectively ranked seventh in the world in number of listed companies, ahead of Euronext, Germany and Hong Kong. When separated, Shanghai was number ten in the world, ahead of Germany, Singapore and South Korea (Table 11.2).

The two Chinese domestic markets with US$452 billion (A$603 billion) ranked fourth in Asia after Tokyo, Hong Kong and Australia by total market capital and at the peak of the stockmarket boom, Shanghai ranked second after Tokyo.

Yet after 13 years of operations, the markets are now at a crossroad where the challenges are greater than the opportunities. The markets are victims of their own successes. When the markets opened in 1991 and 1992, investment in stocks was seen by the investing public as a one-way bet and the Shanghai index rose relentlessly until its peak of 2246 in 2001. Then, equally relentlessly it began to fall and has continued to do so. By 6 June 2005, the index had dropped to 1005 and threatened to break the 1000 level (Renmin Ribao 2005b).

The reasons for the fall are complex and the political and economic repercussions are potentially wide-ranging. The simple explanation for the fall is that Chinese markets have been highly overvalued since establishment. As recently as the end of 2004, the Shanghai Exchange reported the average price/earning ratio for 2002 was 34.4 times, 36.5 times in 2003 and 24.2 times in 2004. These were the ratios after the index had fallen for three years and by the end of 2004, were a little more than one-half the peak in 2001. In comparison with markets subject to different environmental factors, the Hang Seng China-Affiliated Corporations Index had price/earning ratios of 16.2 times, 13.1 times and 18.2 times, respectively, for the same three years.

The inevitable correction was managed by a number of regulatory factors. Prior to reforms in 2001, a quota system for IPOs was rigorously enforced. The founding logic seemed to be a zero-sum game where each yuan subscribed for an IPO was another yuan which could not be subscribed to government bonds or other public purposes.

Candidates for IPO were selected by provincial and provincial-level city governments on the basis of criteria, which by definition were not necessarily commercial as selectors were not underwriting the risk. At the same time, IPO

Table 11.2   **World markets by number of listed companies, 2004**

Toronto	3630
NASDAQ	3229
London	2837
New York	2293
Tokyo	2276
Australia	1582
Shanghai and Shenzhen	1379
Euronext	1333
Hong Kong	1086
Shanghai	837
Germany	759

Source: Shanghai Securities Exchange, 2004. *Shanghai Securities Exchange Fact Book 2004*, Shanghai.

prices were carefully controlled and kept low artificially. When average market price/earning ratios were in the 50s, no IPO could exceed a price/earning ratio of 20, allegedly preventing speculation. Chinese markets have always been short of product and the amount of cash chasing the available product was enormous. RMB deposits in Chinese Banks at the end of 2004 were RMB 24,500 billion (A$4,657 billion) and the ratio of M2 to GDP at 189 per cent was the highest in the world. Despite doubtlessly the best of intentions, when the demand for shares was kept artificially unsatisfied it is not surprising that the overpricing continued. While prices continued to rise, everyone was happy.

These practices led to a series of comfortable and corrupt relationships. Companies, underwriting houses and provincial governments jostled for rationed listing slots that were controlled by the CSRC. Underwriting houses controlled the allocation of shares and as an IPO was a one-way bet, it was a useful lubrication to achieve one's own objectives.

The so-called non-tradable share overhang also influenced market prices. About one-third of shares in listed companies are tradable on the exchanges and the remaining shares are owned by the state, either directly via the State Asset Supervision and Administration Commission or indirectly as legal person shares owned by other SOEs.[14] The gradual removal of the state from business has been on the reform agenda for many years. Privatisation has never been an official policy and often a dirty word, yet over the past 15 years many SOEs have been sold or otherwise found their way into the hands of private and even foreign owners. Whenever possible reforms were officially raised, the prospect of the untradable two-thirds of market capital suddenly flooding the market seriously spooked investors.

Two such events took place within a short period of time in 2001 and the combination initiated the market slide. In April 2001, the IPO quota system was revoked and decisions about IPOs were vested in the CSRC and the underwriters who assumed the financial risk. On 12 June 2001, a very modest proposal was implemented to allow a limited sell-down of state shares. The purpose of the measure was to shore up the State Social Security Fund, which was experiencing liquidity problems. Under the proposal new IPOs of SOEs would sell down a block of 10 per cent of existing state shares with the proceeds going to the Social Security Fund. No existing listed company was affected by the measures sent the market into a tailspin. Between the peak of the market in April and October, the market dropped to 1600, losing one-quarter of its value.

The reaction by the government to the crash is interesting. Share investment in China is a mass phenomenon—Shanghai alone has nearly 37 million A Share individual accounts[15] (Shanghai Stock Exchange Fact Book 2004) and unhappy investors are a threat to political stability. The *Hong Kong Economic Journal* (Heung Gong Gingdzai Yatbou 2001) reported that as the market crisis deepened Zhu Rongji himself intervened and by 22 October had ordered the procedures be revoked (O'Neill 2001).

Another proposal to sell-down state shares prompted the current slump in share prices. In April 2005, the CSRC announced an 'experiment' where the state shares of four companies would be floated. Once again the proposal was modest and very generous to existing shareholders. In the case of Sany Heavy Industry, existing non-State shareholders will get three free shares plus RMB 8 (A$1.50) in cash for every State share sold (Gu 2005). Once again the market sold heavily on the news as everyone knows the meaning of 'experimental'. The markets themselves were 'experimental' long after it was practicable to reverse the 'experiment'.

However the CSRC appears to be standing firm and on 1 June CSRC Chairman Shang Fulin said, '[r]eform of the dual share system is vital to China's capital markets. It has started and the pace will not drop' (Renmin Ribao 2005a). In late July 2005 as this book was going to press, CSRC announced another 42 companies would join the 'experiment'.

Several measures have been proposed to mitigate the effects of the new policy. On 31 May, the *Shenzhen Daily* reported the State Council would abolish the dividend tax. In a meeting of the CSRC in early May, an extraordinary proposal was put for a state-operated fund to support the market (Renmin Ribao 2005b).

The market crash has exposed the weakness of China's securities houses. Most knowledgeable players know securities houses have been breaking the law in myriad ways for a long time. Infractions include trading on their own account using identification cards bought in rural areas, trading on the margin and using investor funds for house account trading. It is generally agreed that with the current market correction as many as half of the 130 houses are technically bankrupt.[16] The most important of these to fail to date is Nanfang Securities whose liquidation was announced on 3 May 2005 (*China Daily* 2005). Nanfang was the fifth largest securities house and largest underwriter in Shanghai in 2004. It is reported to be RMB 10 billion (A$1.9 billion) under water. The possible repercussions of this collapse for the broader social and political peace and stability are large and it will be interesting to observe the inevitable political reaction.

Regulation and supervision

Harsh words have been spoken about the quality of regulation of domestic stockmarkets. The combination of a financial system with its roots in Stalinist bureaucracy and international aspirations, which focuses on the Taiwanese Ministry of Economic Affairs[17] and Korean chaebols, is rarely a felicitous one. However these explanations downplay the significant progress that has been made in regulations, especially under Zhou Xiaochuan.

Zhou Xiaochuan was appointed Chairman of the CSRC in February 2000 and is probably the outstanding economic intellectual of his generation in positions of high state authority, and one of the few with a cohesive view of a market economy. He adds a fine political sense borne out of a career spent in the seat of power in Beijing and close connections to the factions that control power. His career has been spent reforming ministries, including MOFTEC, SCRES, State Administration of Exchange Control and the People's Bank. His connections with the 'Shanghai Clique' go back to his father, the Minister of the First Ministry of Machine Building Zhou Jiannan who was Jiang Zemin's boss and worked closely with Wang Daohan.

On assuming his position he quickly moved to establish the international credibility of his team. He brought back Gao Xiqing from teaching and recruited Hong Kong SFC's vice-chairman, Laura Cha, as a vice-chairman. Laura Cha was a particularly difficult acquisition; she had US citizenship, which she had to renounce to get a vice-ministerial position.

In the two years between his appointment and his promotion out of the job in November 2002, he has
- required that one-third of the boards of listed companies be made up of external and independent directors
- delisted unprofitable companies or those with a poor reporting record
- appointed inspectors and clarified their powers
- required audits by five international auditors
- prohibited the use of external borrowings to finance stock purchases
- abolished the IPO quota system.

Zhou was promoted to Governor of the People's Bank of China after the sixteenth Party Congress in 2002. Whether his successor Shang Fulin will be able to continue Zhou's work remains to be seen. He is a high-flyer and a protégé of Zhu Rongji, who first came to prominence after being appointed by Zhu in 1994 to tackle the triangular debt problem. Most people felt he was largely successful in dealing with a difficult task. When he became Governor of the Agricultural Bank in 2000, he demonstrated an ability to make tough decisions with the closing of 3,000 branches and retrenchment of 50,000 staff. This toughness is demonstrated as he continues to back the decision to sell-down state shares.

However, most observers feel that he does not have Zhou's intellectual fire power—who does?—and there are doubts that he fully understands the implications of a market economy. He has created a bitter atmosphere within the commission by easing out overseas-trained staff favoured by Zhou. Gao Xiqing left very abruptly soon after Shang's arrival, and was followed some time later by Laura Cha who returned to Hong Kong. There is bitterness concerning the CSRC, where some people believe Zhou did not back his protégés sufficiently. But who will get the last laugh here? Cha has been well looked after with an appointment to Hong Kong's Executive Council and with the convergence of reform, Gao's new position as vice-chairman in charge of the social welfare fund may make him one of the largest institutional investors in the market and possibly more important than Shang.

Conclusion

It has become fashionable to deride the Chinese equity markets as a 'Mickey Mouse casino'—the 'casino' accusation is a curious one. Does everybody who invests in the New York stock exchanges know exactly which way the market will move? As with so many other aspects of modern Chinese life, the markets are complex and multifaceted. Far from being a 'Mickey Mouse casino', the supervision of the markets has evolved into a system recognisable to any international investor. Supervision and regulation have become more important as the market matures. Different sections of the market have different views of risk, and as the A, B, H share structure allows discrete observation of each segment, conclusions can be drawn about supervision of the market. Domestic investors remain unconcerned about the quality of Chinese supervision and may blame better supervision for the drop in the market and would rather it did not happen (Rong 2002). However international institutions have clear and negative views about the quality of supervision by Chinese officials. The differential between the H and B Share prices demonstrates that institutional investors will continue to invest in Chinese companies through Hong Kong markets.

Chinese regulators and politicians must receive the clear message—the opening-up of currency markets means China will become part of the world capital market, and to be able to hold its head up high must continue the reforms initiated in 2001. As retail investors recover from the current market corrections, company information and proper regulation will become more central to investment decisions.

Hong Kong will continue to benefit as it continues with the current regulations that will secure its future as one of the world's great markets. As China continues to grow, Hong Kong may become the New York of the twenty-first century. The real challenges and opportunities available depend on whether Hong Kong can become an intermediary between the mainland and Taiwan, and integrate the equity and other markets from the three components of China. Together the four Greater

China markets have 3,169 listed companies, only fifty fewer than NASDAQ and rank third in the world ahead of NYSE and London. More Taiwan investment money goes to the mainland than anywhere else and one million Taiwanese now live and work in China. Populations on both sides of the Taiwan Straits pay more attention to business than political visits or panda exchanges, and an integrated equity market based in Hong Kong could have much wider political and social implications. Could share trading become the ping-pong diplomacy of the twenty-first century?

In theory Shanghai should have every bit as much chance as Hong Kong to become the New York of the twenty-first century if it can overcome the difficult and fundamental problems of political interference. A significant proportion of the new middle class are share owners and a stable market is viewed by many politicians as an important part of political stability and, by extension, of maintaining power. Can a relatively closed political system respond to the imperatives of a relatively open market? Can it afford not to find a way? These are key questions that become more important with greater liberalisation. Government bodies argue public companies must behave in an open and transparent fashion. Can the question of how the government behaves be far behind? Will market reform be a catalyst for political reform?

The question of supervision also goes to the issue of minority rights. Under the current system most companies are majority state-owned and the issue is treated as redundant. It appears privatisation is again to the fore and equity markets will play a key role in the process. The process is 'experimental' but the number of experiments has, at the end of June 2005, been expanded ten times. On the record of previous 'experiments' it appears this can only increase, and means the question of minority rights must be addressed urgently.

Notes

[1] The following is compiled from notes from the author's discussions between 1988 and 1992 with the following institutions: PBOC Head Office, PBOC Shanghai, PBOC Shenzhen, Shanghai City Government, Shenzhen City Government, Stock Exchange Executive Council, Hai Tong Securities, Jing'an Securities, Jun'an Securities, Shanghai Securities Exchange, Shenzhen Stock Exchange, Shanghai Vacuum Electron Device Ltd, Shenzhen Development Bank.

[2] Notes from the author's discussions with members of the Shenzhen Stock Exchange in 1991.

[3] The minimum level of foreign participation for joint venture status was 25 per cent. The subscription was probably illegal.

[4] Notes of the author's meetings with Shenzhen Vanke, Shenzhen City Government, Shenzhen Stock Exchange and Sun Hung Kai Securities between December 1988 and June 1989.

⁵ Notes from the author's meetings with members of the Shenzhen Stock Exchange in October 1991.

⁶ The market's property bias gave the lie to Hong Kong's other pretension—that it was a pure market-based free-enterprise economy. High property prices were largely fuelled by the public finance system of Hong Kong. Land sales finance the Hong Kong Government. Income tax is low and there are a small number of excises. The majority of the government income is raised through stamp duties, largely on land sales, and the sale of land which is released in a notably niggardly fashion. Hong Kong is one of the few places in the world where the government is proud to announce each year that land prices have risen. This has fuelled the development of artificially large land development companies.

⁷ Interestingly, the principles of Tian An were closely associated with both Zhao Ziyang and Milton Friedman.

⁸ In a nod to tradition, it included a small amount of Hong Kong property.

⁹ The author was involved in the process to list the Shenyang textile company on the Hong Kong Stock Exchange.

¹⁰ The author arranged and was involved in the meetings preparing for the Hong Kong listing.

¹¹ Notes from meetings between the author and SCRES Chairman Liu Hongru in 1991.

¹² Note that the official listing dates of several Red Chips date back to the 1970s. This is a result of the use of listed shell companies for backdoor listings.

¹³ These statistics do not include many small industrials based around China that do not fit into either category.

¹⁴ The state has been accused acting as a monolithic owner of state shares, but this does not emphasis the local nature of SASAC intervention or the high degree of autonomy enjoyed by SOE management. The primary purpose of the SASAC is negative—to prevent the alienation of state assets and intervention is rarely made in the positive sense of securing the economic benefit for the owner, the state. Equally, intervention of a political nature can affect non-state companies every bit as much as it affects SOEs.

¹⁵ This statistic does not necessarily mean that there are 37 million individual investors. A current ID card is needed to open a trading account and for various reasons securities house have visited rural areas where ID cards are rarely needed, to purchase ID cards to open new accounts.

¹⁶ Notes from discussions with current and former CSRC staff in May 2005.

¹⁷ Chinese regulators have been asked why they prefer to use Taiwanese precedents as the basis for new regulations and have been intrigued at how often the answer is 'Zhonghua minzu' (Chinese race).

References

China Daily, 2005. 'China to liquidate number 5 securities broker', 10 May 2005, accessed 14 July 2005. Available online at http//www2.chinadaily.com.cn/English/doc/2005-05/10/content_440683.htm.

China Regulatory Securities Commission, 2004. Available online at http://www.csrc.gov.cn/en/homepage/index_en.jsp.

Crow, C., 1933. *Handbook for China*, Kelly and Walsh, Shanghai.

Green, S. and Wall, D., 2000. *This Little Piggy Becomes a Market*, OECD, Paris.

Gu, G.Z., 2005. 'China's stockmarket reforms', Asia Times Online May 24 2005, accessed week of June 6 2005. Available online at http://www.atimes.com/atimes/China/GE24Ad03.html.

Guillermaz, J., 1972. *Le Parti Communiste Chinois au Pouvoir*, Payot, Paris.

Heung Gong Gingdzai Yatbou, 2001. 'Jüjung Geimaan Paaibun Kau Si, Wan Sewui', *Hong Kong Economic Journal*, 24 October.

Hong Kong Exchanges and Clearing. 2005. Accessed week of 6 June 6. Available online at www.hkex.com.hk/.

Liu, S. and Wu, O. (eds), 1986. 'Shehuizhuyi Jingji Jian Shi [China's socialist economy: an outline history 1949–84]', *Beijing Review*, Beijing.

Ministry of Foreign Economic Relations and Trade, 1979. *Regulations for the Establishment of Sino-Foreign Joint Ventures*, Ministry of Foreign Economic Relations and Trade, Beijing.

O'Neill, M., 2001. 'Beijing pulls plug on sales of state holdings in listed firms, easing fears of heavy dilution', *South China Morning Post*, October 24.

Pott, F. L., 1928. *A Short History of Shanghai*, Kelly and Walsh, Shanghai.

Renmin Ribao, 2005a, 'China's stock index hits eight-year lowest after new round reform starts', 2 June 2005, accessed week of 6 June 2005. Available online at http://english.people.com.cn/200506/2/eng20050602_188178.html.

—— ,2005b 'Shanghai composite index falls below 1000 points', 6 June 2005, accessed week of 6 June 2005. Available online at http://english.people.com.cn/200506/06/eng20050606_188735.html.

Rong, F., 2002. 'Chinese investors dislike market regulation'. Available online at http://journalism.berkeley.edu/projects/greaterchina/story-stock.html.

Rowley, A., 1987. 'Asian Stock Markets', *Far Eastern Economic Review,164(47)*:125–56.

Rule, T., 1990. 'Zhengjuan Shichang ji qi zai Jingji Fazhanzhongde Zuoyong', *Fazhan Zhengjuan Shichang Guoji Yantaohui Ziliao Huibian*, Zhengjuan Jiaoyisuo Yanjiu Sheji Lianhe Ban'gongshi, Beijing.

Shanghai Online Finance Press, 2003. 'Guowuyuan ren mian renyuan, mianqu Gao Xiqing Zhenglinhui fuzhuxi yizhi', 3 January 2003, accessed week of June 6 2005. Available online at http://finance.sina.com.cn/y/20030103/0830297713.shtml.

Shenzhen Fact Book, 2003 *Shenzhen zheng quan jiao yi suo bian [Shenzhen Fact Book],* Nankai University Press, Tianjin.

— —, 2004, *Shenzhen zheng quan jiao yi suo bian [Shenzhen Fact Book],* Nankai University Press, Tianjin.

State Statistical Bureau, 1959. *Ten Great Years: statistics of the economic and cultural achievements of the People's Republic of China*, People's Publishing House of Peking, Beijing.

Sun Hung Kai Securities, 1991. *Shanghai Vacuum Electron Device Limited Information Memorandum*, Shanghai.

Woodhead, H.G.W. (ed), 1929 *The China Yearbook 1928*, Tientsin Press, Tianjin.

12

Recent developments in the social security system

Tim Murton

Many of the far-reaching economic and social reforms since 1978 have resulted in structural changes to the economy, particularly in the transition from a centrally-planned to a socialist-market economy.

A significant focus of China's economic reform agenda has been the reform of state-owned enterprises (SOEs). In a bid to improve efficiency, SOEs are now no longer required to provide the same level of services once expected. The change for social security provisions has been direct and significant. SOEs are no longer required to provide cradle-to-grave welfare in pensions, childcare and other social services. Consequently, since the mid to late 1990s, the Chinese government has been exploring alternative sources of social security provision.

Coupled with a rapidly ageing population that is beginning to affect the demand for social security, the government has recognised the need to strengthen the social security system. It considers social security reform to be a key component of the overall reform process. The Chinese government also believes that social security reform underpins economic growth and is necessary to social stability in the process of rapid, market-oriented growth.

Social security in China commonly refers to social insurance and social relief. The purpose of this chapter is to discuss developments in these areas since January 2004. Most attention in social insurance reform is paid to pensions, which is the most active area of social security reform. The major pension reforms include the introduction of the occupational pension scheme, and developments regarding the National Social Security Fund, the sale of state-owned shares and the Liaoning social security pilot program. Social relief emphasises the urban minimum livelihood guarantee scheme, which is discussed in this chapter. Although not regarded as a core component of the social security system, the issue of social welfare is addressed, specifically the increasingly important role of communities in providing basic social services to the local population.

Before proceeding to outline the major reforms to China's social security system since January 2004, it is necessary to understand exactly the meaning and context of 'social security' (*shehui baozhang*).

Context of social security

Social security in the Chinese context is a broad term and comprises five components

- social insurance (*shehui baoxian*), which includes pension insurance, unemployment insurance, health insurance, work injury insurance and maternity insurance
- social relief (*shehui jiuzhu*), which includes the social safety net called the urban minimum livelihood guarantee (*zuidi shenghuo baozhang*), and which is known colloquially in China as 'Dibao'[.1]
- social welfare (*shehui fuli*), which includes the provision of community services and other social services, such as aged care
- preferential treatment and resettlement (*youfu anzhi*), which involves the provision of services to soldiers both currently serving in and demobilised from the People's Liberation Army
- mutual assistance (*shehui huzhu*), which involves people helping out others for the benefit of society. Generally speaking, this component refers to the encouragement and promotion of volunteerism (Murton 2003a).

The government considers there to be a sixth component—individual savings— in the social security system (Ministry of Civil Affairs 2004). Although this component proposes that people should be more responsible for the provision of their own welfare, it is not yet considered a formal part of the social security system. It is expected that individual savings will play an increasingly important role in social security provision in the future, especially as the shortfall in social security funding becomes more difficult to address.

By engaging in social security reform, the government aims to develop a social security system that is

- independent of work units, in that employers should not be required to bear the main responsibility for the provision of social security

- varied in terms of its sources of funding, in that it does not depend solely on the finances of the central government, and that funding comes from other avenues such as the welfare lottery and the sale of state-owned shares
- standardised across the country, in that policies and regulations are implemented in a similar way throughout China, and
- is socially based in terms of administration and services, in that social organisations, such as banks, the post office and communities, provide services and implement social security policies and regulations (Ministry of Labour and Social Security 2001).

The main principles underpinning reforms of social security are sustainability and affordability. Sustainability refers to the long-term viability of the pension system, in that it is adequately funded and can be maintained over the long term, as well as being flexible enough to respond to future challenges. Affordability refers to the issue of cost. The social security system must be designed in such a way that it is not so costly for employers, employees or the government that they shirk their responsibility to contribute.

Social security reform is currently confined mostly to urban areas and reforms in rural areas remain unaddressed. Although the government is often criticised for focusing social security reforms on urban areas, it is a prudent course of action at present. It is easier to expand social security coverage to employees in urban areas who may have no recourse to alternative sources of income in the case of retirement or unemployment. Rural populations, on the other hand, are able to till their land on a subsistence basis, which affords them a measure of protection.

Latest developments in pension reform

White paper on social security

In September 2004, the central government issued a white paper on labour and social security entitled 'White Paper on China's Social Security Situation and Policies' (Ministry of Labour and Social Security 2004) prior to the General Assembly of the International Social Security Association in Beijing. The purpose of the document was to provide a general overview of the current state of the social security system. It provided much statistical information and defined the broad context of social security in China. Most interestingly, the White Paper was situated largely in the present and discussion of future directions in social security was limited. For example, discussion on pension insurance was limited to stating that the government would continue its work on the separation of funds in the social pool and individual accounts. Other future developments included the extension of social security coverage to all employees in urban areas, and transferring fund pools based at the municipal government level to the provincial governments (Ministry of Labour and Social Security 2004). Having said that, the White Paper provides a good description of the policy priorities of the government for social security reform, among which, the most important were responding to the impacts of SOE reform and population ageing, as well as the need to increase social security coverage among employees in urban areas.

Major factors driving social security reform

The most significant drivers for social security reform are the reform of SOEs, population ageing and the need to increase pension coverage.

Prior to the late 1990s, most social security-related services, such as pensions, childcare and health-related services and benefits, were provided by work units (*danwei*), many of which were SOEs. This was called the 'iron rice bowl', which denoted the lifelong welfare that such enterprises once provided (Murton 2003a:11). However, in the transition from a centrally planned to a socialist-market economy, the government determined that work units should shed those responsibilities that were not part of their core business in a bid to make them more efficient and competitive in a global environment. It is on this basis that the government is exploring and piloting other means of providing social security services. Based on experiences trialling other means of service provision, social security has now become the responsibility of the government, employers, employees and the general public.

Population ageing is a significant challenge for the government, and has been exacerbated by the one-child policy. Improvements in the health area mean that the elderly are living longer. Some commentators, such as Leckie (Reuters 2004), have mentioned that western populations got rich before they got old, whereas the Chinese population will get old before it gets rich. This comment highlights that China is experiencing rapid population ageing that is occurring in a period of economic transition. Whereas the transition occurred in Italy and Sweden over 79 and 89 years respectively, it will occur in China over only approximately 26 years (Leckie and Pai 2005). It is currently estimated that more than 10 per cent of the population is already aged 60 years or more (Xinhua News Agency 2005). Future projections suggest that by 2030 the number of elderly people, aged 60 years or more, will comprise approximately 16 per cent of the world's elderly, and approximately 24.5 per cent of China's own population (Xinhua News Agency 2005).

The government also recognises the need to increase pension coverage. Pension reform is taking place in urban areas, where approximately 40 per cent of the population resides. However, pension coverage is still not high enough, with only about 15 per cent of the total population covered by the existing pension scheme (*Beijing Morning News* 2005). As the social security system still operates on a pay-as-you-go basis, where employees pay contributions for current retirees on the implicit promise that future employees will contribute to their retirement, this will create significant funding pressures. It has already created a significant shortfall, largely because such schemes can only be maintained on the basis of extensive coverage.

Current shortfall in pension funding

Keeping the pension scheme sustainable without a high degree of social unrest continues to be a major challenge, especially since the funding shortfall in pension funding is estimated to be approximately 2.5 trillion RMB (A$400 billion) (*Beijing Morning News* 2005), which includes an amount of approximately 1 trillion RMB (A$180 billion) of funds raided from individual accounts to pay for current pensions (Information Times 2005). Moreover, commentators such as Leckie (Reuters 2005) believe the government has a 10-year window of opportunity to fund a US$2 trillion (A$2.67 trillion) liability before the whole scheme becomes unaffordable due to population ageing. Although the difficulties in funding the shortfall can be resolved, it will take much political will to do so. The government has already recognised the seriousness of the problem and has begun to adopt a holistic approach to the provision of social security in that country.[2]

The government is exploring a number of options to address the considerable shortfall in funding. Some of the newer ideas being considered are the use of land taxes and charging a levy on mobile phone users. The thinking on both of these options is still in its preliminary stages. A more immediate option at this stage is to sell off state-owned shares in businesses.

Sell-off of state-owned shares

The current drive to sell-off state-owned shares demonstrates that the government is serious about funding its pension liabilities and developing its stockmarkets. On at least two previous occasions, the government attempted to sell its shares on the stockmarket. Investors responded badly to this move, resulting in its value declining sharply. On both occasions, investors feared that the new shares could flood the market and reduce the value of their investments.

The present value of state-owned shares in listed firms is impressive, representing approximately A$346 billion (Lague 2005) or two thirds of the total capitalisation of domestic stockmarkets (*The Economist Magazine* 2005). As these shares gradually come onto the market, a shock is likely to occur and the value of the market is expected to fall, as Chinese investors are likely to respond in a similar fashion to the way they did previously (see Chapter 11). The level at which the market bottoms out will probably reflect a more realistic pricing of the companies listed on the stockmarket.

In order to prevent a massive shock to the stockmarkets, the government is proceeding slowly through a pilot program. The details of the pilot program have not yet been finalised, but it is likely to consist of selling or gifting shares in a small number of companies. Minority shareholders are expected to have the power to approve the conversion and buyers of shares would not be able to sell them within one year. In the future, they will be allowed to sell at most five per cent of a company's equity (*The Economist Magazine* 2005). Alternatively, the government is exploring a vehicle similar to Hong Kong's Tracker Fund, which was an Exchange Traded Fund set up by the government during the East Asian financial crisis to stabilise domestic markets. The Hong Kong government bought shares in a range of companies and sold-off parcels to investors with a range of stringent conditions. Another possibility is that state-owned shares be transferred to the National Social Security Fund, which is currently lobbying the government on this matter. Such a move would increase the value of that fund substantially. Regardless of the path chosen, the greatest challenge for the government in selling its state-owned shares will be to balance supply and demand to ensure market stability.

Occupational pension schemes

Since the process of pension reform began in earnest in 1997, the government has consistently tried to encourage enterprises to introduce occupational pension[3] schemes. Such schemes have existed in China since at least 1991, when they were known as enterprise supplementary pensions. In 1995, the government issued the 'Opinion on the establishment of the enterprise supplementary pension insurance system' in an attempt to set guidelines on occupational pension schemes. The take up of such schemes was not high and only after 2000 did the government really encourage enterprises to offer such schemes. The most significant development in relation to occupational pension schemes came on 1 May 2004, with the promulgation of Regulations 20 and 23.[4]

Regulations 20 and 23 were an attempt to codify occupational pension schemes. It is clear that they are intended to be enterprise based and define the contribution and accumulation type pension funds. They operate under trust arrangements in a manner similar to Australia's superannuation system and Hong Kong's Mandatory Provident Funds, in that the services provided by trustees, custodians, investment managers and administrators are intended to be separate. Payments from occupational pension schemes can be made either as lump sums or as pensions. The major difference between Chinese occupational pension schemes and the Australian and Hong Kong models is that they are voluntary and negotiated directly between employers, employees and unions. In this regard, they also contain elements of American 401(k) schemes.

The purpose of occupational pension schemes is to provide retirees with a higher level of retirement income than is available under the basic pension scheme, which comprises funds from the social pool and a person's compulsory individual account. When combined they form the first pillar of the pension system. Whilst occupational pension schemes can be viewed as the third pillar of the retirement incomes system, because of the involuntary nature, they should more properly be considered the second pillar of the pension system. The third pillar comprises individual savings, which if used for retirement, are taxed at a concession.

Regulation 25 was issued in September 2004, subsequent to the government's issuing Regulations 20 and 23. Regulation 32 was issued in December 2004. Regulation 25 stipulated guidelines for the investment of occupational pension schemes in an attempt to guarantee their safety and promote the continued development of such schemes. Regulation 32 strengthened the management of occupational pension schemes through an attempt to lay down rules regarding the administration of such schemes.[5]

The scope of investment of occupational pension schemes is broad but subject to some restrictions. At present, occupational pension schemes must invest no less than 20 per cent of assets in liquid investments such as demand deposits, money-market funds and treasury bills and up to 50 per cent in fixed-income securities. At least 20 per cent must be maintained in government treasury bonds and up to 30 per cent of assets can be invested in equities and insurance products and funds, with stock investments limited to 20 per cent of assets (Leckie and Pai 2005:81). The purpose of allowing such investment is to maximise the potential returns by such schemes while ensuring funds are invested in accordance with the principles of safety, liquidity and diversity. Safety refers to investing funds in a prudent manner, liquidity refers to ensuring that enough cash is available to meet payment needs and diversity refers to investing in such a manner to spread risk over a range of asset classes.

The current scope of investment for occupational pension schemes reflects the state of financial markets and the currently limited availability of products for investment by pension funds. However once assets from occupational pension schemes enter the market, they can be expected to contribute significantly to the future development of capital markets. Moreover, Regulations 20 and 23 indicate that current limitations may be lifted in the future, as the products available for investment increase and as changes and improvements in the financial services industry occur. These decisions are expected to be made by the Ministry of Labour and Social Security, the body responsible for regulating the scheme at present. The ministry has a high degree of discretion in the decisions it can make.

Occupational pension schemes are expected to play a key role in pension reform, especially in wealthier areas of China because of the financial pressures placed on the basic pension scheme. Although it has never been stated explicitly, it is clear that the government does not want occupational pension schemes to fail. It has underwritten the scheme.[6] The prospect of negative returns is unlikely. Financial markets may not operate as effectively as they should in allocating capital, but at least the government guarantee provides an assurance for employees that their assets will be protected. In offering a guarantee of protection, the government will ensure the scheme works while staving off any social unrest that may result from the collapse of such schemes.

The introduction of occupational pension schemes can be expected to have benefits for the emerging financial services industry by

- strengthening China's emerging funds management industry. Occupational pension schemes can be expected to promote the development of competition in the industry, particularly when domestic and international fund managers are able to manage funds from next year, as per accession commitments to the World Trade Organization.
- strengthening China's stockmarkets. The occupational pension schemes should increase the number of institutional investors in stockmarkets, which is likely to stabilise. Pension funds by their nature invest assets over the long term and are not as path dependent as individual investors
- encouraging innovation and professionalism in the financial sector, particularly in the continued development of China's capital markets. In a bid to maximise returns for investors, fund companies are expected to develop new investment strategies. Occupational pension schemes also provide opportunities to strengthen the role of actuaries and to establish a specialist pension funds industry
- encouraging flexibility and competition within China's labour market. Companies are likely to establish occupational pension schemes to encourage talented and valuable staff members to remain with the company. In addition, it will provide a means to attract talented staff.

At present, the size of the occupational pension fund market is approximately 50 billion RMB (A\$9.5 billion) (Sun 2004a), and the government expects the value of assets in occupational pension schemes to grow rapidly. It is estimated that the market for schemes could expand by 100 billion RMB a year until 2010, to total assets of about 1 trillion RMB (A\$180 billion) (Di Biasio 2004). These figures correspond with those of the Ministry of Finance, which has suggested that the value of occupational pension funds is expected to increase by 100 billion RMB per year (A\$19 billion) over the next three years (China Labour Network 2002).

The predicted rapid growth in occupational pension schemes is probably over-optimistic for a number of reasons. First, employers that wish to set up occupational pension schemes must have a sound financial base and meet current pension liabilities under the basic pension scheme. They may view the establishment of such schemes as an additional expense for employees. Moreover, employers can be selective about the staff entitled to an enterprise's occupational pension scheme. The number of people covered by such schemes may not grow as rapidly as predicted.

Assets in occupational pension schemes cannot be pooled in multi-employer funds, such as master trusts, because they are established by individual enterprises. As a consequence, occupational pension schemes are expected to remain small in scale. They may not yet be profitable enough for investment managers, as the fee structure is capped between 0.8 and 1.2 per cent of fund assets. However the government is expected to allow the investment of occupational pension scheme assets to be pooled at some time in the future. This development would increase the diversification of assets and spread risk more widely, especially across a range of employers. Funds could still invest with due consideration to the principles of diversity, safety and liquidity while maximising the potential returns. Moreover, the large size of multi-employer funds would lead to specialisation within the emerging funds industry, especially as specialist fund managers could be selected to manage a particular asset class in which they have expertise. The poor returns of one fund manager could also offset the high returns from other fund managers. In addition, the pooling of funds would reduce costs from economies of scale and allow benefits to be transferred when workers change jobs.

The lack of clarity regarding tax concessions to, and licensing of, companies able to provide services for occupational pension schemes is likely to constrain growth in occupational pension schemes. Although enterprises that establish occupational pension schemes receive tax concessions, tax regimes for schemes differ throughout China. For example, the highest rate of tax concession is in Hebei at 12.5 per cent, whereas most provinces maintain rates of around four to five per cent (Shen 2004). Much is made of the need to standardise tax concessions and the northeast social security pilot program is a trial for this.

Discussion within the government to date suggests that current thinking recognises the need for a nationwide rate of tax concession, and that it should not exceed 8.33 per cent (Shen 2004). Whether this is a sufficient tax concession to encourage employers to introduce occupational pension schemes is not yet clear. It is likely that greater clarity and further tax breaks will be needed to stimulate the market (Di Biasio 2004).

The Ministry of Labour and Social Security has begun accepting applications for the licensing of service providers.[7] Understandably, the procedure is slow because the selection and eligibility criteria for licensing have not been clearly communicated to potential service providers.

National Social Security Fund

The National Social Security Fund (NSSF) was established in 2001 as a fund of last resort. It is designed as a medium to long-term reserve to meet the pension shortfalls of provincial governments when they cannot meet pension liabilities and when the impact of population ageing is most severe.[8] Currently, there is no official legislation on the timing and conditions under which the NSSF would make payments. Li Keping of the NSSF has indicated that the fund is not ready to make any major expenditure at this time or in the foreseeable future. He does not expect there to be any disbursements for the first ten years (Asia Asset Management 2005).

The NSSF is one of China's largest institutional investors. It is often used as a test case for expanding the scope of the investment of social security funds and its experiences and developments are watched closely by the funds management industry. It is often used to pilot government initiatives for social security reform and is an indicator of developments in domestic capital markets.

Funding for the NSSF comes from the finances of the central government, share sales, the welfare lottery and investment returns. As at the end of 2004, NSSF assets were estimated to total 170 billion RMB, comprising approximately 115 billion RMB in funding from the finances of the central government, 26 billion RMB from initial public offerings on Chinese companies listed on overseas stockmarkets, 13 billion RMB from the lottery and approximately 4.6 billion RMB in investment returns. Of the value of the NSSF, approximately 67 billion RMB in bank deposits, 74 billion RMB in bonds, 11 billion RMB in equities, and 18 billion RMB in stocks (Xinhuanet 2005).

By 2015, it is estimated that the NSSF will make payments of 100 billion RMB per year to top up underfunded pension plans, and will need approximately RMB

2.5 trillion to make any headway in alleviating the pension shortfall, assuming a three per cent real rate of return (Clifford 2005). This will be challenging but not impossible to achieve. Last year, the rate of return was 3.3 per cent, while inflation was 3.9 per cent (China Securities Network 2005), meaning the fund realised a real rate of return of -0.6 per cent. Although the fund appears to be underperforming, the accumulated returns are 11.5 per cent, while inflation has totalled five per cent, meaning a real rate of return over the previous three years of 6.4 per cent or 2.13 per cent per year (China Securities Network 2005).

Since 2003, most NSSF funding has come from share sales rather than government funding. The State Council under the then Premier, Zhu Rongji, made a number of sizeable allocations setting up the NSSF. However, the State Council under the current Premier, Wen Jiabao, has not been so keen to make allocations. In 2003, the NSSF received no money from central government finances (Leckie and Pai 2005), while in 2004 it is believed that the NSSF only received 7.6 billion RMB (A\$1.44 billion) in government funding.

The NSSF is presently exploring ways to secure a stable source of funding because it cannot rely on handouts from the government. Options being explored include a mechanism to secure appropriations through the State Budget by using a formulaic approach (Asia Asset Management 2005). However, it is not clear how this might be achieved. The NSSF is also keen to invest more of its assets in domestic capital markets in order to maximise returns. Other options being explored include transferring all of the state-owned shares to the NSSF as tradeable shares, and amending the legislation that governs the fund so as to broaden its scope of investment.

In the most significant development to date, the NSSF was granted permission in 2004 to invest in overseas stockmarkets. Preparations are underway, particularly with respect to reviewing its asset allocation and investment strategy, determining its liabilities, managing risk associated with offshore investing and selecting global fund managers and custodians. It is not yet clear when the fund will begin to invest in overseas markets, but it is expected that the NSSF will invest between US\$500 million (A\$658 million) and US\$1 billion (A\$1.3 billion) in the Hong Kong stockmarket in late 2005 (Chung 2005). Many domestic Chinese fund management companies are watching the NSSF's preparations and experiences with interest. They view the NSSF as the vanguard of the Qualified Domestic Institutional Investor scheme, which would allow Chinese funds management companies to invest in overseas capital markets. Should the NSSF's foray into the Hong Kong stockmarket be successful, it can be expected to invest more widely in other markets as well, such as those in America, Europe and Australia.

Liaoning pilot program on perfecting the urban social security system

The Liaoning pilot program with an urban social security system was introduced in 2001 to experiment with measures designed to strengthen the pension system and to ensure its sustainability and affordability. Liaoning was selected because a high proportion of the population live in urban areas and it contained many SOEs.

The main task of the Liaoning pilot program was to rectify the shortfall in pension funding and learn lessons concerning the management of social security funds, particularly the separation of funds in the social pool and those in individual accounts. Although the pilot program was doomed to failure because it was under-funded, the government did learn many crucial lessons from it. Lessons were learned regarding the need to ring fence monies being held in individual accounts from those in the social pool and the need to expand the scope of investment of pension funds. Because of the lessons learned, the pilot project was able to accumulate funds in individual accounts, to the value of 11 billion RMB (A$2.09 billion) throughout the three years of the project (*People's Daily* 2004). Moreover, it led to changes in the system, whereby employees are now required to pay eight per cent of salaries to the basic pension scheme. It is expected that the lessons learned from the Liaoning pilot program will be applied progressively throughout China.

In 2004, the second iteration of the Liaoning pilot program, called the Northeast Social Security Pilot Program, was launched, with the remaining two north-eastern provinces, Jilin and Heilongjiang, being included. The expanded pilot program will focus on similar issues to the Liaoning pilot program and build upon the lessons learned. Additionally, the northeast social security pilot program is expected to focus more on stimulating the development of the occupational pension scheme by trialling a tax concession of four per cent of an enterprise's payroll.

The Urban Minimum Livelihood Guarantee scheme[9]

State-owned enterprise reform and population ageing have led to an increase in urban and rural poverty. To alleviate poverty, in 1999, the government implemented the urban minimum livelihood guarantee scheme to ensure urban residents whose total average family income was below the standard for the local area could obtain assistance with their living costs.

The urban minimum livelihood guarantee scheme is a new social relief system, replacing the 'five guarantees'[10] scheme in urban areas. Approximately 20 million people receive payments, which are calculated on the basis of the average family income for a given area and average living costs, and are indexed to inflation. To provide further assistance, supplements for education, housing and health[11] are available to recipients of payments under the urban minimum livelihood guarantee scheme.

Under the scheme, three groups of people are targeted including

- urban residents categorised as belonging to the 'three withouts',[12] namely without the means to live, without labour ability and without dependants
- urban residents that either receive unemployment benefits or who have done so and not yet found job, and whose family income is below the urban minimum livelihood guarantee standard for that locality. People in this category are required to undertake some compulsory form of work. For instance, unemployed plumbers in receipt of urban minimum livelihood guarantee payments may undertake unpaid plumbing jobs in their communities
- urban residents who are either in work, 'laid-off' or retired, and whose average family income is less than the urban minimum livelihood guarantee standard after receiving their wages, basic living allowance or pension (Ministry of Civil Affairs 2004).

Targeting ensures that access is available to all people in urban areas, provided family circumstances allow it.

All funds required for the urban minimum livelihood guarantee scheme come from the budgets of the central, provincial and municipal governments, while policy responsibility for it lies with the Ministry of Civil Affairs. Administrative responsibility for the scheme rests with communities at the street office and community residents' committee levels.[13] Representatives at these levels receive applications for payment under the scheme and carry out an investigation into the family's income and actual standard of living, based on information provided by the family and by questioning neighbours and other relevant people. The district level Civil Affairs Bureau will approve applications.

The urban minimum livelihood guarantee scheme is an integral part of the current social security system and is likely to play an increasingly important role in the future, especially as the pension shortfall becomes more severe. The government is expected to become more reliant on the urban minimum livelihood guarantee scheme to provide people with a basic standard of living. However, there are a number of challenges that must first be addressed, particularly the measurement of poverty and integrating the supplementary payments into the main payment. The most significant of these is the standardisation of the poverty line.

Although more than 20 million people receive urban minimum livelihood guarantee payments, the government recognises that there are many more people in poverty.

However, due to funding constraints, it cannot provide assistance to all who need it. In a recent speech, Bo Xilai, China's Minister for Commerce, mentioned that at least 90 million people in China live on less than US$1 per day[14] (AFP 2005). In the case of the Urban Minimum Livelihood Guarantee scheme, the poverty line has been raised higher than necessary to take into account the fact that the government does not have enough funds to offer assistance to all the urban poor.[15] In some cases, arbitrary measures of poverty determination are used, particularly the consideration of assets. For example, if applicants from Shanghai keep a dog, they are not eligible to receive the Urban Minimum Livelihood Guarantee payment because dogs are considered to be something that the rich have. As a further example, if an applicant from the central or western regions applies for payment, they may be rejected if they own an air conditioner.[16]

Social welfare and the role of communities

Communities play an important role supporting the social security system in China.

Prior to 1985, work units were responsible for providing the bulk of the social services to which a person might require access. Leung writes

> Each work unit of the state sector functioned as a self-sufficient 'welfare society' within which an individual received employment and income protection, and enjoyed heavily subsidised benefits and services, such as housing, food, education, recreation, childcare, and social security benefits for sickness, maternity, work injury, invalidity and death, and old age (2000:425).

Nowadays, communities play a much more important role in the provision of social services as a result of SOE reform and the need to 'socialise' such services, particularly for vulnerable populations such as the elderly, the disabled and the urban poor. Communities are responsible for, *inter alia*, improving the living standards of the people and maintaining social stability (National Development and Reform Commission 2001).

Many of the services that communities now provide occur at either the Street Office or the Community Residents' Committee[17] level, particularly those services that communities are required to provide because of policies formulated by the central government. Street Offices are responsible for marriage registration, household registration, crime patrols, family planning, childcare centres and playgroups, labour and social security services, aged care, and health, as well as recreational and cultural activities. Community Residents' Committees are also responsible for providing these services but do so in a much more limited fashion. In order to provide services, communities may receive a specific but often insufficient allocation of funds. Leung writes, 'The municipal government allocation for community services only accounts for less than thirty per cent of the total expenses' (2000:426). However, communities have considerable discretion to decide the way services are delivered.

To provide services to residents, communities also rely on their own efforts. Provided there is a demand and residents are prepared to pay on a user-pays basis, they can provide a wide range of additional services. Examples of such services include matchmaking and helping families with chores such as cleaning, ironing, shopping and paying bills. The services that one community may provide, when compared to others across the country, can vary markedly.

Importantly, communities do not just provide social services to people; they also play an important role in ensuring the smooth progress of economic and social reforms. In particular, they are responsible for absorbing some of the unemployment in that country by offering paid employment in the community. Communities are expected to provide referrals to employment services and, at the Street Office level, may provide training for employment purposes, as well as job-matching services. Although communities play an important role in addressing unemployment, they are limited in what they can do.

Conclusion

Each of these reforms demonstrates the government is responding actively and realistically in the social security field and that it has already made great strides in this area. The introduction of occupational pension schemes and the Northeast Social Security Pilot Project are two key examples. These reforms have taught the government a number of critical lessons that provide guidelines to be followed throughout the country. However, significant challenges such as the funding shortfall and the sale of state-owned shares remain and continue to put pressure on the sustainability of the social security system.

Social security reform will remain one of the top domestic concerns for the Chinese government. It has recognised the importance of a holistic approach to such reform and has already begun to adopt such an approach. The social security system is likely to develop as a comprehensive system with each component interacting as one cog in a larger machine. In particular, the Urban Minimum Livelihood Guarantee scheme and social welfare are likely to play increasingly important role in the social security system, especially as means of staving off social unrest and ensuring a basic standard of living for populations residing in urban areas. Of most significance, each of the reforms has a key role to play in deepening economic reform in China.

Acknowledgments

The views expressed in this paper are those of the author and not necessarily those of the Minister for Family and Community Services or the Department of Family and Community Services.

Notes

[1] My own translation, it is also commonly referred to as the Minimum Living Guarantee. There is no standard translation for this scheme. People familiar with the scheme and the Chinese language will also refer to it as 'Dibao' for want of a standardised term.

[2] Information obtained from interviews with officials from the Ministries of Civil Affairs and Labour and Social Security, July 2004. The officials stated openly that the pension system in China is in danger of collapse if nothing is done.

[3] In China, occupational pension schemes are known as *Qiye Nianjin*, which is more properly translated as Enterprise Annuities. Enterprise Annuities is a common term, but I have chosen to use the preferred translation of the Ministry of Labour and Social Security in this paper.

[4] A copy of the unofficial English translation of Regulations 20 and 23 can be found in Appendixes C and D in Leckie and Pai (2005).

[5] Regulations 25 and 32 are available in Chinese only. They are available at the following web addresses: Regulation 25 http://www.molss.gov.cn/news/2004/1110.htm. Regulation 32: http://www.molss.gov.cn/news/2005/0204a0.htm

[6] Information obtained from interview with an official from the China Insurance Regulatory Commission.

[7] The China Merchants Bank has applied for a Trustee licence (Sun 2005b), and Boshi Funds Management has applied for an Investment Manager and Trustee licence (Chan 2005).

[8] For more information about the structure of the National Social Security Fund, see Murton 2003b.

[9] The author's own translation.

[10] The 'five guarantees' were food, housing, medical, clothing, and funeral expenses.

[11] Under the urban minimum livelihood guarantee scheme, the health supplement is provided to access government-subsidised medical services and the education supplement is provided for cheaper school fees for the children of recipients of urban minimum livelihood guarantee payments.

[12] The author's own translation. More commonly these people are referred to as the 'three nos'. However, I believe that the 'three withouts' is a more accurate translation.

[13] For information on the roles of the various levels of government in the social security context in China, see Murton (2003a).

[14] This is the standard poverty measure of the World Bank and the United Nations.

[15] Information obtained from interview of officials from the Ministry of Civil Affairs, 9 March 2005.

[16] Information obtained from interview of officials from the Ministry of Finance, 9 March 2005.

[17] Community Residents' Committees were previously known as Neighbourhood Committees.

References

Agence France-Presse, 2005. '90 million Chinese below poverty line', Australian Broadcasting Commission 29 May 2005, accessed 30 May 2005. Available online at http://www.abc.net.au/news/newsitems/200505/s1379327.htm.

Asia Asset Management, 2005. 'NCSSF's Li Keping speaks to Asia Asset Management', *Asia Asset Management Magazine,* May: 29–32.

Beijing Morning News, 2005. 'Woguo yanglao baoxian jijin zhifu yali shenzhong', China Labour Network Website, 20 May 2005, accessed 23 May 2005. Available online at http://www.labournet.com.cn/ldnews/fileview.asp?fileno=46071.

Chan, P., 2005. 'Boshi eyes corporate pensions', *Asia Asset Management Magazine,* June:6.

China Labour Network, 2002 .'Caizheng Bu Xuezhe: 2010 Nian Qiye Buchong Yanglaojin Ke Da Wanyi', China Labour Network Website, 28 November 2002, accessed 29 November 2002. Available online at http://www.labournet.com.cn/ldnews/fileview.asp?fileno=1418.

China Securities Network, 2005. 'Shebao Jinnian Touzi Gupiao 88 Yi Zhi 178 Yi', China Securities Network Website, 29 March 2005, accessed 20 March 2005. Available online at http://cs/xinhuanet.com/sylm/03/t20050329_623204.htm.

Chung, O., 2005. 'China fund pledge lifts Hang Seng', The Standard Website, 20 January 2005, accessed 20 January 2005. Available online at http://www.thestandard.com.hk/stdn/std/Business/GA20Ae03.html.

Clifford, M., 2004. 'Pension fund plans US$2.9b market first', The Standard Website, 2 April 2004, accessed 2 April 2004. Available online at http://www.thestandard.com.hk\thestandardnews_detail_frame.cfm?articleid=46400&intcntid=1.

Di Biasio, J., 2004. 'China's El Dorado', *Asian Investor Magazine,* August/September:40–42.

Information Times, 2005. 'Woguo Shebao Geren Zhanghu Quekou 1 Wanyi', China Labour Network, 27 April 2005, accessed 2 May 2005. Available online at http://www.labournet.com.cn/ldnews/fileview.asp?fileno=45420.

Lague, D., 2005. 'China share sale isn't a quick fix', *International Herald Tribune,* 18 May 2005, accessed 19 May 2005. Available online at http://www.iht.com/bin/print_ihub.php?file=/articles/2005/05/17/business/shares.php.

Leckie, S. and Pai Y., 2005. *Pension funds in China–a new look,* ISI Publications, Hong Kong.

Leung, J.C.B., 2000. 'Community building in China: from welfare to politics', *Community Development Journal,* 35(4):425–27.

Ministry of Civil Affairs, 2004. *Proposal for a program of technical assistance in the area of the urban minimum livelihood guarantee scheme*, AusAID China-Australia Governance Program, Beijing.

Ministry of Labour and Social Security, 2001. *Guojia Wanshan Chengzhen Shehui Baozhang Shidian Zhengshi Zai Liaoning Zhankai*, Ministry of Labour and Social Security, 8 July 2001, accessed 13 July 2001. Available online at http://www.molss.gov.cn/news/2001/07091.htm.

— —, 2004. *Zhongguo de Shehui Baozhang Zhunagkuang He Zhengce Baipishu (Quan Wen)* [*White Paper on China's Social Security Situation and Policies (Full Text)*], Ministry of Labour and Social Security, 7 September 2004, accessed 8 September 2004. Available online at http://www.molss.gov.cn/news/2004/0907c.htm.

Murton, T., 2003a. 'New perspectives on pension reform: The People's Republic of China', *International Studies Asian Occasional Papers*, Department of Family and Community Services, Canberra.

— —, 2003b. 'The national social security fund', in Garnaut, R., and Song, L., (eds.) *China: New Engine of World Growth*, Asia Pacific Press, Canberra.

National Development and Reform Commission, 2001. *Report on Australian Community Development*, Beijing.

People's Daily, 2004. 'Woguo Yanglao Baoxian Geren Zhanghu Kongzhang Jin 6000 Yi Yuan', China Labour Network, 21 September 2004, accessed 22 September 2004. Available online at http://www.labournet.com.cn/ldnews/fileview.asp?fileno=37040.

Reuters, 2005 'China facing pensions crunch', The Standard Website, 14 December 2004, accessed 14 December 2004. Available online at http://www.thestandard.com.hk/stdn/std/Markets?FL14Ag01.html.

Shen, X., 2004. 'Qiye Nianjin Shichang Kaiju Dare Jigou Moma Libing Jingdai Shiji' Xinhuanet, 27 September 2004, accessed 27 September 2004. Available online at http://news.xinhuanet.com/stock/2004-09/27/content_2026885.htm.

Sun, M., 2004a. 'Firms vie for occupational pension funds', *China Daily*, 13 September 2004, accessed 14 September 2004. Available online at http://www.chinadaily.com.cn/english/doc/2004-09/13/content_373895.htm.

— —, 2004b 'China Merchants Bank to play pension trustee', *China Daily*, 25 September 2004, accessed 27 September 2004. Available online at http://www.chinadaily.com.cn/english/doc/2004-09/25/content_377731.htm.

The Economist Magazine, 2005 'Hangover cure', The Economist, 5 May 2005, accessed 6 May 2005. Available online at http://www.economist.com/finance/displayStory.cfm?story_id=3945544.

Xinhuanet, 2005 'China social security fund totals 170.8 Billion Yuan: Chairman' China Economic Net, 29 March 2005, accessed 30 March 2005. Available online at http://en.ce.cnMarketsEquities2005032920050329_3452657.shtml.

Xinhua News Agency, 2005 'Xiang Huaicheng Biaoshi Zhongguo Yanglao Tixi Mianlin Yanjun Tiaozhan', China Labour Network, 22 April 2005, accessed 2 May 2005. Available online at http://www.labournet.com.cn/ldnews/fileview.asp?fileno=45279.

13

Component trade and China's regional economic integration

Prema-Chandra Athukorala

International fragmentation of production—cross-border dispersion of component production/assembly within vertically integrated manufacturing industries—has been an important feature of the deepening structural interdependence of the world economy in recent decades.[1] With a modest start in electronics and clothing industries in the late 1960s, international production networks have gradually evolved and spread into many industries such as sport footwear, automobiles, televisions and radio receivers, sewing machines, office equipment, electrical machinery, power and machine tools, cameras and watches. At the formative stage of product fragmentation, outsourcing predominantly involved locating small fragments of the production process in a low-cost country and reimporting the assembled components to be incorporated in the final product. Over time, production networks have begun to encompass many countries involved in the assembly process at different stages, resulting in multiple-border crossing of product fragments before getting incorporated in the final product. As the supply of parts and components through international networks became firmly rooted, producers in advanced countries began to move final assembly of an increasing range of consumer durables (for example, computers, cameras, television sets and motor cars) to overseas locations in order to be physically closer to their final users and/ or to take advantage of cheap labour.

There is a sizeable literature which points to the growing importance of fragmentation-based specialisation for China's dramatic economic transformation under market-oriented policy reforms over the past two decades (Borrus 1997 and

1999, Naughton 1999, McKendrick et al. 2000, Brown and Linden 2005). However, the implications of China's increasing involvement in this new form of international specialisation for regional and global trade patterns have not yet been systematically examined. Much (if not all) of the literature on China's integration into the global economy and the perceived competitive threat to countries in the region is based on the traditional notion of horizontal specialisation scenario in which countries trade goods that are produced from start to finish in just one country (IMF 2004, Eichengreen et al. 2004, Ahearne et al. 2003, Lall and Albaladejo 2004). In a context where trade in parts and components (middle products) is growing rapidly, the standard trade flow analysis naturally runs the risk of ignoring complementarities in trade relations on the supply side. This is because intra/extra regional patterns of trade in parts and components and trade in related final goods (final trade) are unlikely to follow the same patterns.

The purpose of this paper is to assess the implications of China's evolving role in the process of international fragmentation of production for trade patterns in East Asia, based on a systematic separation of trade in parts and components from total trade flows using a new data set extracted from the UN trade database.

Data

The data for this paper are compiled from the UN Comtrade database based on the Revision 3 of the Standard International Trade Classification (SITC, Rev 3). The data relate to the eleven-year period from 1992 to 2003. The year 1992 was selected as the starting point because by this time countries accounting for over 95 per cent of total world manufacturing trade had adopted the new system. The analysis ends in 2003 which is the most recent year for which trade data are available for all reporting countries. Given the prohibitive cost of data covering the entire period, 1992, 1996 and 2003 are chosen for the inter-country/region comparison of trade patterns.

In its original form (SITC, Rev 1), the UN trade data reporting system did not provide for separating parts and components from final manufactured goods. The SITC Revision 2 introduced in the late 1970s (and implemented by most countries only in the early 1980s) adopted a more detailed commodity classification, which provided for separation of parts and components within the machinery and transport sector (SITC 7). There was, however, considerable overlap between some advanced-stage assembly activities and related final goods within the sector in the Revision 2, making it difficult to separate fragmentation trade from total trade (Ng and Yeats 2001)[2]. Revision 3 introduced in the mid1980s marked a significant improvement over Revision 2. In addition to redressing overlaps within SITC 7, this new version of SITC provided for separation of parts and components trade in the 'miscellaneous goods' sector (SITC 8). These two sectors together accounted for around 70 per cent of total world manufacturing trade (defined as goods belonging to SITC 5 though 8 less SITC 68 (non-ferrous metals)) during the period under study.

SITC Revision 3, despite its significant improvement over the previous version, does not provide for the construction of data series covering the entire range of activities involving production fragmentation. Data reported under SITC 7 do provide a comprehensive coverage of fragmentation trade. But data for SITC 8 does not seem to capture fully fragmentation trade within that commodity category. For instance, for some products such as clothing, furniture, and leather products in which outsourcing is prevalent (and perhaps has been increasing), the related components are recorded under other SITC categorising (for example, pieces of textile, parts of furniture, parts of leather soles). The SITC data system does not provide adequate information to separate these components and relate them accurately to the related final product. Moreover, there is evidence that international production fragmentation has been spreading beyond SITC 7 and 8 to other areas, in particular pharmaceutical and chemical products (falling under SITC 5) and machine tools and various metal products (SITC 6). Assembly activities in software trade too have recorded impressive expansion in recent years. These are lumped together with 'special transactions' under SITC 9. So the movements of trade in parts and components reported used in this paper are presumably downward biased. These factors cause our estimates to be downward biased, and perhaps the degree of bias may have increased over the years with the gradual spread of production fragmentation to other areas of products beyond SITC 7 and 8. The list of parts and components identified for these two sectors contains a total of 225 five-digit products—168 products belonging to SITC 7 and 57 belonging to SITC 8. [3]

East Asia is defined here to include the newly industrialised economies (NIEs) in North Asia (South Korea, Taiwan and Hong Kong), China and members of the Association of Southeast Asian Nations (ASEAN) Free Trade Area (AFTA). Among the AFTA member countries, only the six largest economies—Indonesia, Malaysia, the Philippines, Thailand, Singapore and Vietnam—are covered in the statistical analysis. Brunei, Cambodia, Laos and Myanmar are ignored because of lack of data. The UN data system does not cover Taiwan (because it is not a UN member). Vietnam has not yet started contributing to the UN trade data reporting system. Singapore has not been reporting data on its bilateral trade with Indonesia from 1964 onwards because of political reasons. In these cases data are extracted from partner-country records.

Table 13.1   World trade in parts and components, 1992–2003 (per cent)

	Exports			Imports			Trade		
	1992	1996	2003	1992	1996	2003	1992	1996	2003
East Asia	34.7	38.7	42.8	27.5	35.2	41.4	31.2	37.0	42.1
Japan	16.9	15.7	11.2	3.7	5.0	4.4	10.4	10.4	7.8
Greater China	7.8	9.5	14.9	10.1	10.7	19.8	8.9	10.1	17.3
China	0.8	1.3	5.7	2.6	2.7	9.9	1.7	2.0	7.8
Hong Kong	3.4	3.8	6.0	4.2	4.8	6.7	3.8	4.3	6.3
Taiwan	3.6	4.4	3.2	3.4	3.2	3.2	3.5	3.8	3.2
Republic of Korea	2.8	3.8	4.1	3.2	3.5	3.4	3.0	3.7	3.8
AFTA	7.2	11.9	12.5	10.4	15.5	12.0	8.8	13.7	12.3
Indonesia	0.1	0.3	0.4	1.0	1.0	0.3	0.5	0.6	0.4
Malaysia	2.5	3.4	3.2	2.9	4.1	3.5	2.7	3.8	3.4
Philippines	0.2	1.2	2.0	0.5	1.6	1.8	0.4	1.4	1.9
Singapore	3.3	5.7	5.4	4.2	6.4	4.7	3.7	6.0	5.1
Thailand	1.0	1.2	1.5	1.8	2.5	1.6	1.4	1.8	1.6
Vietnam	0.0	0.0	0.1	0.2	0.3	0.3	0.1	0.1	0.2
South Asia	0.1	0.2	0.2	0.8	0.4	0.6	0.4	0.3	0.4
Australia and New Zealand	0.1	0.4	0.4	0.3	1.4	1.0	0.2	0.9	0.7
NAFTA	28.8	24.3	21.6	27.5	27.7	22.3	28.2	25.9	21.9
United States	23.1	18.9	16.3	19.0	19.0	14.4	21.1	18.9	15.4
Canada	4.0	3.3	2.6	6.4	5.6	4.0	5.1	4.4	3.3
Mexico	1.7	1.9	2.7	2.2	3.1	3.9	1.9	2.5	3.3
Europe	51.3	54.5	36.3	50.3	53.3	34.7	50.8	53.9	35.5
European Union	48.7	38.4	32.3	46.8	36.2	30.1	47.8	37.3	31.2
World	100.0	100.0	100.0	100.0	100.0	100.0	100.0	100.0	100.0
US$ billion[1]	447.0	729.0	1048.0	408.0	756.9	1044.0	n.a.	n.a.	n.a.

Note: [1] By definition world exports and imports in a given year should be identical. The minor differences seem to reflect recording errors and differences in measurement arising from the use of CIF price for reporting imports and FOB price for reporting exports.
Source: Compiled from *UN Comtrade Database*.

Trends and patterns of trade in parts and components

World trade in parts and components (henceforth referred to as 'components') increased from US$400 billion in 1992 to over US$1000 billion in 2003, recording an annual average growth rate of 3.7 per cent (Table 13.1). The share of these products in total world manufacturing trade increased from 17 per cent to 23 per cent between 1992 and 2003. Components accounted for one fourth of the total increment in world manufacturing trade between these two years.

The share of East Asia (including Japan) in total world exports of components increased persistently from 31 per cent in 1992 to 43 per cent in 2003. The corresponding increase on the import side was even faster, from 27.5 per cent to 41.4 per cent. In 1992, China was a small player in world component trade, with import and export shares smaller than most of the major trading nations in the region. However, China's trading position increased dramatically during the ensuing decade (Figure 13.1). In 2003, China's share in world import of components (9.9 per cent) was the largest among all countries in the region. The combined import and export shares of Greater China (China + Hong Kong + Taiwan) increased from 10.7 per cent to 19.8 per cent, and 7.8 per cent to 14.9 per cent respectively between 1992 and 2003[4]. Contrary to the popular perception of Greater China 'crowding out the rest', this increase has occurred against the backdrop of an overall increase in exports from other countries in the region.

The degree of dependence on this new form of international specialisation is proportionately larger in East Asia than in North America and Europe (and other regions in the world). In 2003, components accounted for 28 per cent of total manufacturing exports from developing East Asia, compared to the world average of 21 per cent, 25 per cent for the North American Free Trade Area (NAFTA) and 17 per cent for the European Union (EU) (Table 13.2). Of the total increment in manufactured exports from East Asia between 1992 and 2003, over a third came from component exports. The comparable figures for NAFTA and the EU were 26 per cent and 18 per cent per cent respectively. The share of components in China's manufacturing trade is still low by regional standards, but is growing fast. Between 1992 and 2003, the share of components in total manufacturing exports from China more than tripled (from 5.5 per cent to 15.2 per cent). On the import side, the increase was much faster, from 16.2 per cent to 33.5 per cent. Within East Asia, countries belonging to AFTA, in particular Malaysia, Philippines, Singapore and Thailand, stand out for their heavy dependence on production fragmentation for export dynamism. In 2003, components accounted for over 40 per cent of total manufacturing exports in AFTA, up from 24 per cent in 1992.

Figure 13.1 **China's trade in parts and components**

(a)   Value of parts and components, US$ billion

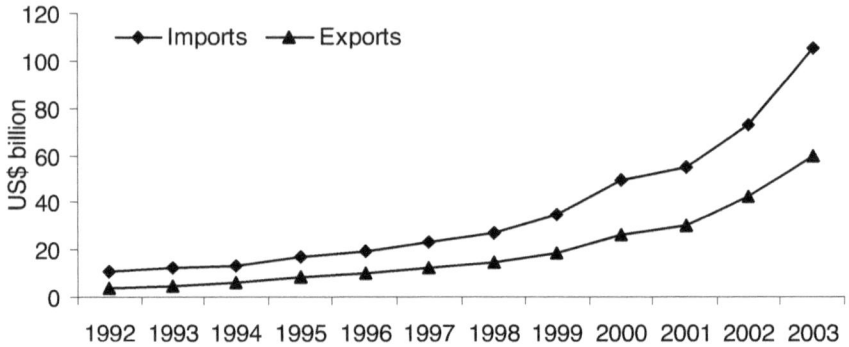

(b)   Share of parts and components in China's manufacturing trade

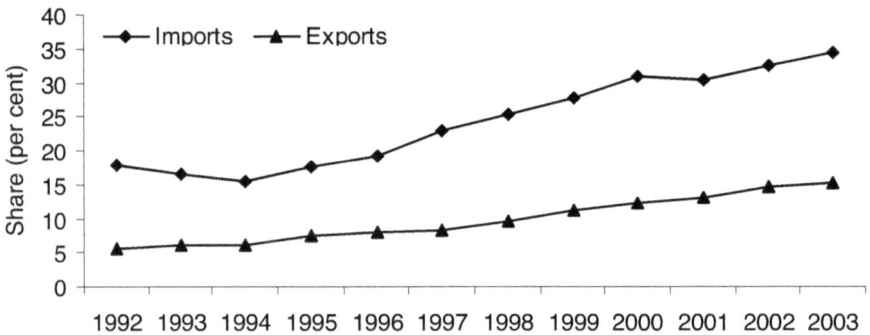

(c)   China's share in world trade in parts and components

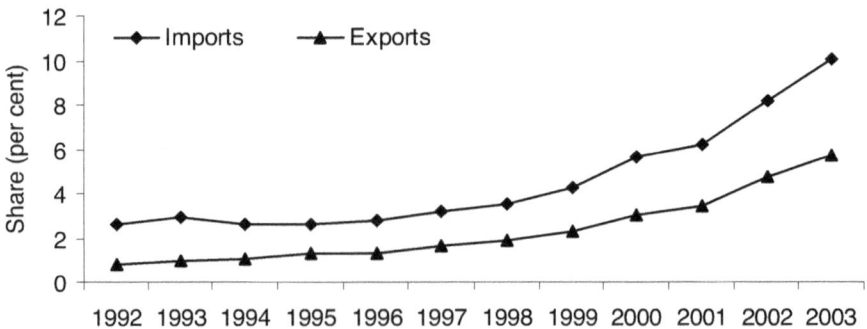

Source: Compiled from *UN Comtrade Database.*

Component trade and China's regional economic integration

Table 13.2a **Parts and components in the manufacturing trade, exports**

	Share of P&C in mfg exports			Growth of mfg exports 1992–2003	Growth of P&C exports 1992–2003	Contribution of P&C to mfg export growth 1992–2003
	1992	1996	2003			
East Asia	19.2	28.0	27.9	3.2	4.8	34.9
Japan	21.2	30.2	27.9	1.2	2.3	47.1
Greater China	13.9	18.8	22.5	4.7	6.7	26.5
China	5.5	9.8	15.2	7.2	12.5	20.0
Hong Kong	12.9	18.7	29.3	2.8	6.2	47.8
Taiwan	28.3	28.8	39.5	2.5	3.9	52.4
Republic of Korea	17.1	25.2	25.5	3.8	5.4	30.9
AFTA	24.7	35.0	40.6	4.1	6.2	49.5
Indonesia	3.7	7.4	13.9	2.7	8.3	24.5
Malaysia	38.7	42.6	42.7	4.5	4.9	44.6
Philippines	19.8	52.5	63.8	8.6	13.7	70.0
Singapore	27.0	39.7	46.7	3.7	6.0	59.8
Thailand	19.1	23.4	26.7	4.1	5.4	31.0
NAFTA	25.3	27.2	25.6	2.7	2.7	26.0
United States	26.8	30.5	29.2	2.2	2.5	32.5
Europe	15.5	16.2	16.6	2.2	2.5	18.0
European Union	15.9	17.7	16.7	2.1	2.2	17.9
World	17.9	20.3	21.1	2.8	3.4	24.4

Source: Compiled from *UN Comtrade Database.*

Table 13.2b Parts and components in the manufacturing trade, imports

Country/region	Share of P&C in mfg exports			Growth of mfg exports 1992–2003	Growth of P&C exports 1992–2003	Contribution of P&C to mfg export growth 1992–2003
	1992	1996	2003			
East Asia	19.8	27.9	34.6	3.5	5.8	45.4
Japan	14.2	19.3	21.5	3.1	4.8	27.7
Greater China	14.2	19.3	21.5	4.1	7.3	44.1
China	16.2	17.8	33.5	6.7	9.8	37.7
Hong Kong	14.0	18.7	32.4	2.6	6.1	52.5
Taiwan	16.9	35.0	37.3	2.8	6.1	57
Republic of Korea	25.2	27.4	33.6	3.1	4.3	40.7
AFTA	28.2	39.3	47.1	2.6	4.7	67.8
Indonesia	18.5	23.8	18.5	-0.5	-0.5	18.5
Malaysia	35.2	47.5	55.7	3.0	4.9	74.4
Philippines	24.8	43.6	63.1	5.5	9.4	76.5
Singapore	30.0	42.8	49.2	2.6	4.6	70.8
Thailand	24.7	32.9	32.5	2.6	3.7	41
NAFTA	18.9	23.6	17.7	3.5	3.2	16.9
United States	17.5	21.7	15.4	3.5	3	13.8
Europe	15.0	16.6	17.4	2.0	2.6	21.1
European Union	15.3	18.9	17.6	1.7	2.3	21.8
World	16.8	19.8	20.7	2.9	3.8	24.4

Source: Compiled from *UN Comtrade database*.

There is evidence that the formation of NAFTA and the integration of some of the new countries that emerged from the former Soviet Union with the rest of the Europe have set the stage for rapid expansion of international production networks in these regions (Kaminski and Ng 2005, Kierzkowski 2001). Proximity to industrial countries and relatively low wages by regional standards (though not compared to some of the East Asian countries) are considered as added advantages of Mexico and countries in the European periphery compared to East Asian countries in this new form of international specialisation. However, interestingly, East Asia's pre-eminent position in fragmentation trade has remained remarkably resilient to the entry of these newcomers.

The explanation for the continued pre-eminence of East Asia seems to lie in powerful supply-side factors such as relatively more favourable trade and investment policy regimes which facilitate international production, better ports and communication systems that facilitate trade by reducing the cost of maintaining 'services links', and considerable inter-country wage differentials in the region, and the regional confluence of a large number of fast-growing countries which are at different stages of economic advancement (Jones et al. 2005, Athukorala and Yamashita 2005). Rapid economic expansion also seems to have brought about 'market thickness' (the economic depth of trading nations) which positively impacts on the location of outsourcing activity (Grossman and Helpman 2005). Part of the explanation also seems to lie in economic history—the early choice of the region (first Singapore and subsequently Malaysia and other countries) by multinational enterprises (MNEs) as a location of outsourcing activities. It is well known that there is a general tendency for MNE affiliates to become increasingly embedded in host countries the longer they are present there and the more favourable the overall investment climate of the host country becomes over time. Moreover, site selection decisions of MNEs operating in assembly activities are strongly influenced by the presence of other key market players in a given country or neighbouring countries (Rangan and Lawrence 1999). Against the backdrop of a long period of successful operation in the region, many MNEs (particularly United States-based MNEs) have significantly upgraded technical activities of their regional production networks in East Asia and assigned global production responsibilities to affiliates located in more mature countries (Singapore and Taiwan in particular, and also Malaysia in recent years) (Borrus 1997, Borrus et al. 2000).

Table 13.3 provides data on the composition of export and import flows of components. Both component exports and imports of East Asia are heavily concentrated in electronics and electrical industries. Semiconductors and other electronics components (components within SITC 77) alone accounted for more than half of component exports from East Asia in 2003. Adding to these items components of telecommunication equipment (SITC 76) and office and automated data processing machines (SITC 75) increases the concentration ratio to almost 90 per cent of total exports of components. The degree of concentration of component trade on electronics is much larger in AFTA (over 60 per cent) compared to the regional average and trade composition of China is much in line with that of the rest of developing East Asia. Electronic and electrical products are also the major areas of activity in NAFTA, EU and rest of the world. But trade patterns of these countries/regions are characterised by a greater presence of other items such as engines and motors (SITC 714), specialised industrial machinery (SITC 728), and internal combustion machines (SITC 713), for which transportation cost is presumably an important consideration for production location. In sum, China and East Asia are unique for the heavy concentration of parts and component trade in electronics.

Fragmentation of production and regional trade patterns

We have noted two important peculiarities of trade patterns in East Asia compared with total global trade and trade of European Union and NAFTA. First, component trade has played a much more important role in trade expansion in East Asia relative to the overall global experience and experiences of countries in other major regions. Second, China, in spite of late entry into this form of specialisation, has begun to replicate the overall regional patterns. In this section we proceed to examine intra-regional trade patterns in the region by explicitly taking into account these important developments in the regional economic landscape.

Table 13.4 compares the share of components in bilateral manufacturing trade flows of China with that of total East Asia and Japan. The share of components in intra-East Asian trade is much larger and it is growing faster than the region's extra regional trade. This share in intra-East Asian exports increased from 27.6 per cent in 1992 to 36.1 per cent in 2003, compared to a marginal increase from 26.8 per cent to 28.7 per cent in the region's total exports. On the import side, the share in intra-regional trade increased from 23.3 per cent in 1992 to 38.6 per cent in 2003. The corresponding increase on the import side was from 22.5 per cent to 35.7 per cent. The much larger difference in the share of components between intra and extra-regional exports compared to comparable figures on the import side reflects the greater reliance of the region on the rest of the world as a market for final goods.

Table 13.3 Composition of parts and component trade by 2-digit SITC categories (per cent)

(a) Exports

SITC code and description	East Asia	Japan	Korea	China	Hong Kong	AFTA	USA	EU	World
7 Machinery and transport equipment	96.1	94.4	98.8	96.0	93.8	98.1	94.0	94.5	94.6
71 Power-generating machinery and equipment	1.3	2.8	1.1	0.7	0.2	0.7	1.4	6.2	4.0
72 Specialised industrial machinery	2.2	2.9	2.8	2.0	0.9	1.8	4.3	7.6	5.2
73 Metalworking machinery	0.5	1.0	0.4	0.5	0.2	0.1	0.9	1.4	1.0
74 General industrial machinery	2.0	3.0	1.4	3.0	0.9	1.1	4.6	7.2	4.5
75 Office machines and automatic data-processing machines	18.3	12.3	19.1	30.8	25.3	17.1	11.3	9.3	13.1
76 Telecommunications and sound-recording equipment	12.4	8.3	14.5	21.9	21.6	5.3	5.6	5.4	8.2
77 Electrical machinery, apparatus and appliances	50.1	43.8	50.2	29.8	43.8	67.3	38.6	26.7	36.9
78 Road vehicles	8.4	18.8	8.7	6.4	0.5	3.1	17.6	23.4	17.0
79 Other transport equipment	1.1	1.4	0.5	0.8	0.3	1.5	9.7	7.3	4.8
8 Miscellaneous manufactured articles	3.9	5.6	1.2	4.0	6.2	1.9	6.0	5.5	5.4
81 Prefabricated buildings fixtures and fittings	0.1	0.0	0.1	0.1	0.1	0.0	0.1	0.6	0.3
82 Furniture, and parts thereof	0.2	0.4	0.2	0.4	0.1	0.1	1.2	1.1	1.3
83 Travel goods, handbags and similar containers	0.0	0.0	0.0	0.0	0.0	0.0	0.0	0.0	0.0
84 Apparel and clothing accessories	0.2	0.0	0.1	0.4	1.0	0.0	0.1	0.1	0.2
85 Footwear	0.0	0.0	0.0	0.0	0.0	0.0	0.0	0.0	0.0
87 Professional, scientific instruments	1.3	2.9	0.3	0.7	0.6	0.8	3.1	2.4	2.0
88 Photographic apparatus, optical goods and watches and clocks	1.9	2.1	0.4	1.8	4.3	0.9	0.4	0.8	1.1
89 Miscellaneous manufactured articles, n.e.s.	0.2	0.2	0.2	0.4	0.2	0.1	1.1	0.6	0.5
Total (SITC 7+8)	100.0	100.0	100.0	100.0	100.0	100.0	100.0	100.0	100.0
US$ billion	399.0	114.0	43.0	59.0	62.0	132.0	162.0	340.0	1047.0

Table 13.3   Composition of parts and component trade by 2-digit SITC Categories (per cent) cont.

(b) Imports

SITC code and description	East Asia	Japan	Korea	China	Hong Kong	AFTA	USA	EU	World
7 Machinery and transport equipment	96.0	91.5	95.7	97.5	95.5	97.3	92.7	93.8	94.6
71 Power-generating machinery and equipment	1.9	2.2	2.6	2.2	0.5	1.8	3.0	5.8	4.6
72 Specialised industrial machinery	2.7	3.2	2.3	2.4	1.3	3.2	4.2	5.4	4.3
73 Metalworking machinery	0.6	0.7	0.8	0.9	0.4	0.4	0.9	1.1	0.9
74 General industrial machinery	1.8	3.0	2.0	1.6	1.0	1.7	5.0	6.0	4.2
75 Office machines and automatic data-processing machines	13.6	16.1	5.6	11.3	22.9	15.9	17.0	13.4	13.5
76 Telecommunications and sound-recording equipment	9.7	10.4	6.8	11.3	17.0	4.1	6.7	5.6	7.4
77 Electrical machinery, apparatus and appliances	59.6	46.0	69.5	60.6	51.5	63.9	28.6	26.2	39.1
78 Road vehicles	4.8	7.1	5.1	6.1	0.8	4.4	23.9	23.8	16.9
79 Other transport equipment	1.4	2.7	1.0	1.2	0.2	1.8	3.4	6.4	3.7
8 Miscellaneous manufactured articles	4.0	8.5	4.3	2.5	4.5	2.7	7.3	6.2	5.4
81 Prefabricated buildings fixtures and fittings	0.1	0.2	0.1	0.0	0.1	0.0	0.4	0.8	0.4
82 Furniture, and parts thereof	0.3	1.2	0.3	0.2	0.1	0.1	3.5	1.7	1.4
83 Travel goods, handbags and similar containers	0.0	0.0	0.0	0.0	0.0	0.0	0.0	0.0	0.0
84 Apparel and clothing accessories	0.2	0.0	0.0	0.1	0.8	0.1	0.1	0.0	0.1
85 Footwear	0.0	0.0	0.0	0.0	0.0	0.0	0.0	0.0	0.0
87 Professional, scientific instruments.	1.4	3.8	2.2	0.7	0.6	1.2	2.2	2.2	1.8
88 Photographic apparatus, optical goods and watches/clocks	1.7	2.1	0.9	1.4	2.8	1.2	0.8	0.8	1.1
89 Miscellaneous manufactured articles, n.e.s.	0.3	1.2	0.8	0.1	0.2	0.1	0.5	0.7	0.6
Total (SITC 7 + 8)	100.0	100.0	100.0	100.0	100.0	100.0	100.0	100.0	100.0
US$ billion	367.0	46.0	35.0	105.0	66.0	126.0	147.0	317.0	1047.0

Source: Compiled from *UN Comtrade Database*.

Table 13.4   Share of parts and components in manufacturing trade of East Asia, China and Japan, 1992, 1996 and 2003 (per cent)

	East Asia			China			Japan		
	1992	1996	2003	1992	1996	2003	1992	1996	2003
(a) Exports									
Exports to:									
Total East Asia	27.6	25.6	36.1	5.7	9.7	23.1	25.4	29.9	32.4
Japan	23.6	22.0	28.0	4.6	8.7	15.3			
Hong Kong	16.3	17.3	33.6	5.7	8.1	25.3	17.2	22.1	35.0
Taiwan	39.3	36.3	44.0	14.0	19.1	31.7	31.7	32.6	25.9
Korea	31.0	21.5	34.1	5.2	12.9	20.2	27.7	24.1	28.4
AFTA	41.9	39.8	50.0	7.5	15.3	31.3	29.5	37.1	37.8
Rest of the world	26.2	26.0	22.9	3.5	6.9	13.1	23.8	29.9	27.6
NAFTA	23.4	20.8	15.1	3.3	5.6	10.6	22.4	25.3	20.3
EU	17.8	17.5	17.9	2.3	4.5	12.0	15.9	19.5	20.3
World	26.8	25.8	28.7	5.0	8.4	17.4	24.3	29.9	29.7
(b) Imports									
Imports from:									
Total East Asia	23.3	30.3	38.6	7.6	17.1	34.2	11.7	17.5	23.3
Japan	30.9	42.3	45.8	16.7	21.7	31.9			
Hong Kong	24.9	33.0	41.9	0.0	18.3	33.4	14.2	21.6	28.3
Taiwan	18.4	25.4	45.2	10.3	10.9	32.9	13.7	24.1	45.0
Korea	20.5	30.7	38.5	9.8	11.2	27.9	14.9	34.4	44.1
AFTA	34.2	37.9	49.5	5.6	23.5	47.4	17.5	20.0	28.9
Rest of the world	21.4	26.5	29.1	31.3	19.5	31.3	14.0	17.7	17.7
NAFTA	25.3	32.0	36.7	12.4	13.1	20.9	19.6	24.5	23.1
EU	14.9	18.4	23.3	18.5	13.9	22.0	6.6	7.6	10.3
World	22.5	28.8	35.7	16.1	17.8	33.5	13.1	17.6	21.1

Source: Complied from *UN Comtrade Database*.

The share of components in regional exports of China increased from 5.7 per cent in 1992 to over 23 per cent in 2003. On the import-side, the increase was even faster between the two years, from 7.6 per cent to 34.2 per cent. By 2003, intra and inter-regional difference in parts and component shares in Chinese imports was broadly similar to the overall East Asian patterns. However, on the export side the shares were much lower both in intra and extra-regional exports. This difference reflects the increasingly important role of China as a final product assembler for advanced-country markets using middle-products procured from the region. For the same reason there is a clear difference between China and Japan in terms of the relative importance of components in export and import flows. China's parts and component shares on the export side are notably smaller across all trading partner countries/regions compared to that of Japan, whereas more or less the reverse pattern holds on the import side.

The growing importance of components in intra-regional trade points to the need for separating final trade from trade in components in order to gain a clear understanding of the on-going process of China's trade integration and its implications for other countries in the region. Table 5 presents data for 1992, 1996 and 2003 on percentage shares of East Asia in China's manufacturing trade with this disaggregation.

The shares of Chinese imports of total manufacturing coming from East Asia increased from 64.3 per cent in 1992 to 76.2 per cent in 2003. This increase was dominated by components. The regional share of total imports of components increased from 30.3 per cent to 77.7 per cent between these two years, compared to a mild increase in final imports from 70.5 per cent to 75.4 per cent. Parts and component imports accounted for over 90 per cent of the total increment in total Chinese regional imports between 1992 and 2003. Japan has continued to be the major regional source country. But when it comes to imports of components, there has been a notable diversification of source countries (Figure 13.2). The most notable development is the rapid growth of the combined share of AFTA, from a mere 1 per cent in 1992 to 19.3 per cent 2003. Within AFTA, import shares of Malaysia and the Philippines have increased at a faster rate compared to that of Singapore. By 2003, Malaysia's share in total Chinese imports of components stood at 8 per cent compared to Singapore's of 3.5 per cent. Import shares of Taiwan and Korea also have increased persistently. However, the share of Hong Kong has declined as much of manufacturing activities carried out by Hong Kong businesses relocated to Mainland China. Overall, the data clearly suggest that China's trade integration through fragmentation trade is not predominantly a phenomenon limited to Greater

China (or the 'China Circle', see Naughton 1997). The procurement network has rapidly expanded to cover other countries in the region.

On the exports side, the aggregate regional share has declined persistently for total manufacturing as well as the two sub-categories of components, and final goods. Overall, China's evolving export patterns exhibit a clear extra-regional bias (the degree of which has increased over the year), in contrast to greater regional integration on the import side. However, the aggregate figure, being dominated by the dramatic decline in exports to Hong Kong, camouflages some noteworthy differences among individual countries/country groups. For instance, export share of AFTA has increased persistently throughout the period under study reflecting the growing importance of two-way trade in components. The share of AFTA in total component exports from China increased from 4.8 in 1992 to 11.2 per cent in 2003.

A comparison of data reported in Tables 13.5 and 13.6 reveals some noteworthy differences between intra-regional trade patterns of China and Japan. The share of intra-regional imports in manufacturing imports of Japan has increased over the year. The increase in the share of parts and components is particularly noteworthy. However, overall the degree of regional bias in Japanese imports is small compared to China. On the export side, Japan's regional shares in final goods have increased, in contrast to the persistent trend noted above for China. However, the regional share of China's component exports is much larger and growing faster (when the exceptional case of Hong Kong is excluded) compared to that of Japan. This reflects China's rising role as a key player in regional production networks.

From 1997 China has maintained a net importing position (a widening trade deficit) with the region. If Hong Kong is excluded the average deficit over the past six years would have been even larger (Table 13.7, Figure 13.3). The prime source of the widening deficit has been increasing reliance on countries in the region for sourcing parts and components for fuelling booming domestic final good assembly activities. Net parts and components trade with the region increased persistently from about US$2 billion in 1997 to over US$50 billion in 2003. The import position in final goods trade also has recorded a mild but persistent increase from 1999 onwards. China's net trade position in favour of the region has in fact widened in recent years. By contrast, Japan has persistently recorded a large trade surplus, reflecting the heavy involvement of Japanese companies in overseas assembly activities to maintain their competitiveness in final trade in third country markets. Put simply, Japan's trade relations with the rest of East Asia is predominantly in the form of using the region as an assembly base for meeting demand in the region and, more importantly for exporting to the rest of the world.

Figure 13.2 **China's regional manufacturing trade** (shares in total trade)

(i) Parts and components

(a) Exports

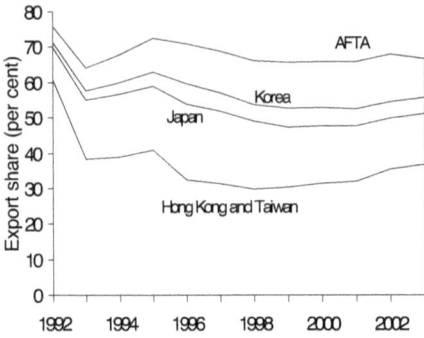

(b) Imports

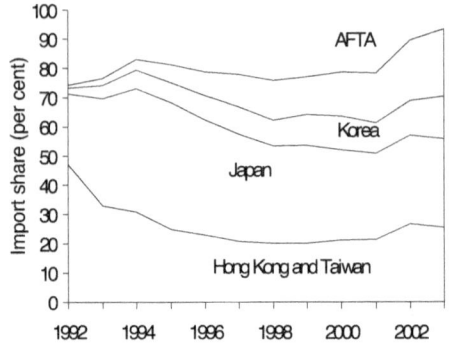

(ii) Final manufacturing

(a) Exports

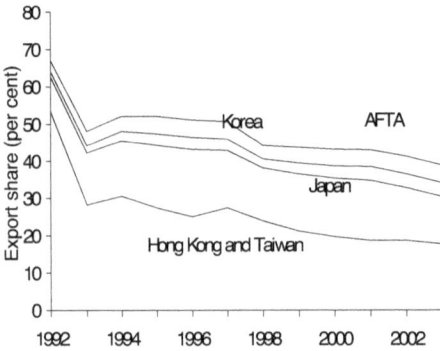

(b) Imports

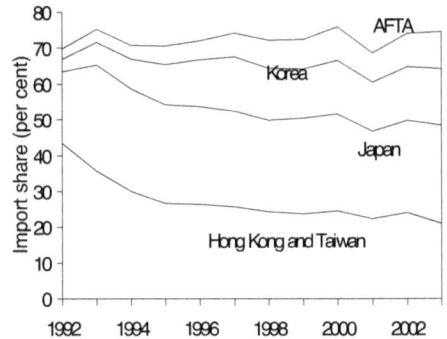

Total manufacturing

(a) Exports

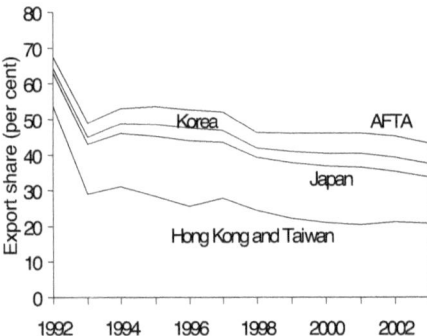

(b) Imports

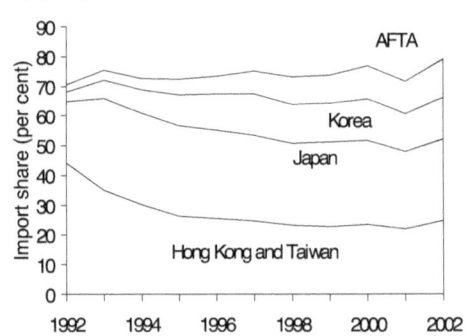

Source: Compiled from *UN Comtrade Database*.

Table 13.5   **Share of East Asia in Chinese exports and imports of manufactured goods, 1992, 1996 and 2003** (per cent)

	Exports			Imports		
	1992	1996	2003	1992	1996	2003
(a) Parts and components						
Japan	8.6	18.8	11.1	24.2	35.0	25.3
Hong Kong	61.0	22.9	27.0	5.3	8.6	4.2
Taiwan	1.7	3.7	3.6	5.3	10.4	16.9
Republic of Korea	1.5	5.4	4.3	1.9	7.6	12.2
AFTA	4.8	10.4	11.2	0.9	7.5	19.3
Indonesia	0.7	1.4	0.8	0.0	0.1	0.5
Malaysia	1.0	2.4	3.8	0.1	1.7	7.9
Philippines	0.3	0.7	1.1	0.0	0.3	4.7
Singapore	2.4	5.2	3.9	0.7	4.2	3.5
Thailand	0.5	0.8	1.6	0.1	1.3	2.7
Vietnam	0.1	0.3	0.3	..	..	..
Total East Asia	77.6	61.1	57.2	30.3	69.1	77.7
(b) Final goods						
Japan	9.3	18.1	13.0	20.4	27.3	27.2
Hong Kong	52.7	23.7	16.8	33.2	8.3	4.0
Taiwan	0.6	1.4	1.6	10.6	18.4	17.4
Korea	1.4	3.3	3.5	3.4	13.0	15.8
AFTA	3.1	5.2	5.2	2.9	5.3	10.8
Indonesia	0.4	0.7	0.8	1.5	1.1	1.5
Malaysia	0.5	0.7	0.9	0.5	1.4	2.3
Philippines	0.2	0.5	0.5	0.1	0.1	1.0
Singapore	1.3	2.2	1.6	0.6	1.8	3.5
Thailand	0.7	0.7	0.7	0.2	0.9	2.4
Vietnam	0.1	0.5	0.5	..	..	0.2
Total East Asia	67.2	51.9	40.1	70.5	72.4	75.4
(c) Total manufacturing						
Japan	9.2	18.2	12.7	20.5	28.7	26.6
Hong Kong	53.1	23.7	18.5	27.9	8.4	4.3
Taiwan	0.6	1.6	2.0	9.9	17	17.3
Korea, Rep of	1.4	3.5	3.7	3.1	12.1	14.6
AFTA	3.2	5.7	6.2	2.6	5.7	13.7
Indonesia	0.4	0.7	0.8	1.1	0.7	1.0
Malaysia	0.5	0.9	1.4	0.4	1.3	3.9
Philippines	0.2	0.5	0.6	0.1	0.1	2.1
Singapore	1.4	2.4	2.0	0.6	2.0	3.1
Thailand	0.6	0.7	0.8	0.2	0.9	2.3
Vietnam	0.1	0.5	0.5	..	..	0.1
Total East Asia	67.6	52.7	43.0	64.3	71.8	76.2

Source: Complied from *UN Comtrade Database*.

Conclusion

There is clear evidence that fragmentation-based specialisation has become an integral part of the economic landscape of East Asia. Trade in components has been expanding more rapidly than conventional final-goods trade. The degree of dependence on this new form of international specialisation is proportionately larger in East Asia than in North America and Europe.

Over the past decade or so, China has been rapidly integrating into the regional production networks. This development is an important counterpoint to the popular belief that China's global integration would crowd out other countries' opportunities for international specialisation. The estimates presented in this paper support our hypothesis that, in a context where fragmentation-based trade is expanding rapidly, standard trade flows analysis can lead to an understatement of the trading significance of China in the process of economic integration through trade. China's imports of components from East Asia have grown rapidly, in line with rapid expansion of manufacturing exports mostly to North America and the European Union. Reflecting this evolving pattern of international specialisation, China has run a persistent and widening net trade position with East Asia (excluding Japan). By contrast Japan has maintained a persistent, net surplus in its regional trade. The surplus has, however, marginally narrowed in recent years because of growing assembly imports from the region, from China in particular to Japan.

Increasing intra-regional economic interdependence in East Asia through international product fragmentation does not, however, mean that the process has contributed to lessoning the regions' dependence on the global economy. The region's growth dynamism based on this new form of specialisation depends inexorably on its extra-regional trade in final good, and this dependence has in fact increased over the years. While the growing importance of China both as a regional exporter and importer has begun to change the picture in recent years, extra-regional trade is likely to remain the engine of growth of the region in the foreseeable future. Growing trade in components has made the East Asian region increasingly reliant on extra-regional trade for its growth dynamism.

Is China's reliance on other countries in the region for sourcing components for its burgeoning electronics and electrical industries a structural feature of the ongoing process of its rapid economic integration? Or is it a passing phenomenon which will last only until China develops its own domestic production capabilities? Some analysts (for example, Lall and Albaladejo 2004) allude to the latter possibility, arguing that China has the potential to build a strong electronics industry based predominantly on locally produced components within its boundaries, combining

Table 13.6   **Share of East Asia in total Japanese exports and imports, 1992, 1996 and 2003**

	Exports			Imports		
	1992	1996	2003	1992	1996	2003
(a) Parts and components						
China	1.4	2.9	12.3	2.3	6.9	18.3
Hong Kong	4.3	4.3	7.4	2.2	1.5	0.7
Taiwan	7.7	6.4	5.7	6.3	8.3	12.4
Republic of Korea	5.7	5.3	6.5	9.3	11.6	12.8
AFTA	14.0	22.3	15.4	13.7	17.4	21.7
Indonesia	1.3	1.8	1.7	0.5	1.0	1.4
Malaysia	3.6	4.9	3.1	3.3	4.2	5.6
Philippines	1.2	2.6	3.0	1.6	3.8	5.7
Singapore	4.8	5.6	3.6	3.9	5.5	4.1
Thailand	3.2	4.0	4.0	4.5	2.9	4.9
Vietnam	0.0	0.1	0.3	0.0	0.0	0.3
Total East Asia	33.3	41.2	47.2	33.4	45.8	65.9
(b) Final goods						
China	3.7	5.8	11.4	12.4	19.8	34.6
Hong Kong	6.6	6.5	5.8	1.8	1.1	0.5
Taiwan	5.3	5.6	6.8	6.0	5.6	4.1
Korea	4.7	7.2	6.9	8.0	4.8	4.3
AFTA	10.8	16.1	10.7	9.8	14.8	14.3
Indonesia	1.6	2.3	1.4	2.5	2.8	2.7
Malaysia	1.9	2.9	1.8	1.8	3.7	3.1
Philippines	1.0	1.8	1.4	0.7	1.4	2.0
Singapore	3.4	4.5	2.6	1.6	2.7	1.5
Thailand	2.7	4.3	2.8	3.1	3.6	3.8
Vietnam	0.2	0.4	0.6	0.1	0.6	1.1
Total East Asia	31.2	41.2	41.6	38.1	46.1	57.8
(c) Total manufacturing						
China	3.2	4.9	11.7	11.1	17.5	31.2
Hong Kong	6.1	5.8	6.3	1.8	1.2	0.5
Taiwan	5.9	5.8	6.5	6.0	6.1	5.8
Korea	5.0	6.6	6.7	8.2	6.0	6.1
AFTA	11.6	18	12.1	10.3	15.3	15.8
Indonesia	11.6	17.7	12.3	2.2	2.4	2.3
Malaysia	1.6	2.2	1.5	1.9	3.6	3.5
Philippines	2.3	3.7	2.2	0.8	1.7	2.7
Singapore	1.0	2.1	1.9	1.8	3.0	1.9
Thailand	3.7	5.1	2.9	3.1	3.3	3.8
Vietnam	2.8	4.4	3.2	0.1	0.4	0.9
Total East Asia	31.6	41.2	43.3	37.4	46.1	59.5

Source: Complied from *UN Comtrade Database*.

Table 13.7   **China and Japan: net trade with East Asia, 1992, 1996 and 2003** (Export minus imports as a percentage of exports)

Imports	China			Japan		
To:	1992	1996	2003	1992	1996	2003
(a) Parts and components						
Japan	−718.6	−284.2	−297.7	..	..	..
China	..	..	..	72.5	25.8	42.2
Hong Kong	100.0	22.4	74.0	91.2	89.2	96.3
Taiwan	−1101.8	−483.7	−729.2	84.5	59.0	14.0
Korea	−324.5	−190.3	−399.1	69.0	31.8	22.2
AFTA	38.6	−48.8	−202.7	81.6	75.6	44.8
Total East Asia	−29.1	−133.2	-138.0	81.0	65.3	45.4
(b) Final manufacturing						
East Asia	4.9	−21.4	−37.5	51.2	30.2	14.1
Japan	−98.6	−31.4	−53.5	..	..	..
China	..	..	..	−33.0	−112.5	−88.0
Hong Kong	43.0	69.5	82.4	89.1	88.9	95.0
Taiwan	−1615.7	−1021.2	−686.1	55.0	37.7	63.3
Korea	−112.0	−239.4	−226.8	32.3	58.7	60.9
AFTA	15.9	12.6	−53.2	63.6	42.7	17.3
Total East Asia	4.9	−21.4	−37.5	51.2	30.2	14.1
(c) Total manufacturing						
Japan	−127.3	−53.2	−90.9	..	..	..
China	..	..	..	−21.9	−88.1	−47.1
Hong Kong	46.2	65.7	80.2	89.4	89.0	95.5
Taiwan	−1543.5	−918.7	−699.8	64.4	44.6	50.5
Korea	−122.9	−233.1	−261.7	42.5	52.2	49.9
AFTA	17.6	3.2	−100.0	68.9	54.9	27.7
Total East Asia	3.0	−32.2	−60.8	58.8	40.7	24.3

Source: Complied from *UN Comtrade Database.*

a high export competitiveness with an import substitution policy for an enormous domestic market. However, China's industrial transformation over the past one-and-a-half decades has not yielded any indication of this happening. We have seen that the net trade deficit in components has persistently widened during this period. It seems that firms involved in vertically integrated global industries tend to rely on international networks of production, which embrace difference territories and different forms of cooperation to optimise their competitiveness. Because of technological complexities and intrinsic country-specific cost advantages nations are becoming specialised in specific activity in the value chain and in certain kinds of products. Moreover, over a long period of time many MNEs (particularly United States-based MNEs) have significantly upgraded technical capabilities of their regional production networks in East Asia and assigned global production responsibilities to affiliates located in more mature countries (Singapore and Taiwan in particular). Naturally country risk considerations would have a much greater bearing on any corporate decision to deviate from these well-established global practices compared to simple relative cost considerations.

Is the new-found fondness in China and other East Asian countries for free trade agreements (FTAs) consistent with the objective of maximising gains from the ongoing process of international production fragmentation? Trade in components and final assembly is more sensitive to tariff changes than final trade (or total trade as captured in published trade data) (Yi 2003). Normally a tariff is incurred each time a goods-in-process cross a border. Consequently, with one percentage point reduction in tariff, the cost of production of a vertically-integrated good declines by a multiple of this initial reduction, in contrast to a one per cent decline in the cost of a regular traded good. Moreover, tariff reduction may also make more profitable goods that were previously produced entirely in one country and have now become vertically specialised. Consequently, in theory, the trade-stimulating effect of FTA would be higher for parts and component trade than for normal trade, other things remaining unchanged. However, in reality, much would depend on the nature of 'rules or origin' (ROOs) built into FTAs (Garnaut 2003). Trade distorting effects of ROOs are presumably more detrimental to fragmentation-based trade than for conventional final goods trade, because of the inherent difficulties involved in defining the 'product' for duty exception and the transaction costs associated with the bureaucratic supervision of the amount of value-added in production coming from various sources. Moreover, maintaining barriers to trade against non-members (while allowing free trade among members) can thwart 'natural' expansion of fragmentation of trade across countries. Formation of FTAs would therefore simply result in substituting for the existing tariff concessions rather that generating new

Figure 13.3 **China and Japan:Trade with East Asia^1** (US$ billon)

(i) Parts and components

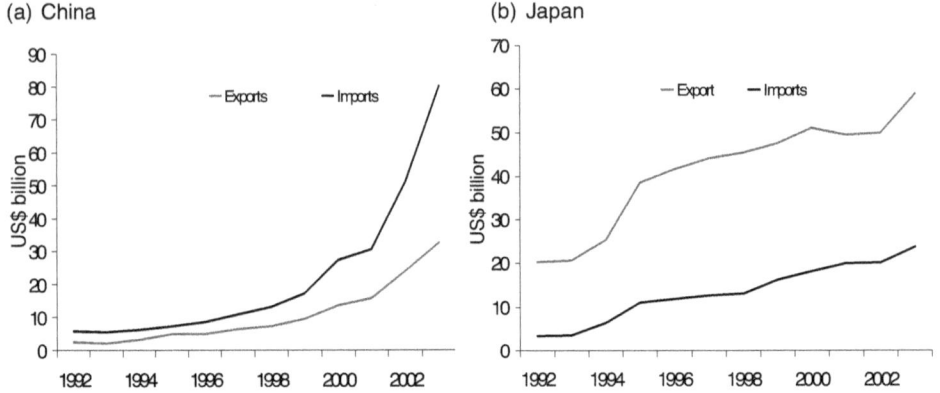

(a) China

US$ billion — Exports — Imports

1992 1994 1996 1998 2000 2002

(b) Japan

US$ billion — Export — Imports

1992 1994 1996 1998 2000 2002

(ii) Final manufacturing

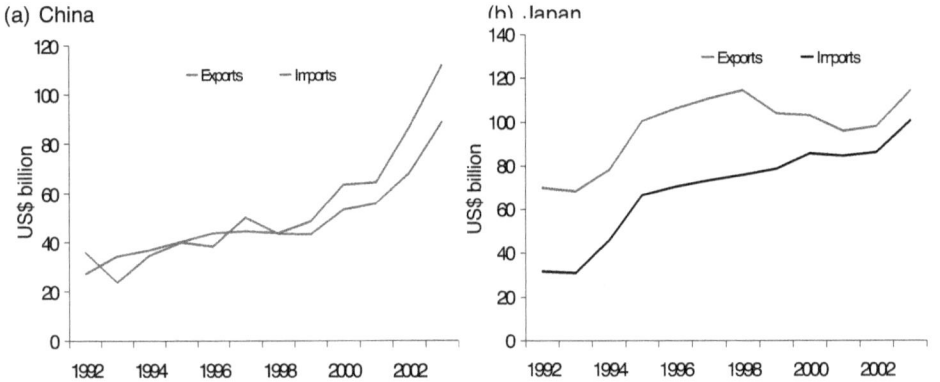

(a) China

US$ billion — Exports — Imports

1992 1994 1996 1998 2000 2002

(b) Japan

US$ billion — Exports — Imports

1992 1994 1996 1998 2000 2002

Total manufacturing

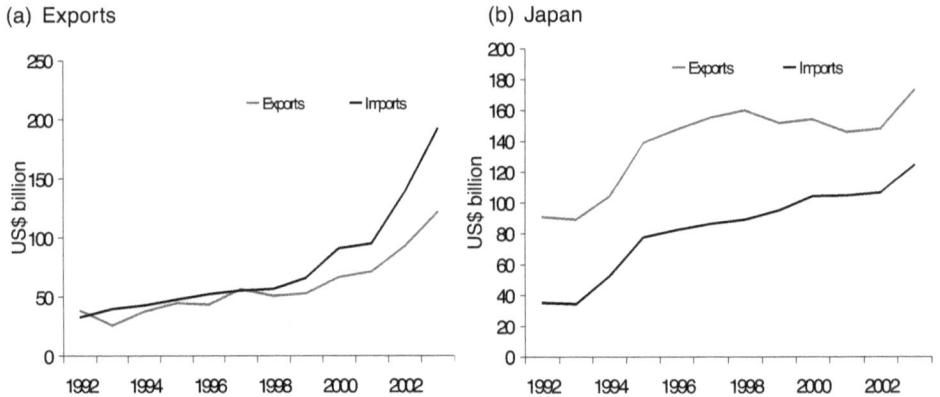

(a) Exports

US$ billion — Exports — Imports

1992 1994 1996 1998 2000 2002

(b) Japan

US$ billion — Exports — Imports

1992 1994 1996 1998 2000 2002

Note: ^{1} East Asia excluding China and Japan
Source: Compiled from *UN Comtrade Database*.

incentives for fragmentation trade. Thus, in terms of opportunities for trade expansion through international product fragmentation, the ideal policy choice appears to be multilateral liberalisation through the WTO process; the ongoing process of product fragmentation seems to have strengthened the case for a global, rather than a regional, approach to trade and investment policymaking.

Notes

[1] Alternative terms include 'vertical specialisation', 'slicing the value chain', 'disintegration of production' and 'international production sharing' and 'outsourcing'.

[2] For instance 'television tubes' were not separable from 'TVc' and ' computer processors' were lumped together with 'computers'.

[3] The list is available in Athukorala (2003), Appendix A-5.

[4] Much of Hong Kong's component trade relates to production fragmentation-based activities in the Mainland China and most (Freenstra et al. 1999).

References

Ahearne, A.G., Fernald, J.G., Loungani, P. and Schindler, J.W., 2003. *China and emerging Asia: comrades or competitors?*, International Finance Discussion Paper No. 789, Board of Governors of the Federal Reserve System, New York.

Arndt, S. and Kierzkowski, H. (eds.), 2001. *Fragmentation: new production patterns in the world economy*, Oxford University Press, New York.

Athukorala, P., 2003. *Production fragmentation and trade patterns in East Asia*, Trade and Development Discussion Paper 2003/21, Division of Economics, Research School of Pacific and Asian Studies, The Australian National University, Canberra.

——, (forthcoming). 'Production fragmentation and trade patterns in East Asia', *Asian Economic Papers*.

—— and Yamashita, N., (forthcoming). 'Production fragmentation and trade Integration: East Asia in a global context', *North American Journal of Economics and Finance*.

Borrus, M., 1997. 'Left for dead: Asian production networks and the revival of USE electronics', in Barry Naughton (Ed.), *The China Circle: economics and technology in the PRC, Taiwan and Hong Kong*, Brookings Institution Press, Washington, DC:139–63.

——, Earnst, D. and Haggard, S., 2000. *International Production Networks in Asia: Rivalry or Riches?*, Routledge, London.

Brown, C. and Linden, G., 2005. 'Offshoring in the semiconductor industry: a historical perspective', in Lael Brainard and Susan M. Collins (eds), *Brookings Trade Forum: 2005*, Brookings Institution Press, Washington, DC.

Eichengreen, B., Rhee, Y. and Tong, H., 2004. *The impact of China on the exorts of other Asian countries*, National Bureau of Economic Research (NBER) Working Paper 10768, NBER, Massachussets.

Feenstra, R.C., Hai, W., Woo, W.T. and Yao, S., 1999. 'Discrepancies in international trade data: an application to China-Hong-Kong entrepot trade', *American Economic Review*, 87(2):338–43.

Lardy, N.R., 2002. *Integrating China into the Global Economy*, Brookings Institution Press, Washington, DC.

Ng, F. and Yeats, A., 2001. 'Production sharing in East Asia: who does what for whom, and why?', in L. K. Cheng and H. Kierzkowski (eds), *Global Production and Trade in East Asia*, Kluwer Academic Publishers, Boston:63–109.

Garnaut, R., 2003. 'Australia and Japan: time to be important to each other again', address to the Australia-Japan Business Committee conference, Kyoto, 5 October.

Grossman, G.M. and Helpman, E., 2005. 'Outsourcing in a global economy', *Review of Economic Studies*, 72(1):135–59.

International Monetary Fund (IMF), 2004. 'China's emergence and its impact on the global economy', *World Economic Outlook*, International Monetary Fund Washington, DC:82–102

Jones, R.W., 2000. *Globalization and the Theory of Input Trade*, MIT Press, Cambridge.

— — and Kierzkowski, H., 2001. 'Globalization and the consequences of international fragmentation', In R. Dornbusch, G. Calvo and M. Obstfeld (eds), *Money, Factor Mobility and Trade: the festschrift in honor of Robert A. Mundell*, Press, Cambridge:365–81.

— — and Chen Lurong, 2005. 'What does the evidence tell us about fragmentation and outsourcing', *International Review of Economics and Finance*, 14(3):305–16.

Kaminski, B. and Ng, F., 2004. 'Production disintegration and integration of central Europe into global markets', *International Review of Economics and Finance*, 14(3):377–90.

Kierzkowski, H., 2001. 'Joining the global economy: experience and prospects of the transition economies', in S.W. Arndt & H. Kierzkowski (eds), *Fragmentation: new production patterns in the world economy*, Oxford University Press, Oxford: 231–53.

Lall, S. and Albaladejo, M., 2004. 'China's competitive performance: a threat to East Asian manufactured exports?', *World Development*, 32(9):1441–66.

Lemoine, F. and Ünal-Kesenci, D., 2004. 'Assembly trade and technology transfer: the case of China', *World Development*, 32(5):829–50.

McKendrick, D.G., Doner, R.F. and Haggard, S., 2000. *From Silicon Valley to Singapore: location and competitive advantage in the hard disk drive industry.*, Stanford University Press, Stanford.

Naughton, B., 1997. 'The emergence of China circle', in Barry Naughton (ed.), *The China Circle: economics and technology in the PRC, Taiwan and Hong Kong*, Brookings Institution Press, Washington, DC:3–37.

— —, 1999. 'The global electronics revolution and China's technology policy', *NBR Analysis*, 10(2):5–28.

Rangan, S. and Lawrence, R., 1999. *A prism on globalization*, Brookings Institution Press, Washington, DC.

Yi, K., 2003. 'Can vertical specialization explain the growth of world trade', *Journal of Political Economy*, 111(1):52–102.

14

China's trade expansion and the Asia Pacific economies

Kunwang Li and Ligang Song

Chinese foreign trade expanded at an average annual rate of 17 per cent from 1979 to 2000, which was twice the average annual growth rate of China's GDP during the same period. Both growth rates have been considerably higher than the respective world averages over the same period. Accession to the WTO in 2001 has given new impetus to expansion of China's external trade. In 2003, China's total external trade reached US$851 billion, an increase of 37 per cent from 2002— China's first year as a member of the WTO. In that year, with total imports reaching US$413 billion, China passed Japan to become the largest import market in Asia. With total external trade surpassing US$1000 billion in 2004, China has exceeded Japan and become the world's third largest trading nation after the United States and Germany.

China's emergence as a major exporter of a wide variety of manufactures in the past two decades has intensified the competitive impact on both industrial and developing economies alike. From the point of view of people in industrial economies who are involved in labour-intensive and other sectors, the Chinese comparative advantage is strong or strengthening and the expansion of China's exports hurts employment, especially for unskilled labour. This contributes to surges in trade protectionism against Chinese exports in industrial countries. Increasingly, these have taken the form of anti-dumping or other safeguard measures such as re-imposing quotas and setting limits on quantities or growth targets for certain Chinese exports entering their markets.[1] Protectionism prompted the Chinese government to lobby intensely to be granted 'market-economy' status by other members of the WTO, especially industrial countries, in order to ease anti-dumping measures.

There are also anxieties among developing economies over China's rising trade. Developing economies are concerned that China's increasing exports will substitute for their exports in third markets. There are also concerns voiced in some developing economies, especially in East and Southeast Asia, that much needed foreign direct investment could be diverted to China, which has become a magnet in attracting FDI, especially in recent years. Developing economies fear that both trends will slow the growth in their exports and incomes (Lall 2004; Shafaeddin 2004; Song 2004; Weiss 2004).

What is the balance between competition and opportunites for China's trading partners? This chapter explores China's contributions to the trade expansion of China's major trading partners in Asia and the Pacific from 1990 to 2003. The economies included are China's major trading partners in East Asia, including Japan, Korea, Hong Kong, Taiwan, and the five major economies of ASEAN— Indonesia, Malaysia, the Philippines, Singapore and Thailand. Given the important role played by the United States in international as well as regional trade, the United States is also covered. The term 'region' in this chapter refers to East Asia plus the United States.

Trade reform, comparative advantage and the rise of Chinese trade

Chinese economy's remarkable international performance is based on the success of its domestic reform. These, together with trade liberalisation, directly affected China's external trade through increased specialisation, increased market size, and technological advance, supported by foreign direct investment (Song and Sun 2003). China's trade expansion has been based on its underlying comparative advantage, relying strongly on exports of labour-intensive products in its early expansionist period. And then the accumulation of capital in the process of growth saw comparative advantage shift progressively towards increasingly capital-intensive and then further to technology-intensive products. The relationships between factor endowments and trade patterns change over time in a dynamic fashion, with comparative advantage shifting as endowments change. These shifts expand export supply potential (Song 1996).

With the Chinese economy increasingly dependent on a high degree of trade, it is less than ever in China's best interest to try to protect its domestic industries by limiting imports (Song and Sun 2003). As pointed out by McKinnon,

> keeping imports out reduces the effective demand for, and consequently the price of, foreign exchange relative to the domestic costs of labour, capital, intermediate inputs, and so on that producers of export products must pay. Since exporters sell in foreign markets at this less favourable 'real' exchange rate, they are caught in a profit squeeze, which reduces traditional exports and blocks new export development—particularly of manufactures (1973:134).

Furthermore, domestic reform conforming with the WTO requirements has further improved China's trading system, and helped facilitate the expansion of its imports through increased transparency and efficiency. Thus China's increasingly important position in world trade provides huge export opportunities for China's trading partners, as it introduces new competitive pressures on these economies.

In the period 1990–2003, China's exports and imports grew at the average rates of 16 and 17 per cent respectively. Exports and imports increased by 6 and 6.7 times respectively. In comparison, the growth rates of exports and imports in all developing economies were 9 and 8.7 per cent respectively. China's shares in world total exports and imports have increased from 1.8 and 1.5 per cent in 1990 to 5.9 and 5.3 per cent respectively in 2003 (Appendix Table C1 in Appendix C).

The rapid growth of China's exports cannot be separated from the growth of its imports. Amongst other reasons, this is because a large part of China's export industries are in processing trade, in which all or part of imported raw materials, intermediate inputs, and other inputs are exported after being processed or assembled. The share of processing trade in exports reached 55 per cent in 2003.

The economies from which China imports are mainly located in the Asia Pacific region, especially in East Asia. From 1990 to 2003, Japan remained the largest exporter to China, with its share of China's imports rising from 14.2 per cent in 1990 to 18 per cent in 2003 (Table 14.1). The second largest exporter to China is the European Union, with its share in China's imports reaching 13.2 per cent in 2003 despite following a declining trend from 1995. The US position has witnessed great changes during these years. It was the third largest exporter to China in 1990 after Japan and the European Union, with its share in China's imports reaching 12.2 per cent. By 2000, however, the United States was overtaken by Taiwan and Korea with respect to its share in China's total imports. In 2003, the United States' share in China's imports fell even further to 8.2 per cent, lagging behind Japan, Taiwan, ASEAN, and Korea.

Table 14.1   **Sources of China's imports from selected economies, 1990–2003** (per cent of the total)

	1990	1995	2000	2003
Asia	41.0	47.1	50.6	54.9
ASEAN	5.6	7.4	8.9	11.0
Hong Kong	27.1	6.5	9.6	2.7
Japan	14.2	21.9	17.8	18.0
Korea	0.4	7.8	10.0	10.5
Taiwan		11.2	11.3	11.6
United States	12.2	12.2	9.6	8.2
European Union	17.0	16.1	13.4	13.2

Source: International Monetary Fund, (various years). *Direction of Trade Statistics Yearbook*, International Monetary Fund, Washington, DC.

The East Asian economies' dependence on exports to the Chinese market has increased in recent years. Except for Hong Kong, the East Asian economies' exports to China grew faster than to other trading partners. By 2003, Taiwan, ASEAN and Korea had risen to become the third, fourth and fifth-largest exporters to China, with their shares in China's imports reaching 11.6, 11 and 10.5 per cent respectively. The trend towards accelerated growth of trade within East Asia has been strengthened in recent years. The emerging Chinese economy, with its strong trade-orientation, has played a pivotal role in boosting the push for closer economic integration in the East Asian region. East Asia's share of China's imports increased from 41 per cent in 1990 to 55 per cent in 2003 (Table 14.1).

There is great variety in the commodity composition of each economy's exports to China. In both 1990 and 2003, capital-intensive products were the largest component of US exports to China, representing around 70 per cent of total exports to China. Agriculture-intensive products were the second largest component at around 20 per cent (Table 14.2). Labour-intensive and minerals-intensive products occupied relatively small shares in China's imports from the United States, although the share of minerals-intensive products rose during this period. Japan's exports to China have been predominantly capital-intensive products, which rose steadily

Table 14.2   **Commodity composition of exports to China from the
regional economies** (per cent)

	Agriculture-intensive	Minerals-intensive	Labour-intensive	Capital-intensive
Indonesia				
1990	51.0	25.5	0.2	23.2
1995	40.3	38.9	4.6	16.1
2000	37.2	26.0	5.4	31.5
2003	30.8	23.9	5.0	40.3
Japan				
1990	4.2	2.5	11.5	81.9
1995	2.7	3.3	12.0	82.0
2000	2.2	3.9	10.7	83.2
2003	1.5	3.4	6.8	88.3
Malaysia				
1990	78.7	7.5	1.4	12.5
1995	66.3	6.2	4.3	23.2
2000	21.5	9.5	2.4	66.7
2003	14.4	7.7	1.3	76.7
Korea				
1990	17.4	1.8	20.3	60.5
1995	13.4	5.4	21.6	59.6
2000	7.5	11.7	13.6	67.4
2003	3.2	6.8	7.5	82.6
Philippines				
1990	31.7	30.1	1.4	36.8
1995	22.0	61.2	3.7	13.1
2000	6.8	12.6	0.7	79.9
2003	2.3	4.6	0.4	92.8
Singapore				
1990	19.5	48.4	3.6	28.4
1995	20.9	31.9	10.5	36.6
2000	1.5	18.1	2.7	77.6
2003	1.3	15.8	2.2	80.7
Thailand				
1990	77.8	1.1	7.3	13.8
1995	37.4	4.7	13.7	44.2
2000	21.2	10.0	3.1	65.6
2003	17.2	8.6	3.0	71.2
United States				
1990	25.7	2.7	2.7	69.0
1995	25.8	4.1	3.5	66.6
2000	16.5	5.2	2.0	76.3
2003	20.1	5.1	2.2	72.7

Source: Authors' calculations using the data from UN Comtrade database.

from 81.8 per cent in 1990 to 88.3 per cent in 2003. Japan's exports of labour-intensive products to China fell continuously from 11.5 per cent in 1990 to 6.8 per cent in 2003. A similar trend can also be observed for Korea, where the share of labour-intensive products in exports to China fell from 20 per cent in 1990 to about 7 per cent in 2003, providing more evidence of shifting comparative advantage in the process of East Asian industrialisation.

The commodity composition of ASEAN's exports to China has changed a great deal over the same period. In the early 1990s, ASEAN's exports to China were mainly of agriculture-intensive and minerals-intensive products, followed by capital-intensive and labour-intensive products. In 2002, however, capital-intensive products had become the major component in ASEAN's exports to China, followed by agriculture-intensive products and minerals-intensive products. The share of capital-intensive products in ASEAN's exports to China continued to rise to 72.1 per cent in 2003, while the shares of agriculture-intensive and minerals-intensive products were falling. The pattern of bilateral trade between China and ASEAN bears further study, including by looking intra rather than inter-industry trade (see Chapter 13).

There are variations in commodity composition within the ASEAN five in relation to China. While agriculture-intensive and minerals-intensive products remained the major components in Indonesia's exports to China, their shares are declining and the share of capital-intensive products rising. At the beginning of the 1990s, Malaysian exports to China were mainly concentrated on agriculture-intensive products, but the share of these goods dropped drastically after 1995 when capital-intensive products' share was on the rise. The situation with the Philippines and Thailand is similar to that of Malaysia. Singapore demonstrated a different pattern from other members in ASEAN as the share of minerals-intensive products in its exports to China was relatively high, due to its role as an important re-exporter of related products.

Despite all the differences, there is similarity among China's imports from the members of ASEAN—all export only low proportions of labour-intensive products to China. To study the bilateral trading relationships between China and ASEAN further, an export similarity index was used, defined as the degree of similarity between the commodity composition of China's exports to ASEAN and that of ASEAN's exports to China. If this index increases, it indicates a convergence of the structure of the two trade partners' exports, and also suggests greater competition between the two partners in third-country markets. On the other hand, a decline in the index suggests that specialisation between them is increasing in a third market. Furthermore, if the convergence occurs between a developing country and an industrial economy, rising indexes can also be interpreted as a reflection of fast growth and industrialisation for the developing country (Xu and Song 2000).

Table 14.3 provides the bilateral export similarity indexes between China and the five members in ASEAN. Except for Indonesia and the Philippines, the bilateral export similarities between China and Malaysia, Thailand and Singapore have been steadily increasing (statistically significant at the 1 per cent, 5 per cent, and 10 per cent levels respectively). Increase in trade overlap between China and the three members of ASEAN indicates that there has been a convergence in their industrial and export structures, and greater competition between them in third-country markets. The increasing similarity in their export structure, together with increased intensity of bilateral trade, suggests that the patterns of trade between China and ASEAN are of intra-industry, rather than inter-industry, trade. For example, the large amount of capital-intensive products among ASEAN exports to China has a great deal to do with multinational corporations' direct investment in East Asia.

The recent surge in bilateral trade between China and ASEAN indicates that a new pattern of trade has begun to emerge between the two, driven primarily by firms seeking economies of scale and product differentiation through the operation of multinational corporations. The formation of the bilateral free trade arrangement (FTA), the so-called '10+1', can be expected to strengthen bilateral trade between

Table 14.3   **The bilateral export similarity index between China and ASEAN countries, 1995–2003**

	Indonesia	Malaysia	Philippines	Singapore	Thailand
1995	0.330	0.520	0.307	0.557	0.435
1996	0.322	0.529	0.256	0.504	0.381
1997	0.274	0.537	0.426	0.513	0.479
1998	0.314	0.561	0.607	0.553	0.509
1999	0.301	0.596	0.664	0.637	0.605
2000	0.243	0.635	0.612	0.650	0.554
2001	0.299	0.634	0.410	0.610	0.514
2002	0.332	0.634	0.419	0.574	0.550
2003	0.369	0.539	0.461	0.585	0.502
Spearman coefficient	0.345	0.770***	0.503	0.588*	0.697**
p-value	0.328	0.009	0.138	0.074	0.025

Note: The estimates with ***, **, * denotes significance at 1 per cent, 5 per cent and 10 per cent levels respectively.
Source: Authors' calculations.

Table 14.4   **Impact of '10+1' gain in regional economies' exports to China**
(change in per cent)

Indonesia	Malaysia	Japan	Korea	Philippines	Singapore	Taiwan	Thailand	US
28.38	29.96	1.19	0.03	36.12	29.75	0.42	30.03	0.51

Source: Calculated by Zhang Bowei based on the GTAP modeling techniques with the base year of 1997.

ASEAN and China further. To assess the potential impact of this regional grouping on region's economies, a simulation analysis is carried out by employing the computable general equilibrium (CGE) model based on the GTAP to examine how China's imports from the regional economies will change after the realisation of free trade between China and ASEAN.

Trade liberalisation between China and ASEAN will enchance ASEAN's exports to China considerably (Table 14.4). This appears especially significant to two members of ASEAN—the Philippines and Thailand. For the economies outside '10+1', while trade liberalisation between China and ASEAN produces no negative effect on their exports to China, the positive effects are minimal, especially for Korea, Taiwan and the United States. Formation of a bilateral FTA between China and ASEAN could reduce their engagement with other regional economies as engagement with each other comes to dominate, yielding new pressures within China, ASEAN and the other economies.

Diminished gains from trade accompany a diminished pressure to adjust. The FTA-induced separation of third countries, including economies in the region, from East Asian dynamism reduces opportunities for rising living standards. This is likely to be most damaging to potential suppliers of the natural resource-based products in which China's comparative disadvantage is most pronounced, and especially in agricultural industries in which trade distortion is endemic. The trade-off between costs of adjustment and gains from trade through the rise of China is affected by the presence of FTAs. For the world as a whole, the trade-off between adjustment costs and gains from trade is more favourable if the movement is towards specialisation according to global comparative advantage, as it is modified by growth and structural change in individual economies (Garnaut and Song forthcoming). This message becomes clearer through China's contributions to regional trade and economic growth.

China's contributions to regional export growth

The Asia Pacific economies continued to perform well above world average in terms of growth of trade from 1990 to 2003. The total exports of the Asia Pacific economies (including the United States) increased 1.4 times over this period. The growth rate of the 10 developing economies was much higher than that of the two industrial countries, the United States and Japan. Within the developing economies, China's exports grew the fastest, followed by ASEAN, South Korea, Taiwan and Hong Kong. What have been the major sources of rapid growth of the regional economies' exports?

Employing the method described in Appendix A, the eleven regional economies' export growth can be decomposed into three components. The first component is the demand effect, which reflects the inducement from overall world trade expansion. The second, a competitiveness effect, represents the improvement in an economy's international competitiveness either through price or product quality. An economy can increase its share in the world market by expanding its exports faster than the world average. Thus, changes in export share in world markets provide an indication of changes in an economy's international competitiveness. The first two effects will basically determine an economy's export growth. However, there is a deviation between the sum of these two parts and the realised-growth rate. The reason for this deviation is that there are some factors, such as geographical proximity, social and cultural ties, special trade arrangements that may lead to an uneven distribution of an economy's exports among its various trading partners. Thus, the third effect is introduced as the location effect, which includes all factors other than the first two.

Table 14.5 reports the results of the decomposition of the three effects for the eleven economies as well as the region's total export growth. First, the demand effect is very prominent in the region's export growth. On the whole, the region's total exports increased by 142 per cent over the period 1990–2003, of which 135 percentage points were brought about by the demand effect. That is, the demand effect contributed 95 per cent of total growth (135 per cent/142 per cent), while the competitiveness effect contributed 25 per cent, and the location effect −18.8 per cent.

Second, the region's developing economies have seen exports grow more through improvements in their international competitiveness—China, Malaysia, the Philippines and Thailand, in particular, benefited more from increased international competitiveness driving export growth. In contrast, for NIEs, the contribution of the demand effect exceeds that of the competitiveness effect. This is especially

Table 14.5   **Decomposition of export growth of the regional economies (per cent)**

	Total	Demand	Competitiveness	Location
(a)1990–2003				
China	598.3	137.2	512.1	−51.0
Hong Kong	172.5	256.1	83.0	−166.5
Indonesia	137.6	117.6	16.3	3.6
Japan	64.7	140.7	−61.3	−14.7
Korea	184.2	116.1	61.8	6.3
Malaysia	256.8	125.1	138.3	−6.7
Philippines	342.1	124.7	224.8	−7.3
Singapore	178.6	140.2	57.3	−18.8
Taiwan	174.6	147.6	60.0	−33.0
Thailand	248.2	121.7	127.6	−1.2
United States	84.1	110.7	−35.2	8.6
Region	142.4	135.8	25.4	−18.8
(b)1990-1995				
China	137.3	85.0	115.6	−63.2
Hong Kong	111.3	74.2	77.7	−40.7
Indonesia	76.9	57.3	33.2	−13.6
Japan	54.0	60.3	8.7	−15.0
Korea	93.6	52.1	49.5	−8.0
Malaysia	150.6	67.3	119.7	−36.4
Philippines	112.0	54.8	69.8	−12.7
Singapore	126.1	74.7	94.5	−43.1
Taiwan	86.7	66.9	46.4	−26.6
Thailand	147.9	55.5	108.4	−15.9
United States	48.4	45.0	2.3	1.1
Region	74.4	57.8	32.7	−16.2
(c)1995–2000				
China	67.3	23.5	37.6	6.2
Hong Kong	16.4	45.8	−13.5	−15.9
Indonesia	36.7	25.3	8.2	3.2
Japan	7.9	31.8	-20.9	−3.0
Korea	30.9	29.2	2.6	−0.9
Malaysia	33.1	25.8	4.8	2.6
Philippines	119.9	32.3	94.5	−6.9
Singapore	17.9	24.1	−11.4	5.2
Taiwan	32.7	32.5	4.5	−4.4
Thailand	20.6	26.4	−7.6	1.8
United States	32.3	22.6	3.9	5.9
Region	27.5	28.4	−1.2	0.3

Table 14.5   **Decomposition of export growth of the regional economies (per cent) cont.**

	Total	Demand	Competitiveness	Location
(d)2000–2003				
China	75.9	10.6	54.4	10.9
Hong Kong	10.8	36.4	−8.2	−17.4
Indonesia	−1.8	12.0	−18.7	5.0
Japan	−0.9	15.2	−18.4	2.3
Korea	12.2	18.5	−5.8	−0.5
Malaysia	7.0	10.3	−10.3	6.9
Philippines	−5.2	9.1	−21.4	7.1
Singapore	4.8	12.8	−13.2	5.1
Taiwan	10.8	20.3	-7.2	−2.2
Thailand	16.5	12.4	−1.4	5.5
United States	−6.3	19.4	−24.5	−1.2
Region	9.0	17.8	−9.4	0.6

Source: Authors' calculations.

so for the United States and Japan, whose export growth was determined by demand rather than competitiveness. This seems to suggest that the more developed the economy, the more likely it is to depend on demand rather than competitiveness to sustain export growth. In fact, for industrialised economies, the contribution of competitiveness to export growth was actually negative as they are losing international competitiveness over a wide spectrum of manufacturing products. In the case of China, the demand effect is important, but the competitiveness effect plays an overwhelming role in sustaining its rapid export growth.

Third, there is a dynamic feature in these three effects over the different periods. The demand effect in regional export growth continued to play an important role in enhancing export expansion in the region's economies over the sub-periods, although its contribution fell over time. The competitiveness effect is falling, presumably because of the strong influence of the industrial economies. Interestingly, the location effect has become more and more important in the regional economies over time, especially during 2000–2003. The next step is to look at how China contributes to the demand effect of regional trade.

China's impact on regional economies' trade expansion can be assessed by looking at China's contribution to the demand effect component of other economies' export expansion. Table 14.6 provides the results of this estimation. For comparison, the estimation also includes the contributions made by the two largest economies in the Asia Pacific region—the United States and Japan.

During the period 1990–2003, the proportion of the US contribution to the regional demand effect was 19.1 per cent, making it the largest contributor among the three, followed by China, which contributed 16.2 per cent. Japan's contribution is comparatively low at a mere 4.6 per cent, reflecting the sluggishness of the Japanese economy and Japan's declining role in leading regional economic growth since the early 1990s.

By looking at the results over different periods, it can be seen that China's contribution to the demand effect has been rising continuously. Before 2000, the US contribution led, but things began to change dramatically after 2000. In the period 2000–2003, China's role increased rapidly to 32.8 per cent, and the US role fell drastically from 33.2 per cent during 1995–2000 to about 5 per cent during 2000–2003. Japan's becomes inconsequential, a mere 0.4 per cent.

Except for the Philippines, to which China and the United States contirbute roughly equal effects in raising the demand for export growth, China has had a more powerful role in the export growth of all other regional economies. Within the region, China's impact in raising NIEs' export growth was stronger than that of ASEAN. Among the NIEs, Hong Kong is the largest beneficiary from rising demand in China, followed by Taiwan and Korea. Compared with the previous period, 1995–2000, China's contributions to the demand effect of export growth of ASEAN increased substantially. China has now become an engine for driving export growth in the region's economies.

Industrial linkages between China and the regional economies through trade

To analyse the impact of China's final demand on regional economies' production, an index of international division of labour (IDL) is introduced. The index is defined as the ratio of each economy's value-added to the total value-added in the region by sector, generated by an extra unit of demand in that sector in China. The index can be constructed by using an input–output methodology, which allows us to calculate and assess China's impact on regional economies through trade at the industrial level (see Appendix 14B for details). The data required are from the *Asian International Input–Output Table 1995*, published by the Institute of Developing Economies.

The degrees of international division of labour between China and other regional economies as defined are shown in Table 14.7. For each sector, the figures across different economies (rows) sum to unity, indicating the extent to which an extra unit of demand from China is being distributed. In sector 1—agriculture, livestock, forestry and fishery—98 per cent of China's demand is met within China and

Table 14.6 **China's contributions to the demand effect of export growth of the regional economies in comparison with the United States and Japan** (per cent)

	China	United States	Japan
(a)1990—2003			
China		9.4	6.7
Hong Kong	64.5	14.4	1.4
Taiwan	15.3	37.1	5.4
Indonesia	18.4	17.0	22.7
Japan	10.1	34.3	0.0
Korea	0.0	10.1	37.6
Malaysia	11.2	20.6	7.7
Philippines	4.0	46.3	10.0
Singapore	7.2	23.1	3.9
Thailand	6.4	28.4	8.9
United States	7.4	0.0	7.0
Region	16.2	19.2	4.6
(b)1990—1995			
China	0.0	4.9	7.4
Hong Kong	48.5	15.7	3.3
Taiwan	7.4	26.4	8.2
Indonesia	8.3	11.2	31.8
Japan	5.2	25.8	0.0
Korea	0.0	27.0	15.3
Malaysia	4.6	12.4	9.7
Philippines	2.0	34.0	15.5
Singapore	3.0	14.0	5.0
Thailand	3.1	20.1	13.3
United States	4.0	0.0	11.8
Region	8.3	14.5	7.4
(c)1995–2000			
China	0.0	42.8	10.5
Hong Kong	51.1	28.8	1.7
Taiwan	25.7	45.3	4.6
Indonesia	10.6	33.3	13.9
Japan	10.9	52.4	0.0
Korea	16.8	38.5	5.8
Malaysia	7.0	48.9	6.3
Philippines	2.6	67.2	6.3
Singapore	6.8	45.9	4.2
Thailand	7.6	40.4	8.1
United States	6.3	0.0	6.3
Region	15.9	33.2	4.2

Table 14.6   **China's contributions to the demand effect of export growth of the regional economies in comparison with the United States and Japan** (per cent) cont.

	China	United States	Japan
(d)2000–2003			
China	0.0	10.7	1.5
Hong Kong	79.2	3.5	0.1
Taiwan	54.2	6.8	0.5
Indonesia	31.1	6.2	1.8
Japan	35.0	10.8	0.0
Korea	48.5	6.5	0.6
Malaysia	25.0	10.8	1.2
Philippines	16.0	17.9	1.5
Singapore	25.4	7.3	0.5
Thailand	27.5	9.4	1.1
United States	8.9	0.0	0.4
Region	32.9	5.0	0.4

Source: Authors' calculations.

about 2 per cent is divided among the other regional economies. Among these, the United States and Japan are benefiting more than the other economies in this sector.

Overall rankings are United States, Japan, Korea, Taiwan, Indonesia, Malaysia, Singapore, Thailand and Philippines, which suggests that increased demand in China benefited industrial economies more than the developing economies in the region. The international division of labour between China and the United States, Japan, South Korea and Taiwan is greater than that between China and all members in ASEAN except Indonesia. This difference in IDL indicates that China's trade dependence on the industrial economies and the NIEs within the region is higher than its dependence on the ASEAN economies.

For individual sectors, China's indices of IDL in transport equipment, machinery, chemicals, paper products, presswork and textiles are relatively low (approximately 90 per cent), suggesting that China's demand for those products is more heavily dependent on world markets. For example, China's demand for both machinery and transport equipment had to be met chiefly by Japan and to a lesser degree the United States in the mid 1990s; and Japan, the United States plus NIEs were relatively more important in providing other manufacturing goods to China.

In comparison, China's indices of IDL in sectors such as agriculture, food, energy and minerals are relatively high, suggesting China relied more on domestic supplies to meet demand at that time. The figures show that China relied relatively more on Malaysia to meet its demand for timber and Thailand to meet its demand for rubber.

In brief, the degree and pattern of international division of labour between China and other regional economies largely reflected underlying comparative advantage. In relation to other regional economies, China relied more on imports of capital-intensive products and on exports of labour-intensive products. This is consistent with the finding that China has been importing increasing amounts of capital-intensive products from other economies in the region.

For energy and mineral sources, the results presented here were obtained based on 1995 data, when China's energy and mineral sectors still had a relatively high degree of self-sufficiency. As China's economy and trade rapidly expand, however, it will depend more and more on foreign resources, including energy and raw materials, to meet domestic demand, as demonstrated by the surge of China's demand for these products in recent years.

Conclusion

This chapter has examined how China has played an important role in enhancing the export expansion of its trading partners, through increasing imports from the regional economies. We examined the sources of export growth of these economies and their international industrial linkages with China. The results show that China has played an increasingly important role in the rapid development of the Asia Pacific region since 1990. China replaced Japan as the engine of regional trade growth in the second half of the 1990s. Since 2000, China has surpassed the United States and become the most powerful engine in the region's trade expansion.

The emergence of China into the world market has resulted in significant competitive pressures on other East Asian economies, but it has at the same time offered enormous opportunities to other Asian and Pacific economies. To take these opportunities, it is important for both China and its regional trading partners to continue to adjust their industrial structures in response to intensifying competition in the regional economies. A closer trading relationship centering on China in the East Asian region is now taking shape. It is imperative for the regional economies to maintain an open trading regime as such a regime underscored the great achievements of the regional economies in the past decades. And there is no doubt that such a regime will continue to play an important role in securing the region's prosperity in the future.

Table 14.7 Indexes of international division of labour (IDL): China versus its trading partners

Sector	Indonesia	Malaysia	Philippines	Singapore	Thailand	China	Taiwan	Korea	Japan	United States
1	0.0010	0.0008	0.0001	0.0004	0.0005	0.9813	0.0009	0.0019	0.0051	0.0075
2	0.0011	0.0008	0.0001	0.0007	0.0004	0.9742	0.0015	0.0031	0.0131	0.0049
3	0.0023	0.0015	0.0002	0.0010	0.0011	0.9610	0.0023	0.0048	0.0187	0.0071
4	0.0013	0.0023	0.0002	0.0008	0.0035	0.9568	0.0008	0.0027	0.0089	0.0218
5	0.0017	0.0019	0.0002	0.0007	0.0017	0.9187	0.0058	0.0206	0.0302	0.0185
6	0.0155	0.0128	0.0003	0.0013	0.0011	0.9342	0.0030	0.0067	0.0163	0.0087
7	0.0090	0.0016	0.0002	0.0014	0.0011	0.9026	0.0056	0.0173	0.0275	0.0337
8	0.0031	0.0038	0.0008	0.0019	0.0014	0.9174	0.0063	0.0143	0.0307	0.0202
9	0.0217	0.0034	0.0001	0.0040	0.0004	0.9508	0.0012	0.0047	0.0094	0.0042
10	0.0063	0.0038	0.0004	0.0014	0.0171	0.9198	0.0048	0.0114	0.0242	0.0108
11	0.0030	0.0013	0.0002	0.0011	0.0007	0.9609	0.0026	0.0055	0.0164	0.0083
12	0.0030	0.0014	0.0005	0.0014	0.0006	0.9396	0.0059	0.0077	0.0282	0.0117
13	0.0020	0.0026	0.0003	0.0011	0.0006	0.9022	0.0013	0.0108	0.0604	0.0176
14	0.0021	0.0023	0.0003	0.0016	0.0013	0.8954	0.0070	0.0095	0.0608	0.0170
15	0.0023	0.0018	0.0003	0.0025	0.0009	0.9199	0.0049	0.0134	0.0359	0.0182
Total	0.0036	0.0022	0.0003	0.0018	0.0016	0.9403	0.0038	0.0085	0.0246	0.0134

Note: Figures are as defined in the text; See Appendix B for the list of these sectors.
Source: Authors' calculation using data from *the Asian International Input-Output Table*, Institute of Developing Economies, 1995.

Acknowledgments

The authors would like to thank Shi Binzhan for his valuable help with processing the data and Zhang Bowei for his input in carrying out the CGE modeling work.

Notes

[1] See the recent trade disputes between China and the European Union over imports of textile/ clothing into the EU markets.

References

Garnaut, R. and Song, L., (forthcoming).'Truncated globalisation: the fate of the Asia Pacific economies?', in H. Soesastro and C. Findlay (eds), *Reshaping the Asia Pacific Economic Order*, Routledge, London.

Institute of Developing Economies (IDE), 2001. *Asian International Input-Output Table 1995*, IDE Statistical Data Series 82, Tokyo.

Lall, S., and Albaladejo, M., 2002. 'The competitive impact of China on manufactured exports by emerging economies of Asia', in C.A. Magarinos, Y. Tu and F.C. Sercovich (eds), *China in the WTO: the birth of a catching-up strategy,* Palgrave Macmillan, Houndmills:76–110.

— —, 2004. 'China's competitive performance: a threat to East Asia manufactured exports?', *World Development,* 32(9):1441–66.

Li, K. and Xue, J. 1998. 'Regional trade growth among APEC: an empirical analysis' (APEC qu yu nei mao yi zeng zhang de yin su fen xi), *World Economy*, 1:43–50.

McKinnon, R.I., 1973. *Money and Capital in Economic Development*, The Brookings Institute, Washington, DC.

Sano, T. and Chihatru T., 1993. *International Industrial Linkages and Economic Interdependency in Asia-Pacific Region*, Institute of Developing Economies, Tokyo.

Shafaeddin, S. M., 2004. 'Is China's accession to WTO threatening exports of developing countries?', *China Economic Review*, 15(2):109–44.

Song, L., 1996. 'Institutional change, trade composition and export supply potential in China', in M.Guitian and R. Mundell (eds), *Inflation and Growth in China*, International Monetary Fund, Washington, DC:190–225.

— — and Song, S., 2003. 'A changing role in world trade', in R. Garnaut and L. Song (eds), *China: New Engine of World Growth*, Asia Pacific Press, Canberra:151–75.

Song, L., 2004. 'The export competitiveness of ASEAN, China and the East Asia NIEs, 1987–2000', proceedings of Rising China and the East Asian Economy conference, The Korea Institute for International Economic Policy, Seoul, 19–20 March.

Weiss, J., 2004. *People's Republic of China and its neighbours: partners or competitors for trade and investment?*, ADB Institute Discussion Paper 12, Asian Development Bank Institute, Tokyo.

Xu, X. and Song, L., 2000. 'Export similarity and the pattern of East Asia development', in P. Lloyd and X. Zhang (eds), *China in the Global Economy*, Edward Elgar, Cheltenham:154–64.

Xue, J. and Zhang B., 2004. 'Free trade agreements in East Asia: a simulation analysis using the computable general equilibrium modeling techniques', *World Economy*, 6:51–59.

Appendix 14A Decomposition of export growth

Let $X=(x_{ij})$ be the trade matrix among the economies in the region, where x_{ij} denotes the trade flow from economy i to economy j.
The sum by row is total exports (X_i) and the sum by column is total imports (M_j) of the economy j as follows

$$\sum_j x_{ij} = X_i \qquad (14A.1)$$

$$\sum_i x_{ij} = M_j \qquad (14A.2)$$

Changes in total imports of economy j between time t and 0 will be expressed as

$$\beta_j = \frac{M^t_j}{M^0_j} \qquad (14A.3)$$

which reflects the changes in domestic demand for imports.

Changes in economy i's position in the world market are reflected in the changes in relative competitiveness of the economy, which can be measured by the change in the share of exports of economy i in the world trade (X_w) as

$$\alpha_i = \frac{s^t_i}{s^0_i} = \frac{X^t_i / X^t_w}{X^0_i / X^0_w} \qquad (14A.4)$$

Assuming that the improvement of economy i's competitiveness prevails in all the markets at the same rate, economy i's exports to economy j expand at the same rate as the growth rate of economy i's total exports. However, the realised export at time t might differ from this assumed level due to such factors as geographical proximity and special trade arrangements between trading economies. The unexplained residual, referred to as the location effect, can be formulated as follows

$$\gamma_{ij} = \frac{x^t_{ij}}{\bar{x}^t_{ij}} = \frac{x^t_{ij}}{\alpha_i \beta_j x^0_{ij}} \qquad (14A.5)$$

Rearranging the above formula, Equation 14A.5 can be expressed as

$$x^t_{ij} = \alpha_i \beta_j \gamma_{ij} x^0_{ij} \qquad (14A.6)$$

Thus, changes in economy *i*'s exports between time *t* and 0 can be decomposed into the following three components

$$\Delta X_i = X_i^t - X_i^0 = \sum_j x_{ij}^t - \sum_j x_{ij}^0 = \sum_j \alpha_i \beta_j \gamma_{ij} x_{ij}^o - \sum_j x_{ij}^0$$

$$= \sum_j \left(\beta_j - 1\right) x_{ij}^0 + \sum_j \left(\alpha_i - 1\right)\beta_j x_{ij}^0 + \sum_j \alpha_i \beta_j \left(\gamma_{ij} - 1\right) x_{ij}^0 \qquad (14A.7)$$

The first component of the right-hand side of Equation 14A.7 is the demand effect, the second one is the competitiveness effect, and the third one is the location effect.

Appendix 14B: The calculation formula on impacts of final demand on regional value added

The intermediate transaction segments, given in the *Asian International Input–Output Table 1995*, include ten economies, namely Indonesia, Malaysia, the Philippines, Singapore, Thailand, China, Taiwan, Korea, Japan and the United States. Let $B=\left(b_{ij}^{\alpha\beta}\right)$ denote the 'Inverse Matrix', known as the 'Leontief Inverse', where

α denotes a supplying economy (α represents the 10 economies)

β denotes a demanding economy (β represents the 10 economies)

i denotes the *i*-th industry of economy α *(1≤i≤n)*

j denotes the *j*-th industry of economy β *(1≤j≤n)*

n is the number of industries

Thus *B* is the matrix with the size of 10n×10n. Herein, the 10n dimensional vector *V* is defined as follows

$$V = [V_1^I, ..., V_n^I, ..., V_1^U, ..., V_n^U] \qquad (14B.1)$$

where V_j^E is defined as the ratio of value added to gross inputs in industry *j* of economy *E*.

The ratio of international division of labour by economy *E*, when one unit of demand for industry *j* of China is created, can be defined as follows

$$IDL_j^E = \frac{\sum_i V_i^E b_{ij}^{EC}}{\sum_E \sum_i V_i^E b_{ij}^{EC}} \qquad (14B.2)$$

where $\sum_E$, $\sum_i$ are summations over 10 economies and all the industries respectively (Table 14B.1).

Appendix table B14.1   **Listed industries by sectors**

Number	Sector
1	Agriculture, livestock, forestry and fishery
2	Crude petroleum and natural gas
3	Other mining
4	Food, beverage and tobacco
5	Textile, leather, and the products thereof
6	Timber and wooden products
7	Pulp, paper and printing
8	Chemical products
9	Petroleum and petro products
10	Rubber products
11	Non-metallic mineral products
12	Metal products
13	Machinery
14	Transport equipment
15	Other manufacturing products

Source: Authors' calculations.

Appendix table C14.1 The trade matrix of the regional economies (US$ million)

	China	Hong Kong	Taiwan	Indonesia	Japan	Korea	Malaysia	Philippines	Singapore	Thailand	US	ROW	Total
1990													
China		27163	320	400	9210	433	370	205	2016	854	5314	16474	62760
Hong Kong	20331		3462	754	4680	1907	578	862	2615	1076	19817	26060	82144
Taiwan	2254	7456		1346	8509	1452	1627	854	2711	1728	23917	14661	66515
Indonesia	834	618	849		10923	1363	253	161	1902	188	3365	5218	25675
Japan	6145	13106	15461	5052		17499	5529	2510	10739	9150	91121	111366	287678
Korea	0	3780	1249	1079	12638		708	500	1805	968	19419	25665	67812
Malaysia	619	934	639	342	4505	1359		394	6753	1033	4986	7856	29420
Philippines	62	331	209	61	1622	229	127		240	156	3104	2054	8194
Singapore	799	3429	1900	1283	4616	1173	6873	671		3490	11215	18587	52753
Thailand	269	1038	335	154	3969	394	575	167	1696		5240	9234	23072
United States	4807	6841	11560	1897	48585	14399	3425	2471	8019	2991	0	288111	393106
Rest of world	17689	17788	17769	9635	126047	34196	9104	4196	22460	11772	329521	1816419	2417881
Total	53809	82482	53753	22005	235307	74405	29169	12993	60954	33407	517020	2341705	
1995													
China		36003	3095	1438	28466	6688	1281	1030	3410	1752	24744	40957	148955
Hong Kong	57861		4619	1062	10596	2803	1546	2009	4944	1615	37851	48648	173556
Taiwan	14785	16710		1550	14329	2560	3952	1534	5116	3421	30158	30093	124208
Indonesia	1742	1657	1650		12288	2917	987	590	3767	703	6322	12806	45428
Japan	21934	27780	28984	9969		31292	16802	7100	23006	19719	122034	134428	443047
Korea	9144	10682	3887	2958	17048		2951	1493	6689	2427	24344	49688	131312
Malaysia	1889	3941	2280	970	9199	2015		651	14960	2868	15313	19638	73724
Philippines	209	822	568	126	2740	442	314		994	799	6217	4139	17371
Singapore	2759	10126	4813	2367	9219	3243	22665	1928		6823	21576	35035	118187
Thailand	1642	2921	1354	811	9476	801	1554	414	7917		10078	20231	57201
United States	11749	14220	17925	3395	64298	25413	8818	5294	15318	6402		410618	583451
Rest of world	8450	67901	25801	15982	158367	56935	16750	6238	38183	27161	472335	2325240	3221711
Total	132163	192765	94976	40629	336027	135110	77620	28282	124394	73692	770972	3131521	

Appendix table C14.1 **The trade matrix of the regional economies** (US$ million) cont.

	China	Hong Kong	Taiwan	Indonesia	Japan	Korea	Malaysia	Philippines	Singapore	Thailand	US	ROW	Total
2000													
China		44520	5040	3062	41654	11292	2565	1464	5761	2243	52161	79431	249195
Hong Kong	69744		5112	950	11195	3827	1806	2011	4717	1837	47084	53707	201990
Taiwan	21669	15975		1270	17891	4701	4611	2255	5965	2895	41907	45661	164800
Indonesia	2768	1554	2378		14415	4318	1972	819	6562	1026	8489	17800	62102
Japan	30356	27187	35977	7607		30703	13886	10257	20830	13634	144009	143736	478179
Korea	18454	10708	8027	3505	20466		3515	3360	5648	2015	37806	58321	171826
Malaysia	3028	4440	3729	1707	12780	3235		1727	18050	3550	20162	25744	98152
Philippines	663	1907	2861	183	5609	1173	1377		3124	1206	11405	8693	38203
Singapore	5377	10841	8225	3788	10404	4916	25041	3387		5872	23891	39977	137932
Thailand	2806	3474	2415	1338	10164	1265	2813	1082	5997		14706	22902	68961
United States	15964	14567	23833	2479	64537	27337	10829	8677	17497	6538		579731	771991
Rest of world	54112	78145	30633	7623	170414	67712	13779	-549	40478	21106	836579	2828026	4148058
Total	224942	213319	128230	33511	379530	160479	82195	34489	134630	61923	1238200	3903731	
2003													
China		76288	9005	4482	59422	20096	6141	3094	8868	3828	92633	154390	438250
Hong Kong	95477		5436	1001	12088	4570	1981	2227	4589	2304	41780	52420	223874
Taiwan	49362	16134		877	14264	5880	4131	1861	6470	3229	33018	47414	182640
Indonesia	3802	1183	2233		13603	4323	2364	945	5399	1392	7386	18362	60995
Japan	57480	29918	31320	7179		34823	11250	9011	14858	16043	117384	144644	473911
Korea	35110	14654	7045	3378	17276		3852	2975	4636	2524	34369	66931	192750
Malaysia	6810	6784	3777	2129	11222	3039		1437	16522	4615	20539	28090	104966
Philippines	2145	3094	2492	296	5768	1313	2462		2431	1234	7274	7714	36224
Singapore	10134	14423	6897	4155	9696	6058	22793	3236		6156	20570	44157	144121
Thailand	5707	4331	2613	2275	11403	1588	3887	1622	5873		13669	27361	80329
United States	28418	13542	17488	2521	52064	24098	10920	7992	16576	5841		544149	723611
Rest of world	118390	52194	32894	4251	176219	73033	12944	3099	41772.26	28636	916626	3651303	5111362
Total	412836	232545	121200	32544	383025	178824	82726	37499	127996	75804	1305250	4786939	

Note: The row denotes exports of a specific economy, and the column denotes imports of a specific economy.
Source: The International Monetary Fund (IMF), (various issues). *Direction of Trade Statistics Yearbook*, The International Monetary Fund,

Index

A Shares, 179–181, 188
ageing of population, 35, 49, 196, 199, 207
agricultural output index, 113
anti-dumping measures, 241
arable land
  amount available, 118
  decline in quantity, 110, 122
Arthur Andersen, 180
ASEAN Free Trade Area (AFTA), 217, 228–233
Asia Pacific economies, China's trade
  expansion, 240–262

B Shares, 179–181
Bank of Japan, 26
Beijing Air Catering, 175
Beijing Tianqiao Department Store, 176
'big four' banks, 159–166
  overstaffing in, 173
bilateral trade, China/ASEAN, 245–247
Bretton Woods system, 20
'bubble economy', 10, 13, 34

CHECKS, 58, 60–66
Chen Yun, 72
China Securities Regulatory Commission
  (CSRC), 181, 188, 190, 191
China's trade expansion, 240–262
  trade reform, 241–247
  industrial linkages with regional economies,
  251–254
Chinese banking
  current performance, 166–173
  current structure, 159–166
  internal governance and supervision, 170
Chinese Communist Party (CCP), xiv, 2, 67,
70, 74, 76, 78, 79
Chu Lap-lik, Victor, 183
class struggle, 175
collective agriculture, 73
communism, 76, 175
comparative advantage, 241, 247
conditional convergence theory, 46
corporate governance, 128–138
covered interest parity (CIP), 29
Cultural Revolution, the, 41, 67, 70, 175
currency revaluation
  'global payments imbalances', 19
  'underlying balance', 19

Database of Political Institutions 2000 (DPI
  2000), 58
decentralisation, 72, 75
demand forces, 113
democracy, influence on development, 59
  and income levels, 63
  index, 62
demographic debt, 49
demographic dividend, 35, 36, 37, 38, 49–50
demographic growth, influence on economic
  development, 34
demographic transition, 34–52
  impact on China's savings rate, 41–45
  effects on growth, 45–49
  and savings rate, 39–45
Deng Xiaoping, 1, 67, 70, 71, 75, 175
dependence ratios, 35, 36
  aged-dependence, 45
  child-dependence, 45
  total dependence, 48
Dickey-Fuller test, 30
discretionary behaviour, 77
  limits on, 75
dual-track price system, 76

263

www.ingramcontent.com/pod-product-compliance
Lightning Source LLC
Chambersburg PA
CBHW040150270326
41928CB00035B/3308